The Life of
General Francis Marion

The Life
of
General
Francis Marion

*A Celebrated
Partisan Officer,
in the Revolutionary War,
against the
British and Tories
in South Carolina and Georgia*

BY
Brig. Gen. P. Horry
and
Parson M. L. Weems

JOHN F. BLAIR PUBLISHER
Winston-Salem, North Carolina

Introduction © 2000 by John F. Blair, Publisher
All Rights Reserved
Manufactured in the United States of America
Copyright 1824 by Joseph Allen
This reprint is taken from an 1854 edition
from J. P. Lippincott, Grambo, & Co.

> The Life of General Francis Marion, a Celebrated Partisan Officer, in the Revolutionary War, against the British and Tories in South Carolina and Georgia by Brig. Gen. P. Horry, of Marion's Brigade, and M. L. Weems, formerly rector of Mount Vernon Parish.

> "On Vernon's Chief why lavish all our lays; Come, honest Muse, and sing great MARION'S praise."

*The paper in this book meets the
minimum requirements of the
American National Standard
for Permanence of Paper for
Printed Library Materials.*

Third Printing, 2004

Library of Congress Cataloging-in-Publication Data

Weems, M. L. (Mason Locke), 1759–1825.
    The life of General Francis Marion: a celebrated partisan officer in the revolutionary war against the British and Tories in South Carolina and Georgia / by P. Horry and M. L. Weems.
        p.   cm.
    Originally published: Philadelphia: M. Carey, 1809. With a new introduction.
    "Though bearing Horry's name on the title-page, this was . . . the production of Weems, to whom Horry . . . furnished the materials"—Cf. Duyckinck, Cycl. Amer. lit., 1875, v. 1, p. 508.
    ISBN 0-89587-196-3 (alk. paper)
    1. Marion, Francis, 1732–1795. 2. Generals—United States—Biography. 3. South Carolina—Militia—Biography. 4. South Carolina—History—Revolution, 1775–1783. 5. Georgia—History—Revolution, 1775–1783. 6. United States—History—Revolution, 1775–1783—Campaigns. I. Horry, P. (Peter) II. Title.

E207.M3 W3 2000
973.3'3'092—dc21   00-021755

INTRODUCTION TO THE 2000 EDITION

In 1824, Reverend Mason Locke Weems, better known as Parson Weems, published a biography of Francis Marion that he purportedly co-wrote with Brigadier General Peter Horry, Marion's fellow soldier. Unfortunately, Horry was not pleased to have his name associated with the work. As he wrote to Weems, "I requested you would (if necessary) so far alter the work as to make it read grammatically, and I gave you leave to embellish the work, but entertained not the least idea of what has happened... You have carved and mutilated it with so many erroneous statements your embellishments, observation and remarks, must necessarily be erroneous as proceeding from false grounds. ... Can you suppose I can be pleased with reading particulars (though so elevated, by you) of Marion and myself, when I know such never existed."

This was not the first time Weems had embellished or exaggerated the facts to make his character seem more noble and moral. It was Weems's *Life of Washington* that was responsible for the oft-told tale about George Washington not telling a lie after chopping down the cherry tree.

Although Weems's treatment of Marion has a romantic flair, the real Marion did lead an exciting life. As William Gilmore Simms noted in his later biography of Marion, "Mr. Weems had rather loose notions of the privileges of the biographer; though, in reality, he has transgressed much less in his *Life of Marion* than is generally supposed. But the untamed, and sometimes extravagant exuberance of his style might well subject his narrative to suspicion."

According to Weems, one of the early examples of Marion's charmed life came when he survived a shipwreck as a teenager. His luck held out when he injured his ankle jumping out of a second-story window in Charleston, reportedly in order to avoid a drinking match. Because of the injury, he was at home on convalescent leave from the state militia when the British invaded Charleston. Thus, he avoided almost certain capture when Charleston surrendered.

Without any standing army left to resist the British, Marion organized a group of volunteers into one of military history's most effective guerrilla forces. Seasoned in wars against the Cherokees, Marion knew how to feed, camp, and move an army in the swampy South Carolina Low Country.

Marion's army struck the redcoats without warning at any time of day or night, then disappeared into the bogs and marshes. According to Weems, it was after chasing Marion and his men for seven hours, over twenty-six miles of swamp, without once catching sight of them, that British colonel Banastre Tarleton said, "Come, my boys! Let us go back. . . . As for this damned old fox, the devil himself could not catch him." The legend of the Swamp Fox was born. Marion's name became a great rallying cry when the fortunes of the patriot cause seemed doomed.

As publicity surrounding the filming of Mel Gibson's epic movie *The Patriot* filtered through the Carolinas, we here at John F. Blair, Publisher, felt it was time to resurrect the original biography. We have retained the flowery wording and the footnotes. To make the text more readable to today's audience, we have taken the liberty of updating some of the creative capitalization and use of italics that appeared in the original edition. For the purists, we beg your indulgence. Our primary goal is to introduce Marion's adventurous life to a whole new generation of admirers. We hope you enjoy the ride.

PREFACE

"*O* that mine enemy would write a book." This, in former times, passed for as sore an evil as a good man could think of wishing to his worst enemy. — Whether any of my enemies ever wished me so great an evil, I know not. But certain it is, I never dreamed of such a thing as writing a book; and least of all a war book. What, I! a man here under the frozen zone and grand climacteric of my days, with one foot in the grave and the other hard by, to quit my prayer book and crutches, (an old man's best companion,) and drawing my sword, flourish and fight over again the battles of my youth.

The Lord forbid me such madness! But what can one do when one's friends are eternally teasing him, as they are me, and calling out at every whipstitch and corner of the streets, "Well, but, sir, where's Marion? where's the history of Marion, that we have so long been looking for?"

'Twas in vain that I told them I was no scholar; no historian. "God," said I, "gentlemen, has made 'many men of many minds;' one for this thing and another for that. But I am morally certain he never made me for a writer. I did indeed once understand something about the use of a broadsword; but as to a pen, gentlemen, that's quite another part of speech.

The difference between a broadsword and a pen, gentlemen, is prodigious; and it is not every officer, let me tell you, gentlemen, who can, like Caesar, fight you a great battle with his sword to-day, and fight it over again with his pen to-morrow."

"Burn Caesar!" replied they, "and his book too. If it were written in letters of gold, we would not read it. What have honest republicans like us to do with such an ambitious cut-throat and robber? Besides sir, your reasoning about scholarship, and fine style, and all that, does not, begging your pardon, apply at all to the case in hand. Small subjects indeed, require great writers to set them off; but great subjects require no such artificial helps: like true beauties, they shine most in the simplest dress. Marion is one of this sort: great in his simplicity. Then give us Marion—plain, brave, honest Marion; that's all we want, sir. And you can do this better than any other man. You have known him longest; have fought closest by his side: and can best tell us of his noble deeds. And surely now, after all, you can't bear to let him die, and all his great actions, and be forgotten forever."

This, I confess, went to the quick, and roused me completely. "What! Marion forgotten?" I exclaimed, "Marion forgotten! and by me!" No, never! never! while memory looks back on the dreadful days of the revolution; when a British despot, not the nation, (for I esteem them most generous,) but a proud, stupid, obstinate, despot, trampling the Holy Charter and constitution of England's realm, issued against us, (sons of Britons,) that most unrighteous edict, taxation without representation! and then, because in the spirit of our gallant fathers, we bravely opposed him, he broke up the very fountains of his malice, and let loose upon us every indescribable, unimaginable curse of civil war; when British armies, with their Hessian, and Indian, and tory allies, overran my afflicted country, swallowing up its fruits and filling every part with consternation; when no thing was to be seen but flying crowds, burning houses, and young men, (alas! too often,) hanging upon the trees like dogs, and old men wringing their withered hands over their murdered boys, and women and children weeping and flying from their ruined plantations into the starving woods! When I think, I say, of these things, oh my God! how can I ever forget Marion, that vigilant, undaunted soldier, whom thy own mercy raised up to scourge such monsters, and avenge his country's wrongs.

The Washington of the south, he steadily pursued the warfare most safe for us, and most fatal to our enemies. He taught us to sleep in the swamps, to feed on roots, to drink the turbid waters of the ditch, to prowl nightly round the encampments of the foe, like lions round the habitations of the shepherds who had slaughtered their cubs. Sometimes he taught us to fall upon the enemy by surprise, distracting the midnight hour with the horrors of our battle: at other times, when our forces were increased, he led us on boldly to the charge, hewing the enemy to pieces, under the approving light of day. Oh, Marion, my friend! my friend! never can I forget thee. Although thy wars are all ended, and thyself at rest in the grave, yet I see thee still. I see thee as thou wert wont to ride, most terrible in battle to the enemies of thy country. Thine eyes like balls of fire, flamed beneath thy lowering brows. But lovely still wert thou in mercy, thou bravest among the sons of men! For, soon as the enemy sinking under our swords, cried for quarter, thy heart swelled with commiseration, and thy countenance was changed, even as the countenance of a man who beheld the slaughter of his brothers. The basest tory who could but touch the hem of thy garment was safe. The avengers of blood stopped short in thy presence, and turned away abashed from the lightning of thine eyes.

O that my pen were of the quill of the swan that sings for future days! then shouldst thou, my friend, receive the fulness of thy fame. The fathers, of the years to come, should talk of thy noble deeds; and the youth yet unborn should rise up and call thee blessed. Fired at the charm of thy virtues, they should follow thee in the path of thy glory, and make themselves the future Marions of their country.

Peter Horry.

The Life of
General Francis Marion

CHAPTER I

Short sketch of an extraordinary French couple, viz., the grandfather and mother of our hero—their early and happy loves—cruel persecution of the priests—final expulsion from their native country—providential settlement in South Carolina—their prosperous and exemplary lives —singular will of old Marion—and birth of his grandson, Francis.

Immortal may their memory be
Who fought and bled for liberty.

One thousand seven hundred and thirty-two was a glorious year for America. It gave birth to two of the noblest thunderbolts of her wars, George Washington and Francis Marion. The latter was born in St. John's parish, South Carolina. His father also was a Carolinian, but his grandfather was a Huguenot or French Protestant, who lived near Rochelle, in the blind and bigoted days of Louis XIV.

The priests, who are the persecutors in all countries except America, could not bear that he should worship God in his own way, or dream of going to heaven but in their leading strings, and therefore soon gave him to understand, that he must either "recant or trot;" that is, quit his heresy or his country.

Too brave to play the hypocrite, and too wise to hope for happiness with a "wounded spirit," he quickly made up his mind, and, like faithful Abraham, forsook his country, to wander an exile in lands unknown. The angel who guides the footsteps of the virtuous, directed his course to South Carolina; and as a reward for his piety, placed him in a land where mighty deeds and honors were ripening for his grandson. Nor did he wander alone. A cherub, in the form of a lovely wife, followed his fortunes, and gave him to know, from happy experience, that where love is, there is no exile.

Previous to his expulsion, the priests had, for some time, suspected young Marion of what they called "heresy." But, learning that he was enamoured of the beautiful and accomplished Mademoiselle Louisa D'Aubrey, and like to win her affections, they withheld for a while, their sacred thunders, hoping, that through fear of them, and love of her, he might yet return to the bosom of the Catholic Church, to which she belonged.

Young Marion's suit to his fair mistress, was fortunate to the full extent of an ardent lover's wishes. The charming girl repaid his passion with such liberal interest, that, in a short time after the commencement of their delicious friendship, she received him for her husband, in spite of all that wealthier wooers could promise, or frowning friends could threaten.

The neighboring clergy now marked the conduct of Marion with a keener eye; and discovering in him no symptoms that pointed to recantation, they furiously pressed the bishop to enforce against him the edict of banishment.

At this time, Marion with his lovely Louisa, were living on a small farm in the vicinity of Rochelle. As he walked one afternoon in the main street of that city, he was very rudely accosted by a couple of officers of the holy inquisition, whose looks and dress were as dark and diabolical as their employment.

"Vous etes nommes Marion?" said they; that is "your name is Marion?"

"Yes, gentlemen, that is my name."

Upon this, they rudely thrust a letter into his hand, and turned away, but with such looks as tigers throw at a tender lambkin, whose well-guarded fold forbids their access. On opening the letter he found as follows:

"Your damnable heresy, well deserves, even in this life, that purgation by fire which awfully awaits it in the next. But, in consideration of your youth and worthy connexions, our mercy has condescended to commute your punishment to perpetual exile.— You will, therefore, instantly prepare to quit your country for ever. For, if after ten days from the date hereof, you should be found in any part of the kingdom, your miserable body shall be consumed by fire, and your impious ashes scattered on the winds of heaven.

"Pere Rochelle."*

Had this dreadful letter been presented to Marion even while a bachelor, it would have filled him with horror; for the heart naturally cleaves to the spot where it awoke into being, and quits, with tearful eyes, the scenes among which were spent the first and happiest days of life. But ties stronger than those of nature bound Marion to his country. His country was the country of his Louisa. How could he live without her? And how could he hope that she would ever consent to leave her parents and friends to wander and die with him in hopeless exile?

But though greatly dejected, yet he did not despair. He still trusted in that parent-power who smiles even under frowns, and often pours his richest showers from the blackest clouds. Cheered with this hope, he put the letter into his pocket, and set out to seek his Louisa.

* I forewarn all my friends from thinking me capable of charging this vile persecuting spirit on the "Old W—e of Rome" exclusively. No, thank God, I have not so learned human nature. And they who are yet to learn, may, by reading the "Catholic Layman", soon get satisfied, that the priests are as apt to abuse power as the people, and that, when "clad with a little brief authority," protestants as well as papists, have committed those cruelties which make milder devils blush. [By way of a note on a note, I would observe, that the "Catholic Layman", is a very sensible and spirited pamphlet; the production, it is said, of Mathew Carey, Esq., of Philadelphia, who though a Roman Catholic, has printed more protestant Bibles and Testaments than half the preachers and printers in America put together.]

With arms fondly interlocked, she had accompanied him that morning to the gate on the back of the garden, through which he generally passed when he went to Rochelle. Soon as his horse was led up, and he about to mount, she snatched the bridle, and laughing, vowed he should not go until he had promised her one thing.

"Well, charmer, what's that?"

"Why that you will return very soon."

"Well, indeed I will; so now let me go."

"Oh no! I am afraid that when you get out of sight you will play truant. You must give me security."

"Well, Louisa, what security shall I give you?"

"Why you must give me that thing, whatever it be, that you hold most dear in all the world."

"Well done! and now, Louisa, I give you yourself, the dearest thing God ever gave me in all this world."

At this her fine face was reddened all over with blushing joy, while her love-sparkling eyes, beaming on his, awakened that transport which those who have felt it would not exchange for worlds. Then, after the fond, lengthened kiss, and tender sigh of happy lovers parting, he rode off.

Soon as he was out of her sight, she turned to go to the house. As she passed along the garden, the sudden fancy struck her to adorn the summer house with evergreens and flowers of the liveliest tints, and there, amidst a wilderness of sweets, to receive her returning lover. Animated with this fond suggestion of conjugal affection, (woman's true life,) which at every quickened pulse diffused an answering rapture through the virtuous breast, she commenced her pleasing task; and with her task she mingled the music of her voice, clear and strong as the morning lark, and sweet as from a heart full of innocence and love. The pleasant sounds reached the ear of Marion, as he drew near the garden. Then, entering the gate without noise, he walked up, unperceived, close to her as she sat all alone in the arbour, binding her fragrant flowers and singing the happy hours away. She was singing her favorite hymn, by Madam Guyon.

"That love I sing, that wondrous love,
Which wak'd my sleeping clay;
That spread the sky in azure bright
And pour'd the golden day," &c. &c.

To see youth and beauty, though in a stranger, thus pointing to heaven, is delightful to a pious heart. Then what rapture to an enlightened soul to see a beloved wife thus communing with God, and becoming every day more and more angelic!

Soon as her song was finished, he called out, "Louisa!"

Startled at the sudden call, she turned around to the well-known voice, presenting a face on which love and sweet surprise had spread those rosy charms, which in a moment banished all his sorrows. "My dearest Gabriel," she exclaimed, dropping her flowers, and running and throwing herself into his arms, "here, take back your security! take back your security! and also my thanks for being such a man of honor. But what brought you back, love, so much earlier than you expected?"

Here the memory of that fatal letter went like a dagger to his heart, bleaching his manly cheeks.

He would have evaded the question; but in vain, for Louisa, startled at the sudden paleness of his looks, insisted the more earnestly to know the cause.

He delayed a moment, but conscious that the secret must soon come out, he took the letter from his pocket, and with a reluctant hand put it into hers.

Scarcely had she run through it, which she did with the most devouring haste, when she let it drop from her hands, and faintly articulating, "Ah, cruel priest!" she fell upon his bosom, which she bathed with her tears.

After some moments of distress too big for utterance, Marion, deeply sighing, at length broke silence.

"Ah, Louisa! and must we part so soon!"

At this, starting up with eyes suffused with tears but beaming immortal love, she hastily replied—"Part!"

"Yes!" continued he, "part! for ever part!"

"No, Marion, no! never! never!"

"Ah! can you, Louisa, leave father and mother, and follow a poor banished husband like me?"

"Yes—yes—father, mother, and all the world will I leave to follow thee, Marion!"

"O blessed priest, I thank you! Good bishop Rochelle, holy father in God, I thank you—your persecution has enriched me above princes. It has discovered to me a mine of love in Louisa's soul, that I never dreamed of before."

"My dearest Gabriel, did you ever doubt my love?"

"Pardon me, my love, I never doubted your love, Oh no! I knew you loved me. The circumstances under which you married me gave me delicious proof of that. To have preferred me to so many wealthier wooers—to have taken me as a husband to the paradise of your arms, when so many others would have sent me as a heretic to the purgatory of the inquisition, was evidence of love never to be forgotten; but that in addition to all this you should now be so ready to leave father and mother, country and kin, to follow me, a poor wanderer in the earth, without even a place where to lay my head—"

"Yes, yes," replied she, eagerly interrupting him, "that's the very reason I would leave all to follow you. For, oh my love! how could I enjoy father or mother, country or kin, and you a wanderer in the earth, without a place whereon to lay your head! That single thought would cover my days with darkness, and drive me to distraction. But give me your company, my Gabriel, and then welcome that foreign land with all its shady forests! Welcome the thatched cottage and the little garden filled with the fruits of our own fondly mingled toils! Methinks, my love, I already see that distant sun rising with gladsome beams on our dew-spangled flowers. I hear the wild wood-birds pouring their sprightly carols on the sweet-scented morning. My heart leaps with joy to their songs. Then, O my husband! if we must go, let us go without a sigh. God can order it for our good. And, on my account, you shall cast no lingering look behind. I am ready to follow you wherever you go. Your God shall be my God. Where you live I will live, and where you die, there will I die, and will be buried by your side. Nothing my beloved, but death, shall ever part me from you."

"Angelic Louisa!" cried Marion, snatching her to his bosom in transports—"Wondrous woman! what do I not owe to God, ever blessed, for such a comforter! I came just now from Rochelle with the load of a mountain on my heart. You have taken off that mountain, and substituted a joy most lightsome and heavenly. Like a ministering angel, you have confirmed me in duty; you have ended my struggles—and by so cheerfully offering to forsake all and follow me, you have displayed a love, dear Louisa, which will, I trust, render you next to my God, the eternal complacency and delight of my soul."

In the midst of this tender scene, a servant came running to inform Louisa that her mother, Madame D'Aubrey, had just arrived, and was coming to her in the garden. This startled our lovers into a painful expectation of another trial. For as Louisa was an only daughter, and her parents dotingly fond of her, it was not to be imagined that they would give her up without a hard struggle. Seeing the old lady coming down the walk towards them, they endeavored to adjust their looks, and to meet her with the wonted smile. But in vain. The tumult in their bosoms was still too visible in their looks to escape her discernment. She eagerly asked the cause. Their changing countenances served but to increase her fears and the vehemence of her curiosity. The bishop's letter was put into her hands. Its effects on the good old lady were truly distressing. Not having, like her daughter, the vigor of youth, nor the fervors of love to support her, she was almost overcome.

Soon as her spirits were a little recovered, she insisted that her daughter and son-in-law should instantly step into her coach and go home with her. "Your father, my dear," said she to Louisa, "your father, Monsieur D'Aubrey, will, I am certain, do something for us."

But in this she was woefully mistaken, for Monsieur D'Aubrey was one of that blind sort who place all their religion in forms and notions. He could smile and look very fond upon a man, though not over moral, provided that man went to his church—praised his preacher and opinions, and abused everybody else; but would look very sour on the best man on earth who differed from him in those things. In short, he was destitute of love, the sole life of religion. And though on account of his wife's importunities and his daughter's repose, he had consented to her marriage with Marion, yet he never liked the young 'heretic', and therefore he read the order of his banishment without any burst of grief, and made no effort to revoke the decrees of the church against him, but abandoned him to his fate.

Such insensibility to her husband's interest distressed poor Louisa exceedingly. However, it had this good effect: It contributed greatly to lessen her regret at parting with her parents.

"O had they but loved me as you do, my Marion," said she, "could they have been so indifferent when my all was at stake? No, indeed," continued she, "they could not," and burst into tears.

"Dearest Louisa!" replied he, tenderly embracing her, "would not I leave father and mother and all for you?"

"Well," returned she, with eyes of love, outshining all diamonds, "and am I not going to leave all for you? Yet a few days and I shall have no father, no mother, no country; cut off from all the world but you, Marion! alas! what will become of me if you should prove cruel to me?"

"Cruel! cruel to you, Louisa! O my God, can that ever be?"

"Ah Marion! but some excellent women have left father and mother, and followed their husbands; and yet, after all have been cruelly neglected by them!"

"Yes, Louisa; and God forgive them for that horrid crime! But to me such a deed were utterly impossible. I live for happiness, Louisa, I live for happiness, my angel. And I find so much happiness in loving, that I would as soon cease to live as cease to love. Some indeed, 'sordid celebutes' for example, seem to exist without love; but it is only a seeming existence, most joyless and imperfect. And they bear the dullness of apathy the better, because they have never known the transports of affection. But with me, my charmer, the case is happily different; for at the moment I first saw those angel eyes, they infused a sweetness into my heart unknown before. And those delicious sparks, fanned by your loves and graces, have now risen to such a flame of bliss, that methinks, were it to go out, my life would go out with it. Then, my first and last, and only sweetheart, I pray you, do not fear that I shall ever cease to love you: for indeed that can never be while you continue even half as lovely as you are at present."

"Well then, Marion," replied she, fondly pressing his ruddy cheeks to her heaving bosom, "if it depends on me, on my constant affection and studiousness to please, you shall never love me less; but more and more every day of your life."

The next morning, accompanied by Madame D'Aubrey, Marion and Louisa returned home in order to make the best preparations, which the shortness of the time would allow, to quit their country for ever.

In choosing his place of exile, it has been said that Marion's thoughts were at first turned towards the West Indies. But it would appear that Heaven had decreed for him a different direction. For scarcely had he reached his home, much agitated about the means of getting off in time, before a letter was brought him from an intimate friend in Rochelle, informing him that a large ship, chartered for the Carolinas, by several wealthy Huguenot families, was then lying at anchor under the Isle de Rhee. Gratefully regarding this as a beckoning from heaven, they at once commenced their work, and prosecuted it with such spirit, that on the evening of the ninth day they embraced their weeping friends and went on board the ship.

It is said that many of the most respectable families of Carolina—the Gourdines, Hugers, Trapiers, Postells, Horrys, &c. came over in the same ship.

The next day, the clouds began to bank the eastern sky, and the winds to whistle from the hills. Pleased with the darkly rippling waters, the ready ship got home her anchors and loosed her sails. Then wheeling before the freshening gale, she bid adieu to her native shores, and on wings of widespread canvas, commenced her foaming course for the western world.

But though mutual love and confidence in heaven were strong in the bosoms of young Marion and his Louisa, yet could they not suppress the workings of nature, which would indulge her sorrows when looking back on the lessening shores; they beheld dwindled to a point and trembling in the misty sky, that glorious land, at once their own cradle and the sepulchre of their fathers.

Some natural tears they shed, but wiped them soon, for the earth was all before them where to choose their place of rest; and Providence their guide.

But Marion and Louisa did not leave their country empty handed. Her Parents, 'tis supposed, gave Louisa money, but what sum, after this long lapse of time, is uncertain. Nor does tradition say for how much Marion sold his little farm. But it is well known that on their arrival in Carolina, they went up into the country, and bought a plantation on Goose Creek, near Charleston, where their dust now sleeps, after a long life endeared by mutual love, and surrounded by every comfort that industry and prudence can bestow.

We have said that Marion left his country for the sake of his religion: which appears to have been of that cheerful sort for which a wise man would make any sacrifice. It was the religion of the gospel, that blessed philosophy which asks not a face of gloom, but a heart of joy. And thereunto enjoin a supreme love of God, and a close walk with him in a pure and benevolent life. From this, the genuine spring of all the sweetest charities and joys of life, Marion derived that cheerfulness which appears never to have failed him. Even in his last will, where most men fancy they ought to be gloomy as the grave whither they are going, his cheerfulness continued to shine with undiminished lustre. It was like the setting of a cloudless sun: which, after pouring its fattening beams on the fields of a live-long summer's day, goes down in smiles to rise a brighter beauty on another day. This will is certainly an amiable curiosity, and as it may be of service to the reader, by showing him how free and easy a good life makes a man with death, I will record it: at least the principal features of it, as I got them from the family.

After having, in the good old way, bequeathed "his soul to God who gave it," and "his body to the earth out of which it was taken," he proceeds in the manner following:

In the first place, as to debts, thank God, I owe none. And therefore shall give my executors but little trouble on that score.

Secondly—As to the poor, I have always treated them as my brethren. My dear family will, I know, follow my example.

Thirdly—As to the wealth with which God has been pleased to bless me and my dear Louisa and children, lovingly we have labored together for it—lovingly we have enjoyed it—and now, with a glad and grateful heart do I leave it among them.

He then proceeds to the distribution. Liberally to his children: but far more so to his wife—and at the end of each bequest assigns his reasons, viz.,

I give my ever beloved Louisa all my ready money—that she may never be alarmed at a sudden call.

I give her all my fat calves and lambs, my pigs and poultry—that she may always keep a good table.

I give her my new carriage and horses—that she may visit her friends in comfort.

I give her my family bible—that she may live above the ill tempers and sorrows of life.

I give my son Peter a hornbook—for I am afraid he will always be a dunce.

But Peter was so stung with this little squib, that he instantly quit his raccoon hunting by nights, and betook himself to reading, and soon became a very sensible and charming young man.

His eldest son, who, after his father, was named Gabriel, married a Miss Charlotte Corde, by whom he had six children—Esther, Gabriel, Isaac, Benjamin, Job, and our hero Francis, the least as well as the last of the family. As to his sister Esther, I have never heard what became of her; but for his four brothers, I am happy to state, that though not formidable as soldiers, they were very amiable as citizens. They bought farms—proved their oxen—married wives—multiplied good children, and thus, very unlike our niggardly bachelors, contributed a liberal and laudable part to the population, strength, and glory of their country. God, I pray heartily, take kind notice of all such; and grant, that having thus done his will in this world, they may partake of his glory in the next.

CHAPTER II

Marion's first appearance—a humble cultivator of the earth—
the great Cherokee war of 1761 comes on—volunteers his
services to his country—is appointed a first lieutenant in the
provincial line—commands a forlorn hope—narrowly escapes
with his life—the Anglo-American and the Indian forces
engaged—bloody battle—the Indians defeated—their country
laid waste—peace made—Marion retires.

*A*mong the Mohawks of Sparta, it was a constant practice on the
birth of a male infant, to set a military granny to examine him, as a butcher
would a veal for the market, and if he were found any ways puny, he was
presently thrown into a horse pond with as little ceremony as a blind puppy.
Had such been the order of the day in 1732, Carolina would never have
boasted a Marion; for I have it from good authority, that this great soldier,
at his birth, was not larger than a New England lobster, and might easily
enough have been put into a quart pot. This puny appearance continued
with him till the age of twelve, when it was removed by the following
extraordinary providence.

On a trip to the West Indies, which his friends put him upon for his health's sake, the little schooner in which he was embarked was suddenly attacked by some monstrous fish, probably a thorn-back whale, who gave it such a terrible stroke with his tail as started a plank. The frightened crew flew to their pumps, but in vain; for the briny flood rushed with such fury into their vessel, that they were glad to quit her, and tumble as fast as they could into their little jolly boat. The event showed that this was as but a leap "out of the frying pan into the fire;" for their schooner went down so suddenly as not to give them time to take a mouthful of food with them, not even so much as a brown biscuit or a pint of water. After three wretched days of feverish hunger and thirst, they agreed to kill a little cabin dog who had swam to them from the schooner just before she sunk. On his raw flesh they feasted without restraint; but the blood they preserved with more economy, to cool their parched lips. In a few days, however, their own blood, for lack of cooling food, became so fiery hot as to scald their brain to frenzy. About the tenth day the captain and mate leaped overboard, raving mad; and the day following the two remaining seamen expired in the bottom of the boat, piteously crying to the last for water! water! God of his mercy forgive me, who have so often drank of that sweet beverage without grateful acknowledgments! Scarcely was this melancholy scene concluded before a vessel hove in sight, standing directly for the boat, as if purposely sent to save the child that was tossing in it on the gloomy waves.

Little Marion was so weak that he could not stir hand or foot to climb up the side of the vessel. The captain, however, soon had him on board; and by means of chocolate and turtle broth, sparingly given him at first, recruited him so fast, that, by the time he reached his native shores, he was in much better health than ever. So that on his return to his friends, it was found, as is often the case, that what was at first looked on as a great misfortune, had proved a very noble blessing. His constitution seemed renewed, his frame commenced a second and rapid growth; while his cheeks, quitting their pale suet-colored cast, assumed a bright and healthy olive. According to the best accounts that I have been able to procure,

Marion never thought of another trip to sea, but continued in his native parish, in that most independent and happy of all callings, a cultivator of the earth, till his twenty-seventh year.

A report then prevailing that the Cherokee Indians were murdering the frontier settlers, Marion turned out with his rifle, as a volunteer under governor Lyttleton. The affair, however, proved to be a mere flash in the pan: for the Cherokees finding that things were not exactly in the train they wished, sent on a deputation with their wampum belts and peace-talks to bury the hatchet and brighten the old chain of friendship with the whites; and the good-natured governor, thinking them sincere, concluded a treaty with them. The troops of course were dismissed, and Marion returned to his plantation.

Scarcely, however, had two years elapsed, before the perfidious Cherokees broke out again in a fresh place, killing and driving the defenceless inhabitants at a most barbarous rate. Marion instantly flew again to the governor with the tender of his services to fight for his afflicted countrymen. His excellency was so pleased with this second instance of Marion's patriotism, that he gave him a first lieutenancy in the provincial line under the brave captain William Moultrie. The reported force and fury of the Indians struck such a terror through the colony, that colonel Grant (of the British) with twelve hundred regulars, was ordered out on a forced march to succor the bleeding frontiers.

On their way they were joined at Ninety-Six, May 14, 1761, by twelve hundred provincials, all men of surest aim with the deadly rifle.

To draw off the enemy from their murderous excursions, Col. Grant wisely determined to push the war at once into their own country; which was no sooner discovered by them, than they instantly collected their whole force to oppose him. The only passage into their country was through a dark defile or gap in the mountain, which it was resolved should be forced as rapidly as possible. A forlorn hope of thirty brave fellows were ordered to explore the dangerous pass: and Marion, though but a young lieutenant, had the honor to be appointed their leader. At the head of his command he advanced with rapidity, while the army moved on to support him. But scarcely had they entered the gloomy defile, when, from behind the rocks and trees, a sheet of fire suddenly blazed forth, which killed twenty-one of his men! With the remainder, he faced about and pushed back with all speed; whereupon great numbers of tall savages, frightfully painted, rushed from their lurking places, and with hideous yells and uplifted tomahawks, pursued and gained upon them so fast, that nothing but the nearness of the advanced guard saved them from destruction. The Anglo-American army then prepared themselves for a serious and bloody conflict.

An enemy in such force, so well posted, and defending the only pass into their country, would, they well knew, fight desperately. And well aware, also what slaughter would follow upon their own defeat, they determined to yield the victory only with their lives. A long summer's day was before them, for the sun had just risen above the hills, a bright spectator of the coming fight. Then, in high spirits, with justice on their side, and an approving conscience, they cheerfully left the event to Heaven. The British were formed in small corps, the more promptly to support the riflemen, who led the van, and now with wide extended wings began to move. In a little time they came in sight of the enemy, who appeared flying backwards and forwards, as if not well satisfied with their ground. The provincial marksmen then rapidly advancing, flew each to his tree, and the action began. From wing to wing, quite across the defile, the woods appeared as if all on fire; while the incessant crash of small arms tortured the ear like claps of sharpest thunder. The muskets of the British, like their native bull-dogs, kept up a dreadful roar, but scarcely did more than bark the trees, or cut off the branches above the heads of the Indians. While, with far less noise, the fatal rifles continued to lessen the numbers of the enemy. The action was kept up with great spirit for nearly two hours, during which the superiority of the American riflemen was very remarkably displayed. For in that time they lost only fifty-one—whereas of the Indians there fell one hundred and three, which so disheartened them that they fled and gave up their country to the conquerors, who prepared immediately to enter it.

Colonel Grant had hoped to surprise their towns, but concluding that their swift-footed runners had given the alarm, he moved on in slow marches through the wilderness towards the settlements, thinking that by the destruction of their towns and corn-fields he should drive them into a disposition for peace.

Marion often spoke of this part of the war, as of a transaction which he remembered with sorrow. "We arrived," said he, in a letter to a friend, "at the Indian towns in the month of July. As the lands were rich and the season had been favorable, the corn was bending under the double weight of lusty roasting ears and pods of clustering beans. The furrows seemed to rejoice under their precious loads—the fields stood thick with bread. We encamped the first night in the woods, near the fields, where the whole army feasted on the young corn, which, with fat venison, made a most delicious treat.

"The next morning we proceeded by order of colonel Grant, to burn down the Indians' cabins. Some of our men seemed to enjoy this cruel work, laughing very heartily at the curling flames, as they mounted loud crackling over the tops of the huts. But to me it appeared a shocking sight. Poor creatures! thought I, we surely need not grudge you such miserable habitations. But when we came, according to orders, to cut down the fields of corn, I could scarcely refrain from tears. For who could see the stalks that stood so stately with broad green leaves and gaily tasseled shocks, filled with sweet milky fluid and flour, the staff of life; who, I say, without grief, could see these sacred plants sinking under our swords with all their precious load, to wither and rot untasted in their mourning fields?

"I saw every where around the footsteps of the little Indian children, where they had lately played under the shade of their rustling corn. No doubt they had often looked up with joy to the swelling shocks, and gladdened when they thought of their abundant cakes for the coming winter. When we are gone, thought I, they will return, and peeping through the weeds with tearful eyes, will mark the ghastly ruin poured over their homes and happy fields, where they had so often played.

" 'Who did this?' they will ask their mothers.

" 'The white people did it;' the mothers reply; 'the christians did it!'

"Thus for cursed Mammon's sake, the followers of Christ have sown the hellish tares of hatred in the bosoms even of pagan children."

The reader will, however, with pleasure remember that these were the dark deeds chiefly of a kingly government. A gloomy monarch, three thousand miles distant, and rolling in all the pomps and pleasures of three millions of dollars per annum, could hardly be supposed to know what was passing in the American wilds; but Washington had known. With bleeding heart he had often beheld the red and white men mingling in bloody fight. The horrors of the cruel strife dwelt upon his troubled thoughts; and soon as God gave him power, (as President of independent America,) he immediately adopted that better system which he had learnt from the gospel. His successors, Adams, Jefferson, and Madison, have piously pursued his plan. In place of the tomahawk, the plough-share is sent to the poor Indians—goods are furnished them at first cost—letters and morals are taught among their tribes—and the soul of humanity is rejoiced to see the red and white men meet together like brothers.—

By this god-like policy, the United States have not only saved an immensity of blood and treasure, but are rapidly adding to the population and strength of the country.

Now to return to Marion's letter.—"After burning twenty towns, and destroying thousands of cornfields,* the army returned to Koewee, where the 'Little Carpenter', a Cherokee chief, met colonel Grant and concluded a peace." The troops were then disbanded: and Marion returned to his plantation in St. John's parish, where, with a few well-fed slaves, he continued to till his parental acres, occasionally amusing himself with his gun and fishing rod, of which he was always very fond.

---

* To this day the Indians cannot bear the name of colonel Grant; and whenever they see a drove of horses destroying a corn-field, they call out "Grant, Grant."

CHAPTER III

War between England and America—Marion appointed a
captain in the Second South Carolina regiment—goes with the
author on the recruiting service—curious anecdote of lieut.
Charnock and captain Johnson—some melancholy and
memorable relations.

Marion continued to tread the peaceful and pleasant walks of life,
as above, till the beginning of May, 1775, when, by a vessel direct from
Boston, news was brought of the gallant battle of Lexington. Instantly the
whole town and country were in a flame for war, and the legislature being
purposely convened, hastened to meet the wishes of the people, who were
clamorous for raising two regiments for the service.

On balloting for officers, Marion's ticket came out for a captaincy in
the second regiment, under command of the brave William Moultrie. In a
little time my name was called out as a captain, also, in the same regiment
with Marion. This to me, was matter of great joy, as I had long courted the
friendship of Marion. For though he was neither handsome, nor witty, nor
wealthy, yet he was universally beloved. The fairness of his character—his
fondness for his relations—his humanity to his slaves—and his bravery in

the Indian war, had made him the darling of the country. It is not, therefore, to be wondered at, that I should have taken such a liking to Marion, but why he should have conceived such a partiality for me, that's the question. But it is no business of mine to solve it. However, very certain it is, that on the first moment of our acquaintance, there was something in his eyes and looks towards me which led me to think there must be truth in the old saying of "people's falling in love at first sight." And when it is considered, that strong attachments generally spring from congenialities, I must confess, that the warm and constant friendship of Marion has ever appeared to me exceedingly flattering.

But to return to my narrative.—Our commissions as captains, were soon made out, and signed by the council of safety, the 21st of June, 1775. As we were a couple of flaming patriots, we could not bear to be idle a single moment—marching, fighting, killing, and taking prisoners, was all that we could think or talk of. But as all this fine sport could not be carried on without men, nor men to be had without recruiting; recruiting, of course, appeared to be the first act and prologue of our play.

"But what shall we do for money, captain Marion?" said I.

"Why," replied he, "we must get it from the assembly."

The assembly was accordingly applied to, but alas! "could not help us to a single dollar!" I wonder whether posterity will ever muster faith to believe that the grey heads of South Carolina, without a penny in pocket, ventured to war with Great Britain, the nation of the longest purse in Europe? Surely it was of him who pitted young David with his maiden sling and pebbles against the giant Goliath.

But though the poverty of the legislature was enough to have thrown a damp on spirits of ordinary heat, yet to a flaming zeal like ours, it only served as water on a fiery furnace, to make it blaze the fiercer.

"Why truly, Horry!" said Marion, "this looks unpromising, but we must not mind it my hero, I'll tell you what—if the assembly can't help us, we must e'en help ourselves! So come let us try what we can do on our own credit."

"With all my heart," I replied.

So away went we to borrow money of our friends in Charleston; I mean hard money. And hard money it was indeed. The gold and silver all appeared as if it had caught the instinct of water-witches, diving at the first flash of the war, to the bottom of misers' trunks and strong boxes. For two whole days, and with every effort we could make, we collected but the pitiful sum of one hundred dollars! However, fully resolved that nothing should stop us, we got our regimentals the next morning from the tailor's, and having crammed our saddlebags with some clean shirts, a stout luncheon of bread and cheese, and a bottle of brandy, we mounted, and with hearts light as young lovers on a courting scheme, we dashed off to recruit our companies. Our course was towards Georgetown, Black River, and Great Pedee. Fortune seemed to smile on our enterprise; for by the time we reached Pedee, we had enlisted thirty-seven men, proper tall fellows, to whom we gave furloughs of two days to settle their affairs, and meet us at the house of a Mr. Bass, tavern-keeper, with whom we lodged. I should have told the reader, that we had with us, a very spirited young fellow by the name of Charnock, who was my lieutenant.

On the second day, a captain Johnson of the militia, came to Bass's, and took lieutenant Charnock aside, and after prattling a great deal to him about the "cursed hardship," as he was pleased to call it, "of kidnapping poor clodhoppers at this rate," he very cavalierly offered him a guinea for himself, and a half joe a-piece for Marion and me to let the recruits go.

Never did a poor silly puppy more completely take the wrong sow by the ear, than did Mr. captain Johnson, in thus tampering with lieutenant Charnock. For Charnock, though remarkably good natured and polite among men of honor, could not bear the least approach of any thing that looked like rascality. Immediately, therefore, on hearing this infamous proposition, he brought Johnson into the dining room where Marion and myself were sitting, and, in his presence, told us the whole affair.

Oh that my young countrymen could all have been there, that they might have seen what a pale trembling, pitiful figure a detected rascal makes!

I am sure they could never have lost that blessed moment's impression in favor of truth and honor.

After much swallowing, Johnson, however, at last, got the better of his conscience, and came on with a stout denial of the fact. Whereupon Charnock, snatching a pair of pistols, ordered him to take one and fight him on the spot. This being refused, the furious lieutenant instantly fell upon him with a cane. Sensible that Johnson had very richly deserved this ignominious chastisement, we gave him up to Charnock, who thrashed him very soundly, until, falling on his knees, he roared out for quarter. Charnock then ordered him to be gone, but with the severest threats in case the recruits were not forthcoming at the appointed time.

On the morrow they came, and "let the cat out of the bag." It appeared then, that that most worthless fellow, Johnson, had told the poor simple recruits such dreadful stories about the war, that in their fright they had offered him all their cows and calves to get them off!

Our success in the recruiting business far exceeded our expectations, for in a very short time we made up our full complement of sixty men each. I have often lamented it as a most serious misfortune that we did not enlist for the war. I am certain we could as easily have enlisted for the war as for six months. We should then have had a host of veterans, masters of their dreadful art, inured to hardships, scornful of danger, and completely able to purge our country of her cruel invaders.

As a place of greater security from the enemy's vessels, Dorchester had been pitched on as a deposite for ammunition and military stores, and put under a guard of militia. But fearing that the tories might rise upon this slender force and take away our powder, an article, at that time, of incalculable value, the council of safety advised to add a company of regulars, under some brave and vigilant officer. Marion had the honor to be nominated to the command, and, on the 19th of November, 1775, marched to the post, where he continued, undisturbed by the tories, until Christmas, when he was ordered down to Charleston to put fort Johnson in a state of defence.

About this time an affair happened in Charleston, which filled with horror all who witnessed it. Captain Fuller, of the second regiment, a gentleman in other respects very amiable and exemplary, gave himself up to hard drinking, and to such an excess as brought on an inflammation in the brain. In this frantic state, with wild rolling eyes, and a face shockingly bloated and red, he would behave for all the world as if he were leading his men into action. "Come on, my brave fellows," he would cry, "now be cool and steady—reserve your fire till I say the word—now give it to them, my heroes—hurra, they run, they run. I thank you, my lads, for your gallantry in your country's cause."

All this time the sweat would roll in torrents down his cheeks. Then, quite exhausted, he would fall on his knees, and with clasped hands, and eyes lifted to heaven, would pronounce the Lord's Prayer and the creed in the most moving manner. For several days the soldiers gathered around him while thus employed: and often with tears in their eyes, would observe the total ruin which intemperance had brought upon this once elegant young gentleman.—His friends in the country, hearing of his deplorable condition, came and took him home, where death soon put an end to all his miseries.

In a short time after this, our regiment was deprived of another very genteel young officer, lieutenant Perrineau; who also fell an early sacrifice to that most shameful and detestable practice of morning slings and mid-day draughts of strong grog.

After these two tragedies, the reader will not, I hope, be displeased with the following farce, which was acted in fort Johnson, while Marion was repairing it, in January, 1776. The principal actors in it, were captain Marion, and a young lieutenant, whose name, delicacy, yet a while, bids me suppress. This officer, though in his person as handsome as Absalom, or the blooming Adonis, was as destitute of soul as a monkey. He appeared to have no idea above that of dress and diversion: and provided he could but compass his own little pitiful ends, which were always of the sensual sort, he cared not how shamefully he prevaricated and lied, but would wink, and grin, and chuckle, as if he had done some great thing. He had served under a score of captains, who had all spoken of him as a slippery, worthless fellow, whom they knew not what to do with. But though most heartily despised, the fool had the vanity to think himself amazingly clever; and actually boasted to me one day, that he would soon let me see how far he was over my famous captain Marion's speed. Presently he hears that there is to be, next week, a great cock-fight at Dorchester. Instantly his childish spirits are all on a fever to see the cock-fight. "Oh heavens! he would not miss the cock-fight for the world!" But how to obtain leave of absence from the fort at this busy time, was the rub; however, for such means as he was capable of using, an invention like his could not long be at a loss. In short, he went to Marion, with a doleful face, and in piteous accents, stated that his father, an excellent old man as ever son was blessed with, was at his last gasp, and only wanted to see him before he died.

The generous Marion, not suspecting that so goodly an outside could cover such falsehood, did not wait to hear the coming petition, but instantly granted his wish, unheard—"To be sure, lieutenant, go, by all means, go and wait upon your father; but return as soon as possible, for you see how much we have to do."

The lieutenant affected to be quite overcome with Marion's generosity, and swore he would be back in two days, or at farthest in three. As he stepped along by me, he thrust his tongue into his cheek, and looked prodigiously arch, as if he had achieved a grand exploit. As soon as he was gone, I told Marion I suspected it was all a trick.

And so it turned out; for instead of hurrying off, as he had pretended, to see his dying father, he slipt over to Charleston, where, for fear of being seen by any of our officers, he skulked about in the lower lanes and alleys until it was time to go up to the cock-fight at Dorchester.

At length after a fortnight's absence, he came over to the fort, and entering the marquee, where Marion was sitting with his officers, he began to bow and scrape. As if not perceiving him, Marion turned his head another way. The lieutenant then, exceedingly embarrassed, came out with his apology,—"I am sorry, sir, to have outstayed my time so long; but—but I could not help it—but now I am returned to do my duty."

Marion turned very quickly upon him, and with a most mortifying neglect, said, "Aye, lieutenant, is that you? Well, never mind it—there is no harm done—I never missed you."

The poor lieutenant was so completely cut up, that he could not say a word, but sneaked off, hanging down his head, and looked much more like a detected swindler than a gentleman soldier.

The officers, who were all prodigiously pleased with his confusion, presently went out and began to rally him—"Ah, ha, lieutenant, and so the captain has given you a set down."

"A set down," replied he, very angrily, "a set down, do you call it! I had rather a thousand times he had knocked me down—an ugly, cross, knock-kneed, hook-nosed son of a b-t-h!"

The officers almost split their sides with laughing. The story soon took wind; and the poor lieutenant did not hear the last of it for many a day. I have often heard him say, that nothing ever so completely confounded him, as did that dry, cutting speech of Marion.

"I was never at a loss before," said he, "to manage all other officers that were ever set over me. As for our colonel, (meaning Moultrie) he is a fine, honest, good-natured old buck. But I can wind him round my finger like a pack thread. But as for the stern, keen-eyed Marion, I dread him."

The truth is, Marion wished his officers to be gentlemen. And whenever he saw one of them acting below that character, he would generously attempt his reformation. And few men, perhaps, ever knew better how to manage truants from duty.

To a coarse, conceited chap, like our lieutenant, Marion gave no quarter, but checked him at once, but still in a way that was quite gentlemanly, and calculated to overawe. He kept him at arms' length—took no freedoms with him—nor allowed any—and when visited on business, he would receive and treat him with a formality sufficient to let him see that all was not right.

The effect of such management evinced the correctness of Marion's judgment. The young lieutenant became remarkably polite, and also attentive to duty. In short, no subaltern behaved better. And this very happy change in his manners, was soon succeeded by as pleasing a change in the sentiments of all around him. The officers of the regiment grew fond of him—Marion spoke of him with pleasure, as an excellent soldier—and he of Marion, as his best friend.

This is sufficient to show the truth of the remark made by Aristotle— "that there is no art so difficult and godlike as that of managing men to their own happiness and glory."

CHAPTER IV

The clouds of danger darker and darker—two additional regiments raised—Marion promoted to a majority—fort Moultrie built—A British fleet and army invade Carolina—grand preparations to receive them—admirable patriotism of the Charleston ladies—heavy attack on fort Moultrie—glorious defence of the garrison.

*T*he cloud of war growing still darker and darker every day, the council of safety determined to raise a regiment of artillery, and another of infantry. In consequence of this, several of the officers of the former regiments were promoted. Among these was my friend Marion, who from the rank of captain, was raised to a majority. His field of duties became, of course, much more wide and difficult, but he seemed to come forward to the discharge of them with the familiarity and alertness of one who, as general Moultrie used to say, was born a soldier. In fact, he appeared never so happy, never so completely in his element, as when he had his officers and men out on parade at close training. And for cleanliness of person, neatness of dress, and gentlemanly manners, with celerity and exactness in performing their evolutions, they soon became the admiration and praise both of citizens and soldiers. And indeed I am not afraid to say that Marion was the 'architect' of the second regiment, and laid the foundation of that excellent discipline and confidence in themselves, which gained them such reputation whenever they were brought to face their enemies.

In March, 1776, I was sent over with my company, to Sullivan's island, to prevent the landing of the British from the men-of-war, the Cherokee and Tamar, then lying in Rebellion road. I had not been long on that station, before Col. Moultrie came over with his whole regiment to erect a fort on the island.

The truth is, the governor had of late become confoundedly afraid of a visit from the British. The great wealth in Charleston must, he thought, by this time, have set their honest fingers to itching—and we also suspected that they could hardly be ignorant what a number of poor deluded gentlemen, called tories, we had among us.

The arrival of colonel Moultrie, with the second regiment, afforded me infinite satisfaction. It brought me once more to act in concert with Marion. 'Tis true, he had got one grade above me in the line of preferment; but, thank God, I never minded that. I loved Marion, and "love," as every body knows, "envieth not." We met like brothers. I read in his looks the smiling evidence of his love towards me: and I felt the strongest wish to perpetuate his partiality. Friendship was gay within my heart, and thenceforth all nature without put on her loveliest aspects. The island of sand no longer seemed a dreary waste. Brighter rolled the blue waves of ocean beneath the golden beam; and sweeter murmured the billows on their sandy beach. My heart rejoiced with the playful fishes, as they leaped high wantoning in the air, or, with sudden flounce, returned again, wild darting through their lucid element. Our work went on in joy. The palmetto trees were brought to us by the blacks, in large rafts, of which we constructed, for our fort, an immense pen, two hundred feet long, and sixteen feet wide, filled with sand to stop the shot. For our platforms, we had two-inch oak planks, nailed down with iron spikes. With glad hearts we then got up our carriages and mounted our guns, of which twelve were 18 pounders—twelve 24's, and twelve French 36's, equal to English 42's.

A general joy was spread over the faces of our regiment, as we looked along our battery of thunderers.

But our glorifying, under God, was chiefly in our two and forty pounders. And indeed their appearance was terrible, where they lay with wide Cerberean mouths, hideously gaping over the roaring waves, and threatening destruction to the foes of liberty.

They were soon called to a trial of their metal.—For on the 31st of May, while we were all busily driving on with our fort, suddenly a cry was heard, "a fleet! a fleet, ho!" Looking out to sea, we all at once beheld, as it were, a wilderness of ships, hanging, like snow-white clouds from the northeast sky. It was the sirs Parker and Clinton, hastening on with nine ships of war and thirty transports, bearing three thousand land forces, to attack Charleston.

Such an armament was an awful novelty, that produced on us all a momentary flutter; but, thank God, no serious fear. On the contrary, it was very visible in every glowing cheek and sparkling eye, as we looked, laughing, on one another, that we considered the approaching conflict as a grand trial of courage, which we rather desired than dreaded. And to their equal praise, our gallant countrymen in Charleston, as we learned daily, by the boats, were all in fine spirits, and constantly making their best preparations to receive the enemy. And still my pen trembles in my hand; even after this long lapse of time, it trembles with wonder and delight, to tell of that immortal fire, which in those perilous days, glowed in the bosoms of the Charleston FAIR. Instead of gloomy sadness and tears, for the dark cloud that threatened their city, they wore the most enlivening looks— constantly talked the boldest language of patriotism—animated their husbands, brothers, and lovers to fight bravely—and, for themselves, they vowed they would "never live the slaves of Britain." Some people in our days, may not believe me, when I add of these noble ladies, that they actually begged leave of their commandant, to let them "fight by the sides of their relatives and friends." This, though a glorious request, was absolutely refused them. For who could bear to see the sweet face of beauty roughened over with the hard frowns of war; or, the warrior's musket, on those tender bosoms, formed of heaven only to pillow up the cheeks of happy husbands, and of smiling babes?

But though the spirits of the ladies were willing, their nerves were weak; for when the British ships of war hove in sight, opposite to the town, they all went down to the shore to view them. And then strong fear, like the cold wind of autumn, struck their tender frames with trembling, and bleached their rosy cheeks. Some, indeed, of the younger sort, affected to laugh and boast; but the generality returned silent and pensive, as from a funeral, hanging their lovely heads, like rows of sickly jonquils, when the sun has forsaken the garden, and faded nature mourns his departed beams. Sisters were often seen to turn pale and sigh, when they looked on their youthful brothers, while tender mothers, looking down on their infant cherubs at the breast, let drop their pearly sorrows, and exclaimed, "happy the wombs that bear not, and the paps that give no suck."

In consequence of a most extraordinary continuation of calms, baffling winds, and neap tides, the enemy's ships never got within our bar till the 27th of June, and on the following morn, the memorable 28th, they weighed anchor on the young flood, and before a fine breeze, with top gallant sails, royals, and sky scrapers all drawing, came bearing up for the fort like floating mountains.

The anxious reader must not suppose that we were standing all this while, with finger in mouth, idly gaping like children on a raree show. No, by the Living! but, fast as they neared us, we still kept our thunders close bearing upon them, like infernal pointers at a dead set; and as soon as they were come within point blank shot, we clapped our matches and gave them a tornado of round and double-headed bullets, which made many a poor Englishman's head ache. Nor were they long in our debt, but letting go their anchors and clewing up their sails, which they did in a trice, they opened all their batteries, and broke loose upon us with a roar as if heaven and earth had been coming together.

Such a sudden burst of flame and thunder, could not but make us feel very queer at first, especially as we were young hands, and had never been engaged in such an awful scene before. But a few rounds presently brought us all to rights again, and then, with heads bound up, and stripped to the buff, we plied our bull-dogs like heroes.

The British outnumbered us in men and guns, at least three to one, but then our guns, some of them at least, were much the heaviest, carrying balls of two and forty pounds weight! and when the monsters, crammed to the throat with chained shot and infernal fire, let out, it was with such hideous peals as made both earth and ocean tremble. At one time it appeared as though, by a strange kind of accident, all their broad-sides had struck us at once, which made the fort tremble again. But our palmettoes stood the fire to a miracle, closed up without sign of splinter, on their shot, which was stopped by the intermediate sand; while, on the other hand, every bullet that we fired, went through and through their ships, smashing alike sailors, timber heads, and iron anchors, in their furious course. And thus was the order of our battle—there, a line of seven tall ships; and here, one little, solitary fort—there, British discipline; and here, American enthusiasm—there, brave men fighting for a tyrant; and here, heroes contending for liberty. I am old now, and have forgotten many things, but never shall I forget the heart-burnings of that day, when I heard the blast of those rude cannon, that bade me be a slave; and still my aged bosom swells with the big joy when I hear, which I often do in fancy's ear, the answer of our faithful bull-dogs, as with deafening roar, lurid flame and smoke, they hurled back their iron curses on the wicked claim. But alas! for lack of ammunition, our opening victory was soon nipped like a luckless flower, in the bud: for the contest had hardly lasted an hour, before our powder was so expended that we were obliged, in a great measure, to silence our guns, which was matter of infinite mortification to us, both because of the grief it gave our friends, and the high triumph it afforded our enemies. "Powder! Powder! millions for powder!" was our constant cry. Oh! had we but had plenty of that 'noisy kill-seed', as the Scotchmen call it, not one of those tall ships would ever have revisited Neptune's green dominion. They must inevitably have struck, or laid their vast hulks along-side the fort, as hurdles for the snail-loving 'sheep's heads'. Indeed, small as our stock of ammunition was, we made several of their ships look like sieves, and smell like slaughter pens. The commodore's ship, the Bristol, had fifty men killed, and upwards of one hundred wounded!

The laurels of the second regiment can never fade—the destructive effect of their fire gave glorious proof, that they loaded and levelled their pieces like men who wished every shot to tell. They all fought like veterans; but the behavior of some was gallant beyond compare; and the humble names of Jasper and M'Donald shall be remembered, when those of proud kings shall be forgotten.

A ball from the enemy's ships carried away our flag-staff. Scarcely had the stars of liberty touched the sand, before Jasper flew and snatched them up and kissed them with great enthusiasm. Then having fixed them to the point of his spontoon, he leaped up on the breast-work amidst the storm and fury of the battle, and restored them to their daring station—waving his hat at the same time and huzzaing, "God save liberty and my country for ever!"

As to sergeant M'Donald, while fighting like a hero, at his gun, a cannon ball came in at the port hole, and mangled him miserably. As he was borne off, he lifted his dying eyes, and said to his comrades, "Huzza, my brave fellows, I die, but don't let the cause of liberty die with me."

The effect of our last gun, and which happened to be fired by Marion, is too remarkable to be lost. It was his lot that day to command the left wing of the fort, where many of our heaviest cannon were planted. As from lack of powder, we were obliged to fire very slow, Marion would often level the guns himself. And now comes my story.— Just after sunset the enemy's ships ceased firing, and slipping their cables, began to move off. Pleased with the event, an officer on the quarter deck of the Bristol man-of-war, called out to his comrade, "Well, d—n my eyes, Frank, the play is over! so let's go below and hob nob to a glass of wine, for I am devilish dry!"

"With all my heart, Jack;" replied the other; so down they whipped into the cabin, where the wine and glasses had been standing all day on the table. At that moment, one of our two and forty pounders being just loaded, Marion called to colonel Moultrie, and asked him if it would not be well enough to give them the last blow. "Yes," replied Moultrie, "give them the parting kick."

Marion clapped the match, and away, in thunder and lightning went the ball, which, entering the cabin windows, shattered the two young friends: thence raging through the bulk-heads and steerage, it shivered three sailors on the main deck, and, after all, bursting through the forecastle into the sea, sunk with sullen joy to the bottom.

We got this story from five British seamen, who ran off with the Bristol's long boat, and came and joined us that very night.

The next day, that noble whig, Mr. William Logan, sent us a couple of fat beeves and a hogshead of rum, "to refresh us," as he was pleased to say, "after our hard day's work." And on the second day after the action, the governor and council, with numbers of the great ladies and gentlemen of Charleston, came over to the fort to visit us. We all put on our "best bibs and tuckers," and paraded at the water's edge to receive them, which we did with a spanking 'feu de joie', and were not a little gratified with their attentions and handsome compliments paid us, for what they politely termed "our gallant defence of our country."

And indeed to see the looks of our poor soldiers, when those great ladies, all glittering in silks and jewels, and powdered and perfumed so nice, would come up to them, with faces like angels, sparkling and smiling so sweet, as if they would kiss them; I say, to see the looks of our poor fellows, their awkward bows and broad grins, and other droll capers they cut, no human being could have refrained from laughing.

Presently that excellent lady, Mrs. Colonel Elliot (of the artillery,) came forward and presented us with a most superb pair of colors, embroidered with gold and silver by her own lily-white hands.

They were delivered, if I mistake not, to the brave sergeant Jasper, who smiled when he took them, and vowed he "would never give them up but with his life."

Poor fellow! he too soon made good his promise, near the fatal walls of Savannah.

But it was not the ladies alone that were attentive to us, for that great man, governor Rutledge, in presence of the regiment, took the sword from his side, and with his own noble hand presented it to sergeant Jasper. He also offered him a commission on the spot; but this, Jasper absolutely refused. "I am greatly obliged to you, governor," said he, "but I had rather not have a commission. As I am, I pass very well with such company as a poor sergeant has any right to keep. If I were to get a commission, I should be forced to keep higher company: and then, as I don't know how to read, I should only be throwing myself in a way to be laughed at!" Parents, who can waste on grog and tobacco, that precious money you ought to educate your children with, think of this!

CHAPTER V

Governor Rutledge harangues the Troops—shows Britain's injustice to have been the cause of the American war—independence declared—great joy on that account.

On the 20th of September, 1776, all the troops in Charleston were ordered to rendezvous without the gates of the city, to hear, as we were told, "Some great news." Soon as we were paraded, governor Rutledge ascended a stage, and in the forcible manner of a Demosthenes, informed, that Congress had dissolved all relation with England, by an open Declaration of Independence.

"You are, no doubt, gentlemen," said he, "surprised, and perhaps shocked at this intelligence. But however painful this measure may be to our feelings, it is absolutely necessary to our safety.

"Under the sacred name of 'mother country', England has long been working our ruin. I need not tell you that our fathers were Britons, who for liberty's sake, came and settled in this country, then a howling wilderness. For a long time they ate their bread, not only embittered with sweat, but often stained with blood—their own and the blood of their children, fighting the savages for a dwelling place. At length they prevailed and found a rest. But still their hearts were towards the place of their nativity; and often with tears, did they think and talk of the white-clifted island where their fathers dwelt. Dying, they bequeathed to us the same tender sentiments, which we cherished with a pious care. The name of England was a pleasant sound in our ears—the sight of their ships was always wont to fill our hearts with joy. We hasted to greet the beloved strangers; and hurrying them to our habitations, spread for them our feast, and rejoiced as men do in the society of their dearest friends.

"Oh! had our mother country but treated us with equal affection—as a tender parent, had she but smiled on our valor—encouraged our industry—and thus exalted the horn of our glory, our union and brotherly love would have been eternal; and the impious name of independence had never been heard! But, alas! instead of treating us in this endearing spirit, she cruelly limited our commerce—compelled us to buy and sell to her alone, and at her own prices—and not content with the enormous profits of such a shameful traffic, she has come, at length, to claim a right to tax us at pleasure.

"But, my countrymen, will you suffer thus rudely to be wrested from you, that goodly inheritance of liberty, which was bequeathed to you by your gallant fathers? Will you thus tamely suffer to be frustrated all the glorious designs of God towards you and your children? For look but around on this great land, which he has given you, and yon bright heavens, which he has spread over your favored heads, and say whether he ever intended those mighty scenes to be the prison-house of slaves?—the trembling slaves of a small island beyond the sea?—hewers of wood and drawers of water, planters of rice and pickers of cotton, for a foreign tyrant and his minions? No, my friends, God never intended you for such dishonor—and can you be so wicked as to bring it on yourselves? I trust you will not. Nay, the voices of your brave countrymen in Congress, have said you will not, and anticipating your heroic sentiments, have already declared you a "free and independent people!"

"And now my gallant friends, are you willing to confirm their glorious deed? Are you willing this day, in the sight of heaven, to swear allegiance to the sovereignty of your country, and to place her in the highest rank of nations, by proclaiming her independent?"

In a moment the air resounded with "Yes! yes! independence! independence for ever! God save the independent states of America!"

The oath of allegiance was then tendered to the troops. The officers with great alacrity took it first, which highly pleased the common soldiers, who readily followed their patriotic example. Soon as the solemn rite was performed, the governor ordered a 'feu de joie'. Instantly at the welcome word, "handle arms", the eager warriors struck their fire-locks, loud ringing through all their ranks; and presenting their pieces, rent the air with fierce platoons; while the deep-throated cannon like surly bull-dogs, rolled their louder thunders along the field; then madly bounding back on their rattling wheels, they told to fancy's ear, "Freedom's sons are we, and d—n the villains that would make us slaves!"

CHAPTER VI

Times growing squally—the author sets out a vagrant hunting—
gets into hot water—narrowly escapes with his life—catches a
host of vagabonds, but learns from experience, that, though a
rascal may do to stop a bullet, 'tis only the man of honor that
can make a good soldier.

"*T*he devil," said George Whitefield, "is fond of fishing in muddy
waters"—hence it is, I suppose, that that grand demagogue has always
been so fond of war—that sunshine and basking time of rogues, which
calls them out, thick as May-day sun calls out the rattle-snakes from their
stony crannies.

In times of peace, the waters are clear, so that if the smallest Jack
(villain) but makes his appearance, eagle-eyed justice, with her iron talons,
is down upon him in a moment. But let war but stir up the mud of confusion,
and straightway the eyes of justice are blinded—thieves turn out in shoals:
and devils, like hungry fishing-hawks, are seen by the eye of faith, hovering
over the wretched fry, screaming for their prey.

This was exactly the case in South Carolina. The war had hardly raged
there above a twelvemonth and a day, before the state of society seemed

turned upside down. The sacred plough was every where seen rusting in the weedy furrows—Grog shops and Nanny houses were springing up as thick as hops—at the house of God you saw nobody—but if there was a devil's house (a dram shop) hard by, you might be sure to see that crowded with poor Lazarites, with red noses and black eyes, and the fences all strung along with starved tackies, in grape-vine bridles and sheep-skin saddles. In short, the whole country was fast overrunning with vagabonds, like ravening locusts, seeking where they might light, and whom they should devour.

"Good heavens!" said Marion to me one day, and with great alarm in his looks, "what's to be done with these wretches, these vagrants? I am actually afraid we shall be ruined by them presently. For you know, sir, that a vagrant is but the chrysalis or fly state of the gambler, the horse-thief, the money-coiner, and indeed of every other worthless creature that disturbs and endangers society."

"Why colonel," replied I, "there's a conceit in my head, which, if it could but be brought to bear, would, I think, soon settle the hash with these rascals."

"Aye," replied he, "well, pray give it to us, for I should be very fond to hear it."

"Why sir," said I, "give me but a lieutenant, sergeant, and corporal, with a dozen privates, all of my own choosing, do you see, and if I don't soon give you a good account of those villains, you may, with all my heart, give me a good suit of tar and feathers."

My demand was instantly complied with. Then taking with me such men as I knew I could depend on, among whom was the brave lieutenant Jossilin, I set out from the Long Bluff, towards Sandhills. The reader will please to take notice, that in our hurry we had not forgot to take with us a constable with a proper warrant.

We had gone but a few miles, before we fell in with a squad of as choice game as heart could have wished, three proper tall young vagabonds! profoundly engaged at all fours, in a log tippling shop, with cards as black as their own dirty hands, and a tickler of brandy before them! and so intent were the thieves on fleecing each other, that they took no manner of notice of us, but continued their scoundrel work, eagerly stretched over the table, thwacking down their cards with filthy knuckles, and at every stroke bawling out, "there's a good trick!"

"That's as good as he."

"And there's the best of the three—huzza, d—n me, at him again my hearties."

"Lieutenant Jossilin," said I, "grab them fellows."

You never saw poor devils in such a fright. But soon as they had recovered the use of their tongues, they swore like troopers that they were the "most honestest gentlemen in all Carolina."

"Aye! well, I am very glad to hear that, gentlemen," said I, "for I love honest men prodigiously, and hope the magistrate will confirm the handsome report you have made of yourselves."

So off we set all together for the magistrate. About dinner time I ordered a halt at the house of one Johnson, a militia captain, who appeared quite overwhelmed with joy to see me.

"Heaven bless us!" said he, "and now who could have believed all this? And have I, at last, to my heart's desire, the great honor of seeing under my humble roof the noble major Horry?"

I told him I was much obliged to him, for his politeness—but, for the present, was rather too hungry to relish compliments. "Like sweetmeats, captain," said I, "a little of them may do pretty well after a good dinner."

"Oh, my dear major!" quoth he, "and how sorry I am now that I have nothing fit for dinner for you, my noble son of thunder—a saddle of fat venison, major; or a brace of young ducks; or, a green goose with currant jelly, and a bottle of old Madeira to wash it down, do you see, major! something nice for you, do you see, major!"

"Nice," said I, "captain Johnson! We soldiers of liberty don't stand upon the nice—the substantial is that we care for—a rasher of fat bacon from the coals, with a good stout lump of an ash cake, is nice enough for us."

"Oh, my dear sir!" replied he, "now don't, don't be angry with me; for I was only sorry that I have nothing half so good for you as I could wish, but such as it is, thank God, we have plenty; and you shall have a bite in a trice." So off he went, as he pretended, to hurry dinner.

Now can any honest man believe that this same man, captain Johnson, who had been, as Paddy says, "sticking the blarney into me at that rate," could have been such a scoundrel as to turn about the very next minute, and try all in his power to trick me out of my vagrants. It is, however, too true to be doubted; for having purposely delayed dinner till it was late, he then insisted that I must not deny him the "very great honor of my company that night." Soon as my consent was obtained, he despatched a parcel of riders, to order in, with their guns, as many of his gang as he thought would do. In the course of the night, snug as master Johnson thought himself, I got a hint of his capers, and told my men to see that their guns were in prime order.

While breakfast was getting ready, (for Johnson swore I should not leave him "on an empty stomach,") lieutenant Jossilin came and told me he did not understand the meaning of so many ill-looking fellows coming about the house with their guns in their hands.

I replied that we should see presently.

Breakfast then making its appearance, we sat down, and while we were eating, (our men all on parade at the door) Johnson's men kept dropping in one after another, till there were, I dare say, as many as thirty of them in the room, all armed.

When breakfast was over, I turned to the constable, and desired him to look to his charge, meaning the three vagrants, for that we would start as soon as our men were all refreshed. Upon this captain Johnson said he believed he should not let the prisoners go.

"Not let them go, sir," said I, "what do you mean by that, sir?"

"I mean, sir," replied he, "that the law is an oppressive one."

I asked him, still keeping myself perfectly cool, if he was not an American soldier?

"Yes, sir," he answered, "I am an American soldier; and as good a one, perhaps, as yourself, or any other man."

"Well, sir, and is this the way you show your soldiership, by insulting the law?"

"I am not bound," continued he, "to obey a bad law."

"But, sir, who gave you a right to judge the law?"

"I don't mind that," quoth he, "but d—n me, sir, if I'll let the prisoners go."

"Very well, captain Johnson," said I, "we shall soon try that; and if you and your people here, choose to go to the devil for resisting the law, on your own heads be the bloody consequences."

With this I gave the floor a thundering stamp, and in a moment, as by magic, in bursted my brave sergeant and men, with fixed bayonets, ready for slaughter, while Jossilin and myself, whipping out our swords, rushed on as to the charge.

A troop of red foxes dashing into a poultry yard, never produced such squalling and flying as now took place among these poor guilty wretches—"Lord have mercy upon us," they cried—down fell their guns—smack went the doors and windows—and out of both, heels over head they tumbled, as expecting every moment the points of our bayonets. The house was quickly cleared of every soul except Johnson and his lieutenant, one Lunda, who both trembled like aspen leaves, expecting a severe drubbing.

"Captain Johnson," said I, "don't tremble; you have nothing to fear from me. A man who can act as you have done, is not an object of anger, but contempt. Go! and learn the spirit that becomes a gentleman and an American soldier."

I should have observed, that as we advanced to charge Johnson's poltroons, one of the party, a resolute fellow, presented his gun to my breast and drew the trigger. Happily, in the very instant of its firing, lieutenant Jossilin knocked it up with his sword; and the ball grazing my shoulder, bursted through the side of the house.

As we rode off, some of Johnson's fugitives had the audacity to bawl out, though from a very prudent distance, threatening us that they would yet rescue the prisoners before we got to the bluff. But they wisely took care not to make good their word, for they were only a pack of poor ignorant tories, who did nothing on principle, and were therefore ready to quit their purpose the moment they saw danger in the way.

Our success at vagrant hunting was marvellous. I hardly think we could, in the same time, have caught as many raccoons in any swamp on Pedee. On counting noses, we found, that in our three week's course, we had seized and sent off to Charleston, upwards of fifty. With the last haul, I returned myself to the city, where I received the thanks of general Howe, for "the handsome addition," as he was pleased to term it, "which I had made to the regiment."

But on trial, it was found that such vermin were not worthy of thanks, nor were any addition to the regiment, except as disgust to the men and vexation to the officers. Destitute of honor, they performed their duty, not like soldiers, but slaves; and, on every opportunity, would run off into the woods like wild beasts.

CHAPTER VII

The brave sergeant Jasper again on the carpet—in disguise visits a British post at Ebenezer—in company of sergeant Newton, makes a second trip thither—affecting view of an American lady and her child, with other whig prisoners at Ebenezer—desperate resolve of Jasper and Newton, to rescue them—their bloody conflict and glorious triumph.

*I*n the spring of 1779, Marion and myself were sent with our commands, to Purysburgh, to reinforce general Lincoln, who was there on his way to attack the British in Savannah, which a few months before had fallen into their hands. As the count D'Estang, who was expected to cooperate in this affair, had not yet arrived, general Lincoln thought it advisable to entrench and wait for him.

While we were lying at Purysburgh, a couple of young men of our regiment achieved an act of generosity and courage, which, in former days, would have laid the ground-work of a heroic romance. One of the actors in this extraordinary play was the brave sergeant Jasper, whose name will for ever be dear to the friends of American liberty.

Jasper had a brother who had joined the British, and held the rank of sergeant in their garrison at Ebenezer. Never man was truer to his country than Jasper, yet was his heart so warm that he loved his brother, though a tory, and actually went over to see him. His brother was exceedingly alarmed at sight of him, lest he should be seized and hung up at once as a spy, for his name was well known to many of the British officers. But Jasper begged him not to give himself much trouble on that head, for, said he, "I am no longer an American soldier."

"Well, thank God for that, William," replied his brother, giving him a hearty shake by the hand—"And now only say the word, my boy, and here is a commission for you, with regimentals and gold to boot, to fight for his majesty."

Jasper shook his head and observed, that though there was but little encouragement to fight for his country, yet he could not find in his heart to fight against her. And there the conversation ended.

After staying with his brother some two or three days, inspecting and hearing all that he could, he took his leave, and by a round about, returned to camp, and told general Lincoln all that he had seen.

Having wasted several weeks longer of tiresome idleness, and no news of the French fleet, Jasper took it into his head to make another trip to Ebenezer.

On this occasion he did not, as before, go alone, but took with him his particular friend, sergeant Newton, son of an old Baptist preacher, and a young fellow, for strength and courage, just about a good match for Jasper himself.

He was received as usual, with great cordiality by his brother, to whom he introduced his friend Newton, and spent several days in the British fort, without giving the least alarm. On the morning of the third day his brother had some bad news to tell him.

"Aye! what is it?" he asked, "what is it?"

"Why," replied his brother, "here are some ten or a dozen American prisoners, brought in this morning, as deserters from Savannah, whither they are to be sent immediately. And from what I can learn, it will be apt to go hard with them, for it seems they have all taken the king's bounty."

"Let's see 'em," said Jasper, "let's see 'em."

So his brother took him and Newton to see them. And indeed it was a mournful sight to behold them, where they sat, poor fellows! all hand-cuffed, on the ground. But all pity of them was forgot, soon as the eye was turned to a far more doleful sight hard by, which was a young woman, wife of one of the prisoners, with her child, a sweet little boy of about five years old. The name of this lady was Jones. Her humble garb showed her to be poor, but her deep distress, and sympathy with her unfortunate husband, showed that she was rich in that pure conjugal love, that is more precious than all gold.

She generally sat on the ground opposite to her husband, with her little boy leaning on her lap, and her coal black hair spreading in long neglected tresses on her neck and bosom. And thus in silence she sat, a statue of grief, sometimes with her eyes hard fixed upon the earth, like one lost in thought, sighing and groaning the while as if her heart would burst— then starting, as from a reverie, she would dart her eager eyes, red with weeping, on her husband's face, and there would gaze, with looks so piercing sad, as though she saw him struggling in the halter, herself a widow, and her son an orphan. Straight her frame would begin to shake with the rising agony, and her face to change and swell; then with eyes swimming in tears, she would look around upon us all, for pity and for help, with cries sufficient to melt the heart of a demon. While the child seeing his father's hands fast bound, and his mother weeping, added to the distressing scene, by his artless cries and tears.

The brave are always tender-hearted. It was so with Jasper and Newton, two of the most undaunted spirits that ever lived. They walked out in the neighboring wood. The tear was in the eye of both. Jasper first broke silence. "Newton," said he, "my days have been but few; but I believe their course is nearly done."

"Why so, Jasper?"

"Why, I feel," said he, "that I must rescue these poor prisoners, or die with them; otherwise that woman and her child will haunt me to my grave."

"Well, that is exactly what I feel too," replied Newton—"and here is my hand and heart to stand by you, my brave friend, to the last drop. Thank God, a man can die but once, and there is not so much in this life that a man need be afraid to leave it, especially when he is in the way of his duty."

The two friends then embraced with great cordiality, while each read in the other's countenance, that immortal fire which beams from the eyes of the brave, when resolved to die or conquer in some glorious cause.

Immediately after breakfast, the prisoners were sent on for Savannah, under a guard of a sergeant and corporal with eight men. They had not been gone long, before Jasper, accompanied by his friend Newton, took leave of his brother, and set out on some errand to the upper country. They had scarcely, however, got out of sight of Ebenezer, before they struck into the piny woods, and pushed hard after the prisoners and their guard, whom they closely dogged for several miles, anxiously watching an opportunity to make a blow. But alas! all hopes of that sort seemed utterly extravagant; for what could give two men a chance to contend against ten, especially when there was found no weapon in the hands of the two, while the ten, each man was armed with his loaded musket and bayonet. But unable to give up their countrymen, our heroes still followed on.

About two miles from Savannah there is a famous spring, generally called the 'Spa', well known to travellers, who often turn in hither to quench their thirst. "Perhaps," said Jasper, "the guard may stop there." Then hastening on by a near cut through the woods, they gained the Spa, as their last hope, and there concealed themselves among the bushes that grew abundantly around the spring.

Presently the mournful procession came in sight, headed by the sergeant, who, on coming opposite to the spring, ordered a halt. Hope sprung afresh in our heroes' bosoms, strong throbbing too, no doubt, with great alarms, for "it was a fearful odds." The corporal with his guard of four men, conducted the prisoners to the spring, while the sergeant with the other four, having grounded their arms near the road, brought up the rear. The prisoners, wearied with their long walk, were permitted to rest themselves on the earth. Poor Mrs. Jones, as usual, took her seat opposite to her husband, and her little boy, overcome with fatigue, fell asleep in her lap. Two of the corporal's men were ordered to keep guard, and the other two to give the prisoners drink out of their canteens. These last approached the spring where our heroes lay concealed, and resting their muskets against a pine tree, dipped up water: and having drank themselves, turned away, with replenished canteens, to give the prisoners also. "Now! Newton, is our time!" said Jasper. Then bursting, like two lions, from their concealment, they snatched up the two muskets that were rested against the pine, and in an instant shot down the two soldiers that kept guard. And now the question was, who should first get the two loaded muskets that had just fallen from the hands of the slain. For by this time the sergeant and corporal, a couple of brave Englishmen, recovering from their momentary panic, had sprung and seized upon the muskets; but before they could use them, the strong swift-handed Americans, with clubbed guns, levelled each at the head of his brave antagonist, the final blow. The tender bones of the skull gave way beneath the furious strokes, and with wide scattered blood and brains down they sunk, pale and quivering to the earth without a groan. Then snatching up the guns which had thus, a second time, fallen from the hands of the slain, they flew between the surviving enemy, and ordered them to surrender, which they instantly did.

Having called the prisoners to them, they quickly with the point of their bayonets, broke off their handcuffs, and gave each of them a musket.

At the commencement of the fray, poor Mrs. Jones, half frightened to death, had fallen to the ground in a swoon, with her little son piteously screaming over her. But when she came to herself, and saw her husband and friends around her, all freed from their fetters and well armed, she looked and behaved like one frantic with joy. She sprung to her husband's bosom, and with her arms around his neck, sobbed out, "Oh bless God!

bless God! my husband is safe; my husband is not hung yet;" then snatching up her child, and straining him to her soul, as if she would have pressed him to death, she cried out—"O praise! praise! praise God for ever! my son has a father yet!" Then wildly darting round her eyes in quest of her deliverers, she exclaimed, "Where! where are those blessed angels that God sent to save my husband?"

Directing her eyes to Jasper and Newton, where they stood like two youthful Samsons, in the full flowing of their locks, she ran and fell on her knees before them, and seizing their hands, kissed and pressed them to her bosom, crying out vehemently, "Dear angels! dear angels! God bless you! God Almighty bless you for ever!"

Then instantly, for fear of being overtaken by the enemy, our heroes snatched the arms and regimentals of the slain, and with their friends and captive foes, recrossed the Savannah, and in safety rejoined our army at Purysburgh, to the inexpressible astonishment and joy of us all

CHAPTER VIII

The count D'Estang, with the French fleet, arrives to attack Savannah—our army marches and joins him—fatal effects of D'Estang's politeness—biographical dash of young colonel Laurens—curious dialogue betwixt him and the French general—unsuccessful attack on Savannah—the brave Jasper mortally wounded—is visited by the author in his last moments—interesting conversation—dies like a Christian soldier.

Could the wishes of our army have availed, those gallant soldiers, (Jasper and Newton) would long have lived to enjoy their past, and to win fresh laurels. But alas! the former of them, the heroic Jasper, was soon led, like a young lion, to an evil net. The mournful story of his death, with heavy heart I now relate.

Scarcely had he returned from Georgia, laden, as aforesaid, with glory, when an express came into camp, and informed that the count D'Estang was arrived off Tybee. Instantly we struck our tents and marched for the siege of Savannah. On arriving near that fatal place, we found that the French troops, with their cannon and mortars, had just come up. Oh! had we but advanced at once to the attack, as became skilful soldiers, we should have carried every thing before us. The frighted garrison would have hauled down their colors without firing a shot. This I am warranted to say by the declaration of numbers of their officers, who afterwards fell into our hands. But in place of an immediate 'coup de main,' the courtly D'Estang sent a flag, very politely inviting the town to do him the extreme honor of receiving their surrender.

The British commander was not much behindhand with the count in the article of politeness, for he also returned a flag with his compliments, and requested to be permitted four and twenty hours to think of the matter.

If the asking such a favor was extraordinary, what must the granting of it have been? But the accomplished D'Estang was fully equal to such douceurs for he actually allowed the enemy four and twenty hours to think of surrendering!

But instead of thinking, like simpletons, they fell to entrenching, like brave soldiers. And being joined that very day by colonel Maitland from Beaufort, with a regiment of Highlanders, and assisted by swarms of negroes, decoyed from their masters under promise of freedom, they pushed on their works with great rapidity. According to the report of our troops who were encamped nearest to them, nothing was heard all that night, but the huzzas of the soldiers, the lashes of cow-hides, and the cries of negroes.

I never beheld Marion in so great a passion. I was actually afraid he would have broke out on general Lincoln. "My God!" he exclaimed, "who ever heard of any thing like this before!—first allow an enemy to entrench, and then fight him!! See the destruction brought upon the British at Bunker's Hill! and yet our troops there were only militia! raw, half-armed clodhoppers! and not a mortar, nor carronade, nor even a swivel—but only their ducking guns!

"What then are we to expect from regulars—completely armed with a choice train of artillery, and covered by a breast-work! For my own part, when I look upon my brave fellows around me, it wrings me to the heart, to think how near most of them are to their bloody graves."

In fact, Marion was so outrageous, as indeed were all of us, that we at length begged colonel Laurens to speak to the count D'Estang.

And here I must beg the reader's pardon a moment, while I inform him that this colonel Laurens (son of President Laurens) was a very extraordinary young Carolinian.

On a trip to London, he fell in love with, and married a celebrated belle of that city. It would seem that he was very much taken with his English relations, and they with him, for after his marriage, they would not suffer him to revisit his parents, who doted on him, being their only son, but detained him with them in London, as gay as a young man well could be, in the gayest city in the world, moving every day in the highest circles of society, and every night encircled in the fond arms of a beauteous wife.

But soon as the war against America broke out, his gaiety all forsook him. The idea of a ruffian soldiery overrunning his native land, preyed incessantly on his spirits, and threw him into those brown studies which cost his lady full many a tear. Unable to bear his disquietude, he fled at length from his wife and infant family, to fight for his country. He presented himself before the great Washington, who was so struck with the fire that beamed from his eyes, that he made him handsome offers of rank in the army. But his favorite service was to lead 'forlorn hopes,' and the daring bands that are destined to carry the enemy's works by storm. Washington often gave him letters to this effect to his generals. And this was his object at Savannah, where a regiment of choice infantry was immediately put under his command. But instead of being permitted his favorite pleasure of seeing his ardent warriors mounting the enemy's works, and rushing down streams of fire, followed by the bayonet, he was doomed to fret and pine in the humble office of interpreter between count D'Estang and general Lincoln.

"But, Monsieur le count," said Laurens to D'Estang, "the American officers say they are afraid you have given the English too long time to think."

At this, as Laurens told us afterwards, the count put on a most comic stare, and breaking into a hearty laugh, replied, "De Engleesh think! ha, ha, ha! By gar dat one ver good parole! De Engleesh tink, heh, Monsieur le colonel! By gar, de Engleesh never tink but for deir bellie. Give de Jack Engleeshman plenty beef—plenty pudding—plenty porter, by gar he never tink any more, he lay down, he go a sleep like vun hog."

"But, Monsieur le count," continued Laurens, "the English are doing worse for us than thinking. They are working away like horses, and will soon get their defences too high for us to scale."

"Eh, heh, Monsieur le colonel! you think-a so? Well den, by gar you no need for tink-a so—by gar my French-a-mans run over de fence just like vun tief horse run over de cornfield fence—mind now I tell-a you dat, Monsieur le colonel."

"Well, but Monsieur le count, the British sometimes fight like the d—l."

"Sacre Dieu!" replied the nettled count, starting and gaping as though he would have swallowed a young alligator—"de Briteesh fight like de diable! Jaun foutre de Briteesh! when they been known for fight like de diable? Ess, ess, dat true enough; dey fight de Americans like de diable— but by gar dey no fight de French-a-mans so—no no, by gar dey no make one mouthful for my French-a-mans—Morbleu! my French-a-mans eat dem up like vun leetle grenoulle."

"Green Owl!" exclaimed one of general Lincoln's aids—"Oh my God! who ever heard of a 'green owl' before?"

Here Laurens, smiling at the officer's mistake, replied, "not 'green owl', sir, but 'grenouille', grenouille, sir, is the French for frog."

"Aye, sure enough, sure enough, frog," continued the count, "frog; grenouille is frog. By gar, Monsieur le colonel, you be vun dam good interpret, I set dat well enough. Well den, now, Monsieur le colonel, you hear-a me speak—my French-a-mans eat dem Jack Engleesh all same like vun leetle frog."

"Oh to be sure!—no doubt of all that, Monsieur le count—but before we eat them up, they may kill a great many of our soldiers."

"Dey kill-a de soldier!" replied the passionate count—"well what den if dey do kill-a de soldier! Jaun foutre de soldier! what dey good for but for be kill? dat deir trade. You give-a vun poor dog soldier, two, three, four penny a day, he go fight—he get kill. Well den, what dat? By gar he only get what he hire for."

"But pardon me, Monsieur le count, we can't spare them."

"Vat! no spare de soldier! de grand monarque no spare de soldier? O mon Dieu! Vy, Monsieur le colonel—for why you talk-a so? Well den, hear-a me speak now, Monsieur le colonel—you see de star in de sky; de leaf on de tree; de sand on de shore—you no see all dat, heh? Well den, by gar, Monsieur le colonel, de grand monarque got soldier more an-a all dat— ess, sacra Dieu! more an-a all dat, by gar."

"Well but, Monsieur le count, is it not cruel to kill the poor fellows notwithstanding?"

"Pooh!" replied the count, throwing back his head, and puffing out his cheeks as when a cigar sucker explodes a cataract of smoke from the crater of his throat; "cruel! vat cruel for kill-a de soldier! by gar, Monsieur le colonel, you make-a de king of France laugh he hear-a you talk after dat fashong. Let-a me tell you, Monsieur le colonel, de king of France no like general Washington—by gar, general Washington talk wi' de soldier—he shake hand wi' de soldier—he give de soldier dram—By gar, de grand monarque no do so—no, sacra Dieu! he no look at de soldier. When de king of France ride out in de coach royale wid de supeerb horses, and harness shining so bright all vun like gold, if he run over one soldier, you tink he going stop for dat? No, sacra foutre! he ride on so, all one like if nothing at all been happen. Jaun foutre de soldier! let him prenez garde for himself; by gar the grand Monarque no mind dat. De grand Monarque only tink of de soldier 'commes des chiens', like de poor dam dog for fight for him."

Thus ended the dialogue between colonel Laurens and the count D'Estang.

The next day, the memorable twenty-four hours being expired, a flag was sent into town to know the determination of the British officer, who very politely replied, that having consulted his pillow, he had made up his mind to defend the place. A regular siege was then commenced, and continued for three weeks: at the end of which an attack was made, and with the success which Marion had all along predicted. After a full hour's exposure to the destructive rage of grape shot and musketry, we were obliged to make a precipitate retreat; leaving the ground covered with the mingled carcasses of 400 Americans and 800 Frenchmen. Marion's corps fighting with their usual confidence, suffered great loss; himself did not receive a scratch. Colonel Laurens raged like a wounded lion. Soon as the retreat was ordered he paused, and looking round on his fallen men, cried out, "Poor fellows, I envy you!" then hurling his sword in wrath against the ground, he retired. Presently, after we had reached our encampment, he came to my marquee, and like one greatly disordered, said, "Horry, my life is a burden to me; I would to God I was lying on yonder field at rest with my poor men!"

"No! no! none of that, colonel," said I, "none of that; I trust we shall live to pay them yet for all this."

And so it turned out. And though for humanity's sake, I ought not to boast of it, yet we did live to pay them for it, and often too: and in the same bloody coin which they gave us that day. And although in that fiery season of my days, and when my dear country was in danger, it was but natural for me to rejoice in the downfall of my enemies, yet I was often witness to scenes, which to this day I can never think of but with sorrow—as when, for example, after dashing upon an enemy by surprise, and cutting one half of them to pieces and chasing the rest, we returned to collect the horses and arms of the slain. Who, I say, without grief could behold those sad sights which then offered themselves, of human beings lying mangled over the crimson ground—some stone dead, some still alive and struggling, with brains oozing from their cloven skulls—and others sitting up, or leaning on their elbows, but pale with loss of blood, running in streams from their mortal wounds, and they themselves looking down, the while, sadly thinking of home and of distant wives and children, whom they shall never see again.

Such thoughts, if often cherished, would much abate the rancor of malice in the hearts of those whose sad destiny it is to kill one another; especially if it were known how short sometimes are the triumphs of the victor. It was remarkably so in the present case: for colonel Maitland, of the Highlanders, who had contributed a large part to this very unexpected victory, was so elated by it, that he took to hard drinking, and killed himself in a single week, and the sickly season coming on, the greater part of the garrison perished of the yellow or bilious fever!!

> *Thus friends and foes the same sad fortune shar'd,*
> *And sickness swallowed whom the sword had spar'd.*

Many gallant men were the victims of count D'Estang's folly in this affair; among the number was that impetuous Polander, the count Polaski.

But none fell more universally lamented than the heroic Jasper. Every reader must wish to hear the last of this brave and generous soldier. And they shall have it faithfully, for I happened to be close by him when he received his death's wound; and I was with him when he breathed his last.

Early in the action, the elegant colors presented by Mrs. Elliot, had been planted on the enemy's works; and the fury of the battle raged near the spot where they waved. During the whole of the bloody fray, Jasper had remained unhurt. But on hearing the retreat sounded, he rushed up to bear off his colors, and in that desperate act, was mortally wounded. As he passed by me, with the colors in his hands, I observed he had a bad limp in his walk.

"You are not much hurt, I hope, Jasper," said I. "Yes, major," he replied, "I believe I have got my furlough."

"Pshaw," quoth I, "furlough indeed, for what?"

"Why to go home," he answered, "to go to Heaven, I hope."

"Pooh!" said I, and having, as the reader must suppose, a good deal to attend to, I turned off and left him. However, his words made such an impression on me, that soon as duty permitted, I went to see him, and found too true what he had predicted; the ball had opened a blood vessel in the lungs which no art could stop, and he was bleeding to slow but certain death.

As I entered the tent, he lifted his eyes to me, but their fire was almost quenched; and stretching his feeble hand, he said, with perfect tranquillity, "Well, major, I told you I had got my furlough."

"I hope not," I replied.

"O yes!" said he, "I am going—and very fast too; but, thank God, I am not afraid to go."

I told him I knew he was too brave to fear death, and too honest to be alarmed about its consequences.

"Why, as to that matter, sir," said he, "I won't brag: but I have my hopes, notwithstanding I may be wrong, for I know I am but a poor ignorant body, but somehow or other, I have always built my hopes of what God may do for me hereafter, on what he has done for me here!"

I told him I thought he was very correct in that.

"Do you, indeed?" said he. "Well, I am mighty glad of that—and now major, here's the way I always comfort myself: Fifty years ago, (I say to myself,) I was nothing, and had no thought that there was any such grand and beautiful world as this. But still there was such a world notwithstanding; and here God has brought me into it. Now, can't he, in fifty years more, or indeed in fifty minutes more, bring me into another world, as much above this as this is above that state of nothing, wherein I was fifty years ago?"

I told him that this was, to my mind, a very happy way of reasoning; and such, no doubt, as suited the greatness and goodness of God.

"I think so, major," said he, "and I trust I shall find it so; for though I've been a man of blood, yet, thank God, I've always lived with an eye to that great hope. My mother, major, was a good woman; when I was but a child, and sat on her lap, she used to talk to me of God, and tell how it was he who built this great world, with all its riches and good things: and not for himself, but for me! and also, that if I would but do his will in that only acceptable way, a good life, he would do still greater and better things for me hereafter.

"Well, major, from the mouth of a dear mother, like her, these things went so deep into my heart, that they could never be taken away from me. I have hardly ever gone to bed, or got up again, without saying my prayers. I have honored my father and mother; and, thank God, been strictly honest. And since you have known me, major, I believe you can bear witness, that though a strong man, I never was quarrelsome."

I told him, nothing afforded me more satisfaction, than to remember that, since he was now going to die, he had always led so good a life.

He answered, with tears in his eyes, that he had a good hope he was going where he should not do what he hád been obliged to do in this world. "I've killed men in my time, major, but not in malice, but in what I thought a just war in defence of my country. And as I bore no malice against those I killed, neither do I bear any against those who have killed me. And I heartily trust in God for Christ's sake, that we shall yet, one day, meet together, where we shall forgive and love one another like brothers. I own, indeed, major, that had it so pleased God, I should have been glad to stay a little longer with you to fight for my country. But however, I humbly hope that my death is of God; which makes it welcome to me, and so I bow me to his blessed will. And now, my good friend, as I feel I have but a little time to live, I beg you will do a few things for me when I am dead and gone."

I could not speak; but gathering my answer from my tears, and the close press I gave his hand, he thus went on, but it was in a low voice and laborious.

"You see that sword?—It is the one which governor Rutledge presented to me for my services at Fort Moultrie—give that sword to my father, and tell him I never dishonored it. If he should weep for me, tell him his son died in hope of a better life. If you should see that great gentlewoman, Mrs.

Elliot, tell her I lost my life in saving the colors she gave to our regiment. And if ever you should come across poor Jones and his wife, and little boy, tell them Jasper is gone; but that the remembrance of the hard battle which he once fought for their sakes brought a secret joy to his heart just as it was about to stop its motion for ever."

He spoke these last words in a livelier tone than usual, but it was like the last kindling of the taper in its oil-less socket—for instantly the paleness of death overspread his face, and after a feeble effort to vomit, with convulsions, the natural effect of great loss of blood, he sunk back and expired.

From this victim of D'Estang's madness, I went with a heavy heart on parade, to take a review of the sad remains of the battle. The call of the roll completed the depression of my spirits. To every fourth or fifth name there was no answer—the gloomy silence which ensued, told us where they were. About twelve o'clock we sent in a flag to the garrison for permission to bury our dead. Curiosity led me to accompany the party destined to this mournful duty. I had prepared myself for a sorrowful sight; but ah! what words can express what I then saw and suffered!

A scattered few lay here and there on the utmost verge of the field, killed by cannon shot, and so mangled, that in some instances, it was hard to tell who they were. As we advanced, they lay thicker and thicker. Some, not quite dead, were constantly crying, "Water! water!—Oh! for God's sake, a little water!"—Others lay quite dead, but still their lifeless visages retained the dark frowns of war. There, on the side of the enemy's breast-work, lay the brave ensign Boushe, covering with his dead body, the very spot where he had fixed the American standard. His face was pale and cold as the earth he pressed, but still it spoke the fierce determined air of one whose last sentiment towards those degenerate Britons was, "There d—n you! look at the stripes of liberty."

Close by ensign Boushe, lay that elegant young man, Alexander Hume, Esq. with his sword still grasped in his stiffened fingers. My heart bled within me, when I looked on young Hume, where he lay in all the pale beauties of death. He was to have been married the week following, to a charming woman; but such was his zeal to serve his country, that he came a volunteer to our camp, and met his death the next morning after he joined us. Gifted with a pretty taste for painting, he had tried his skill, and very successfully too, in sketching the likeness of his lovely mistress. For on opening his bosom, was found, suspended by a blue ribband, (the happy lover's color) a fine likeness of the beautiful Miss ——: the back of the portrait was stained with his blood; but unconscious of her lover's fate, she still wore the enchanting smile with which yielding beauty views the youth she loves.

We then proceeded to bury our dead; which was done by digging large pits, sufficient to contain about a hundred corpses. Then taking off their clothes, with heavy hearts, we threw them into the pits, with very little regard to order, and covered them over with earth.

"Poor brothers, farewell! the storm of your last battle has long ago ceased on the field, and no trace now remains on earth that you ever lived. The worms have devoured your flesh; and the mounds raised over your dust, are sunk back to the common level with the plain. But ah! could your mournful story be read, the youth of America would listen to the last words of Washington, and 'study the art of war,' that their countrymen might no more be murdered by military quacks.

As a hint to American officers, I think it my duty to state the following fact:—Our fatal attack on Savannah was made very early in the morning. A few hours previous thereto, a council of war was held; and while it was deliberating, a deserter and spy had the address to bear a musket, as sentinel at the door of the marquee!! On hearing where the attack was to be made, he ran off in the dark, and gave such intelligence to the enemy, as enabled them very completely to defeat us. The fellow was afterwards taken at the battle of Hobkirk Hill, near Camden, and hung.

Scarcely had we finished burying the dead, before the count D'Estang hurried on board his ships with his troops and artillery, while we, passing on in silence by the way of Zubley's ferry, returned to Carolina, and pitched our tents at Sheldon, the country seat of general Bull.

The theatre of war being, from this period, and for some time at least, removed to the northern states, the governor and council were pleased to reduce the regiments, and dismiss the supernumerary officers. To some of my brethren in arms, this was matter of serious alarm. But for myself, possessing, thank God, a liberal fortune in the country, and feeling no attraction to the camp, except when drawn thither by public danger, I was quite happy to hear of this new arrangement, and waited on his excellency to return my commission.

Perhaps some may say it was pride in me, and that I did not like the idea of being 'unfrocked.' Why, as to that matter, it is not for me to boast of my standing among my superiors in those days. But this I must needs say, that it is joy enough, and glory enough too, for me to know, that I was always the favorite of the great Marion; and that he seldom ever asked the lightning of any other sword than mine, to lead his squadron to the charge. However, the moment I heard, as above, that it was in agitation to reduce the regiments, I waited on the governor, and begged that, as there was nothing doing, he would allow me to return to my plantation. To my plantation I did return, and there continued till spring, 1780, when Charleston was taken by the British; at which time, and for some weeks before, I was grievously afflicted with the rheumatism. Thus by a providence, which, I confess, I did not at that time altogether like, I was kindly saved from being kidnapped by the enemy, and also introduced into a field of some little service, I hope, to my country, and of no great dishonor to myself. However, be this as it may, the reader shall soon see, and then let him judge for himself.

CHAPTER IX

Providential escape of Marion out of Charleston—the British
fleet and army invest and take that place—Tarleton and the
British officers begin to let out—young Scotch Macdonald
comes upon the turf—extraordinary anecdote of him—plays a
very curious trick on a rich old tory.

*H*ow happy it is for man, that the author of his being loves him so
much better than he loves himself; and has established so close a connexion
between his duty and his advantage. This delightful truth was remarkably
exemplified in an event that befell Marion about this time, March, 1780.
Dining with a squad of choice whigs, in Charleston, in the house of Mr.
Alexander M'Queen, Tradd street, he was so frequently pressed to bumpers
of old wine, that he found himself in a fair way to get drunk. 'Twas in vain
he attempted to beat a retreat. The company swore, that that would never
do for general Marion. Finding, at last, that there was no other way of
escaping a debauch, but by leaping out of one of the windows of the dining-
room, which was on the second story, he bravely undertook it. It cost him,
however, a broken ankle. When the story got about in Charleston, most
people said he was a great fool for his pains; but the event soon proved that

Marion was in the right, and that there is no policy like sticking to a man's duty. For, behold! presently Charleston was invested by a large British army, and the American general (Lincoln) finding Marion was utterly unfit for duty, advised him to push off in a litter to his seat in St. John's parish. Thus providentially was Marion preserved to his country when Charleston fell, as it soon did, with all our troops.

The spirits of the British were so raised by the capture of our metropolis with all the southern army, that they presently began to scour the neighboring country. And never victors, perhaps, had a country more completely in their power. Their troops were of the choicest kind; excellently equipped, and commanded by active, ambitious young fellows, who looked on themselves as on the high road to fortune among the conquered rebels. They all carried with them pocket maps of South Carolina, on which they were constantly poring like young spendthrifts on their fathers' last testaments. They would also ask a world of questions, such as, "where lay the richest lands?—and the finest situations?—and who were the warmest old fellows, and had the finest girls?" and when answered to their humor, they would break out into hearty laughs; and flourish their swords, and 'whoop' and 'hoic' it away like young fox hunters, just striking on a fresh trail.

Some of them had Dr. Madan's famous book called "Thylipthora, or a Defence of Polygamy," with which they were prodigiously taken, and talked very freely of reducing the system to practice. Cornwallis, it seems, was to be a bashaw of three tails—Rawdon and Tarleton, of two each—and as a natural appendage of such high rank, they were to have their seraglios and harems filled with the greatest beauties of the country.

"Huzza, my brave fellows!"—they would say to each other; "one more campaign and the 'hash' will be settled with the d——d rebels, and then stand by the girls!—stand by the Miss Pinckneys! and Elliots! and Rutledges! and all your bright-eyed, soft bosomed, lovely dames, look sharp! Egad! your charms shall reward our valor! like the grand Turk, we'll have regiments of our own raising! Charleston shall be our Constantinople!

and our Circassia, this sweet Carolina famed for beauties! Prepare the baths, the perfumes, and spices! bring forth the violins and the rose buds! and tap the old Madeira, that our souls may all be joy!"

'Twas in this way they would rant; and then, brightened up to the pitch, they would look and grin on each other as sweetly as young foxes, who, prowling round a farm yard, had suddenly heard the cackling of the rooster pullets. The reader shall presently see the violent and bloody course of these ruffians, who did such dishonor to the glorious island they came from. But before I begin my tragedy, I beg leave, by way of prologue, to entertain him a moment with a very curious farce that was acted on a wealthy old tory, near Monk's Corner, while colonel Tarleton with the British advance, lay there.

The hero of the play was a remarkably stout, red-haired young Scotsman, named Macdonald, son of the Macdonald of famous defeat at Morris Creek Bridge, North Carolina. Soon after the defeat of his father he came and joined our troops. Led by curiosity, I could not help, one day, asking him the reason: to which he made, in substance, the following reply.

"Immediately on the misfortune of my father and his friends at the Great Bridge, I fell to thinking what could be the cause; and then it struck me that it must have been owing to their own monstrous ingratitude. "Here now," said I to myself, "is a parcel of people, meaning my poor father and his friends, who fled from the murderous swords of the English after the massacre at Culloden. Well, they came to America, with hardly any thing but their poverty and mournful looks. But among this friendly people that was enough.—Every eye that saw us, had pity; and every hand was reached out to assist. They received us in their houses as though we had been their own unfortunate brothers. They kindled high their hospitable fires for us, and spread their feasts, and bid us eat and drink and banish our sorrows, for that we were in a land of friends. And so indeed we found it; for, whenever we told of the woeful battle of Culloden, and how the English gave no quarter to our unfortunate countrymen, but butchered all they could overtake, these generous people often gave us their tears, and said,

"O! that we had been there to aid with our rifles, then should many of these monsters have bit the ground." They received us into the bosoms of their peaceful forests, and gave us their lands and their beauteous daughters in marriage, and we became rich. And yet, after all, soon as the English came to America, to murder this innocent people, merely for refusing to be their slaves, then my father and friends, forgetting all that the Americans had done for them, went and joined the British, to assist them to cut the throats of their 'best friends'!

"Now," said I to myself, "if ever there was a time for God to stand up to punish ingratitude, this was the time." And God did stand up: for he enabled the Americans to defeat my father and his friends most completely. But, instead of murdering the prisoners, as the English had done at Culloden, they treated us with their usual generosity. And now these are, "the people I love and will fight for as long as I live." And so he did fight for us, and as undauntedly too as George Washington ever did.

This was young Scotch Macdonald. Now the curious trick which he played, is as follows.

Soon as he heard that colonel Tarleton was encamped at Monk's Corner, he went the next morning to a wealthy old tory of that neighborhood, and passing himself for a sergeant of Colonel Tarleton's corps, presented that officer's compliments, adding that colonel Tarleton was just come to drive the rebels out of the country, and knowing him to be a good friend of the king, begged he would send him one of his best horses for a charger, and that he should be no loser by it.

"Send him one of my finest horses!" cried the old traitor, with eyes sparkling with joy; "Yes, Mr. Sergeant, that I will, by gad! and would send him one of my finest daughters too, had he but said the word. A good friend of the king, did he call me, Mr. Sergeant? yes, God save his sacred majesty, a good friend I am indeed, and a true. And, faith! I am glad too, Mr. Sergeant, that colonel knows it. Send him a charger to drive the rebels, heh? Yes, egad will I send him one, and as proper a one too, as ever a soldier straddled. Dick! Dick! I say you Dick!"

"Here, massa, here! here Dick!"

"Oh, you plaguy dog! so I must always split my throat with bawling, before I can get you to answer heh?"

"High, massa! sure Dick always answer when he hear massa hallo!"

"You do, you villain, do you?—Well then, run! jump! fly, you rascal, fly to the stable, and bring me out Selim, my young Selim! do you hear? you villain, do you hear?"

"Yes, massa, be sure!"

Then turning to Macdonald, he went on: "Well, Mr. Sergeant, you have made me confounded glad this morning, you may depend. And now suppose you take a glass of peach; of good old peach, Mr. Sergeant? do you think it would do you any harm?"

"Why, they say it is good of a rainy morning, sir," replied Macdonald.

"O yes, famous of a rainy morning, Mr. Sergeant! a mighty antifogmatic. It prevents you the ague, Mr. Sergeant; and clears a man's throat of the cobwebs, sir."

"God bless your honor!" said Macdonald, as he turned off a bumper of the high-beaded cordial.

But scarcely had he smacked his lips, before Dick paraded Selim; a proud, full-blooded, stately steed, that stepped as though he disdained the earth he walked upon.

Here the old fellow brightening up, broke out again: "Aye! there, Mr. Sergeant, there is a horse for you! isn't he, my boy?"

"Faith, a noble animal, sir," replied Macdonald.

"Yes, egad! a noble animal indeed!—a charger for a king, Mr. Sergeant!—Well, my compliments to colonel Tarleton: tell him I've sent him a horse, my young Selim, my grand Turk, do you hear, my son of thunder? And say to the colonel that I don't grudge him neither, for egad! he's too noble for me, Mr. Sergeant. I've no work that's fit for him, sir; no! damme, sir, if there's any work in all this country that's good enough for him, but just that which he is now going on; the driving the d——d rebels out of the land."

And in order to send Selim off in high style, he ordered Dick to bring down his elegant new saddle and holsters, with his silver-mounted pistols. Then giving Macdonald a hot breakfast, and lending him his great coat, as it was raining, he let him go, with a promise that he would come next morning and see how colonel Tarleton liked young Selim.

Accordingly next morning he waited on colonel Tarleton, and told his name, with the smiling countenance of one who expected to be eaten up with fondness. But alas! to his infinite mortification, Tarleton heard his name without the least change of feature.

After recovering a little from his embarrassment, he asked colonel Tarleton how he liked his charger.

"Charger, sir!" replied Tarleton.

"Yes, sir, the elegant horse I sent you yesterday."

"The elegant horse you sent me, sir!"

"Yes, sir, and by your sergeant, sir, as he called himself."

"An elegant horse! and by my sergeant! Why really, sir, I-I-I don't understand all this!"

The looks and voice of colonel Tarleton too sadly convinced the old traitor that he had been 'bit'; and that young Selim was gone! then trembling and pale, cried out, "Why, my dear good sir, did you not send a sergeant yesterday with your compliments to me, and a request that I would send you my very best horse for a charger, which I did?"

"No, sir, never!" replied Tarleton: "I never sent a sergeant on any such errand. Nor till this moment did I ever know that there existed on earth such a being as you."

To have been outwitted in this manner by a rebel sergeant—to have lost his peach brandy—his hot breakfast—his great coat—his new saddle—his silver mounted pistols—and worse than all, his darling horse, his young, full-blooded, bounding Selim—all these keen reflections, like so many forked lightnings, falling at once on the train and tinder of his passions, blew them up to such a diabolical rage that the old sinner had like to have been suffocated on the spot. He turned black in the face; he shook throughout; and as soon as he could recover breath and power of speech, he broke out into a torrent of curses, enough to raise the hair on any Christian man's head.

Nor was colonel Tarleton much behind him, when he came to learn what a noble horse had slipped through his hands. And a noble horse he was indeed! Full sixteen hands high; the eye of a hawk, the spirit of the king eagle; a chest like a lion; swifter than a roebuck, and strong as a buffalo.

I asked Macdonald, how he could reconcile it to himself to take the old poltroon's horse in that way?

"Why, sir," replied he, "as to that matter, people will think differently; but for my part I hold that all is fair in war: and, besides, sir, if I had not taken him colonel Tarleton, no doubt, would have got him. And then, with such a swift strong charger as this, he might do us as much harm as I hope to do to them."

And he did do them harm with a vengeance; for he had no more sense of fear than a hungry tiger. And, as to his strength, it was such, that with one of Potter's blades he would make no more to drive through cap and skull of a British dragoon, than a boy would, with a case-knife, to chip off the head of a carrot. And then, he always kept Selim up so lustily to the top of his metal. He was so fond of him, that I verily believe he would at any time have sold the shirt off his back to get corn for him. And truly Selim was not much his debtor; for, at the first flash and glimpse of a red coat, he would paw and champ his iron bit with rage; and the moment he heard the word "go," off he was among them like a thunderbolt.

And to see how Macdonald would charge, you would swear the fear of death was never before his eyes. Whether it was one or ten against him, it made no odds to this gallant Scotsman. He never stopped to count noses, but would dash in upon the thickest of them, and fall to hewing and cutting down like a very fury incarnate.

Poor Macdonald! the arm of his strength is now in dust; and his large red cheeks have, long ago been food for worms: but never shall I forget when first I saw him fight. 'Twas in the days when the British held

Georgetown; and Marion had said to me, "Go and reconnoitre." I took only Macdonald with me. Before day we reached our place of concealment, a thick clump of pines near the road, and in full view of the enemy's lines. Soon as the bonny grey-eyed morning began to peep, we heard the town all alive, as it were, with drums and fifes; and about sunrise, beheld five dragoons turn out, and with prancing steeds dash up the road towards us. I turned my eye on Macdonald, and saw his face all kindled up with the joy of battle. It was like that terrible joy which flashes from the eyes of an ambushed lion, when he beholds the coming forth of the buffaloes towards his gloomy cave. "Zounds, Macdonald," said I, "here's an odds against us, five to two." "By my soul now captain," he replied, "and let 'em come on. Three are welcome to the sword of Macdonald."

Soon as they were come fairly opposite to us, we gave them a blast from our bugles, and with drawn sabres broke in upon them like a tornado.

Their panic was complete; two we stopped, overthrown and weltering in the road. The remaining three wheeled about, and taking to their heels, went off as if old Nick had been bringing up the rear. Then you might have heard the roar, and seen the dust, which dragoons can raise, when, with whip and spur and wildly rolling eyes, they bend forward from the pursuit of death. My charger being but a heavy brute, was soon distanced. But they could not distance the swift-footed Selim. Rapid as the deadly blast of the desert, he pursued their dusty course, still gathering upon them at every jump. And before they could reach the town, though so near, he brought his furious rider alongside of two of them, whom he cut down. One hundred yards further, and the third also would have been slain; for Macdonald, with his crimson claymore, was within a few steps of him, when the guns of the fort compelled him to retire. However, though quickly pursued by the enemy, he had the address to bring off an elegant horse of one of the dragoons whom he had killed.

CHAPTER X

The abomination and desolation set up in South Carolina—
the author, with sorrowful heart, quits his native land, and flies
to the north in quest of warlike friends—fortunate rencontre
with his gallant friend colonel Marion—curious adventures.

*A*fter the capture of Charleston, with all our troops, the British, as
aforesaid, began to spread themselves over the country. Then was exhibited
a spectacle, which for sadness and alarm, ought never to be forgotten by
the people of America. I mean how easy a thing it is for a small body of
soldiers to overrun a populous and powerful country. The British did not,
after Sir Henry Clinton's return to New York, exceed three thousand men;
and South Carolina alone, at the lowest computation, must have contained
fifty thousand! and yet this host of poor honest men were made to tremble
before that handful of ruffians, as a flock of sheep before the wolf, or a
household of little children before a dark frowning pedagogue. The reason
is immensely plain. The British were all embodied and firm as a rock of
granite; the Carolinians were scattered over the country loose as a rope of
sand: the British all well armed and disciplined, moved in dreadful harmony,

giving their fire like a volcano; the Carolinians, with no other than birding pieces, and strangers to the art of war, were comparatively feeble, as a forest of glow-worms: the British, though but units in number, were so artfully arranged that they told for myriads; while, for lack of unity, the Carolinians, though numerous as myriads, passed only for ciphers. In short, the British were a handful of hawks; the poor Carolinians a swarm of rice-birds, and rather than be plucked to the pin feather, or picked to the bone, they and their little ones, they were fain to flatter those furious falcons, and oft times to chirp and sing when they were much in the humor to hate and curse.

Oh! blind indeed, and doubly blind is that people, and well worthy of iron yokes, who, enjoying all the sweets of liberty, in a land of milk and honey, can expose to foreign Philistines, that blessed Canaan, unguarded by Military science. Surely those who thus throw "their pearl before swine," richly deserve that the beast should turn again and trample them, and their treasures too, into the mire. Yes, and had it not been for a better watch than our own, at this day, like the wretched Irish, we should have been trampled into the mire of slavery; groaning under heavy burdens to enrich our task-masters; and doomed on every fruitless attempt at freedom, to fatten the buzzards with our gibbeted carcasses.

For lack of this habitual military preparation on our part, in a few days after the fall of Charleston, Col. Tarleton, with only one hundred and fifty horse, galloped up to Georgetown, through the most populous part of the state, with as much hauteur as an overseer and his boys would gallop through a negro plantation! To me this was the signal for clearing out. Accordingly, though still in much pain from the rheumatism, I mounted my horse, and with sword and pistol by my side, set out for the northward, in quest of friendly powers to aid our fallen cause. In passing through Georgetown, I saw a distant group of people, to whom I rode up, and with great civility, as I thought, asked the news. To which a young fellow very scornfully replied, that "Colonel Tarleton was coming, and that the country, thank God, would soon be cleared of the continental colonels."

I was within an ace of drawing a pistol and shooting the young slave dead upon the spot. But God was pleased to give me patience to bear up under that heavy cross; for which I have since very heartily thanked him a thousand times and more. And indeed, on thinking over the matter, it has often struck me, that the man who could speak in that way to one who had on, as he saw, the American uniform, must be a savage, and therefore not an object of anger, but of pity. But though my anger was soon over, nothing could cure the melancholy into which this affair threw me. To see my native country thus prostrate under foreign usurpers, the generality quite disheartened, and the few, who dared to take her part, thus publicly insulted, was a shock I was not prepared for, and which, therefore, sunk my spirits to the lowest ebb of despondence. Such was the frame of mind wherein I left my native state, and set out, sick and alone, for the northward, with scarce a hope of ever seeing better days. About the middle of the second day, as I beat my solitary road, slowly winding through the silent, gloomy woods of North Carolina, I discovered, just before me, a stranger and his servant. Instantly my heart sprang afresh for the pleasures of society, and quickening my pace, I soon overtook the gentleman, when lo! who should it be but the man first of all in my wishes, though the last in my expectations; who, I say, should it be but Marion! Our mutual surprise was great. "Good heavens!" we both exclaimed in the same moment, "Is that colonel Marion?" "Is that Horry?" After the first transports of that joy, which those who have been long absent from dear friends, can better conceive than I describe, we began to inquire into each other's destinations, which was found to be the same; both flying to the north for troops to fight the British. We had not rode far when Marion, after looking up to the sun, who was now past his half-way house, came suddenly to a halt, and said, "Well, come Horry, I feel both peckish and weary, and here is a fine shade, so let us go down and rest, and refresh ourselves a while."

Whereupon I dismounted; and with the help of his servant, for his ankle was yet very crazy, got him down too. Then, sitting side by side, on the trunk of a fallen pine, we talked over the mournful state of our country;

and came at last, as we had always done, to this solemn conclusion, that we would stand by her like true children, and either conquer or die with her.

After this, a piece of dried beef was paraded, from Marion's saddle-bags, with a loaf of Indian bread and a bottle of brandy. The wealthy reader may smile at this bill of fare; but to me it was a feast indeed. For joy, like a cordial, had so raised my spirits, and reinvigorated my system, that I fed like a thresher.

I shall never forget an expression which Marion let fall during our repast, and which, as things have turned out, clearly shows what an intimate acquaintance he had with human nature. I happened to say that I was afraid "our happy days were all gone."

"Pshaw, Horry," he replied, "don't give way to such idle fears. Our happy days are not all gone. On the contrary, the victory is still sure. The enemy, it is true, have all the trumps in their hands, and if they had but the spirit to play a generous game, would certainly ruin us. But they have no idea of that game; but will treat the people cruelly. And that one thing will ruin them, and save America."

"I pray God," said I, "it may be so."

"Well, don't be afraid," replied he, "you will assuredly see it."

Having despatched our simple dinner, we mounted again and pursued our journey, but with feelings so different from what I had before this meeting, as made me more sensible than ever what a divine thing friendship is. And well indeed it was for us that our hearts were so rich in friendship, for our pockets were as bare of gold and silver as if there were no such metals on earth. And but for carrying a knife, or a horse-fleam, or a gun-flint, we had no more use for a pocket than a Highlander has for a knee-buckle. As to hard money, we had not seen a dollar for years; and of old continental, bad as it was, we had received but little, and that little was gone away like a flash; as the reader may well suppose, when he comes to learn, that a bottle of rum would sweep fifty dollars.

And so here were two continental colonels of us, just started on a journey of several hundred miles, without a cent in pocket! But though poor in gold, we were rich in faith. Burning patriots ourselves, we had counted on it as a certainty, that every body we met, out of reach of the British, were as fiery as we, and that the first sight of our uniforms would command smiling countenances, and hot suppers, and downy beds, and mint slings; and in short, everything that our hearts could wish. But, alas and alack the mistake! For instead of being smiled on every where along the road as the champions of liberty, we were often grinned at as if we had been horse thieves. In place of being hailed with benedictions, we were frequently in danger from the brick bats; and in lieu of hot dinners and suppers, we were actually on the point of starving, both we and our horses! For in consequence of candidly telling the publicans that, "we had nothing to pay," they as candidly declared, "they had nothing to give," and that "those that had no money had no business to travel." At length we came to the resolution to say nothing about our poverty, but, after getting such things as we wanted, to give our 'due bills.' In this we felt ourselves perfectly warranted; for we had, both of us, thank God, very sufficient estates; and besides, turning out, as we did, to fight for our country, we thought we had, even by sacred precept, a very fair claim on that country for a little food.

I remember, one evening, after dark, we reached a tavern, the owner of which at first seemed very fond of accommodating us. But as soon as a lighted wood torch had given him a glimpse of our regimentals, the rogue began to hem and ha, to tell us of a 'mighty fine tavern' about five miles further on.

We begged him to recollect that it was night, and also very rainy, and as dark as pitch.

"Oh!" quoth he, "the road is mighty plain; you can't miss your way."

"But consider, sir, we are strangers."

"Oh! I never liked strangers in all my life."

"But, sir, we are your countrymen, American officers, going to the north for men to fight your battles."

"Oh! I wants nobody to fight my battles; king George is good enough for me."

"But, sir, we have travelled all day long without a mouthful for ourselves or horses."

To this also the brute was preparing some fit answer, when his wife, who appeared to be a very genteel woman, with a couple of charming girls, her daughters, ran out and declared that "take us in he could, and should, that he should; and that he might as well consent at first, for they would not be said nay."

Even against all this, he stood out for some time; till at length his wife reminded him, that though the British were carrying every thing before them in South Carolina, yet that Washington was still in the field, and the issue of the war unknown; and that at any rate it was good to have a friend at court.

On this he came to a pause; and at length reluctantly drawled out, "Well—I suppose—you must—come—in."

I have related this story, partly to show what a savage man would be without that softening, polishing friend, a good wife.

Observing that we were wet and cold, this amiable woman and her daughters soon had kindled up for us a fine sparkling fire, to which their own sweetly smiling looks gave tenfold cheerfulness and comfort. And while the husband went poking about the house, silent and surly as an ill-natured slave, the ladies displayed towards us the most endearing attentions. The mother brought out from her closet a bottle of nice family cordial, to warm and cheer us; while the girls presented basins of water and towels, that we might wash and refresh ourselves after our fatigue. And all these seasonable hospitalities they did, not with that ungracious silence and reserve, which so often depress the traveller's spirits, but with the charming alacrity of daughters or sisters, so sweetening every thing with smiles and sprightly chat as almost made us feel ourselves at home.

As with deep struck thought, I compared our present happy condition with that a few minutes before, benighted, wet and weary, I could not help exclaiming, "O my God! what pity it is that among so many labors which poor mortals take under the sun, they do not labor more for that which alone deserves their care. I mean that love, which at once diffuses and enjoys all the happiness both of earth and heaven."

At supper, the poor creature of a husband strove very hard to draw Marion into a dispute, about what he was pleased to call our "rebellion." I expected to have heard him lashed very severely for such brutality; for few men ever excelled Marion in the 'retort abrupt.' But every time the subject was introduced, he contrived very handsomely to waive it, by some pretty turn to the ladies, which happily relieved their terrors, and gave a fresh spring to general and sprightly conversation.

As our excellent hostess and her fair daughters were about to retire, we bade them good night, and also adieu, telling them that we meant to ride very early in the morning. To this they stoutly objected, urging that, from our fatigue and fasting, we ought to pass a day or two with them, and refresh ourselves. But if we could not do this, we must at any rate stay and give them the pleasure of our company at breakfast.

When we retired to our chamber, I asked Marion why he had not given that brute, our landlord, a proper set down.

"I am surprised at you, Horry," he replied; "when you see that your fellow man is wretched, can't you give him quarter? You must have observed, ever since we darkened his door, that with spleen and toryism, this poor gentleman is in the condition of him in the parable, who was possessed of seven devils. Since we have not the power to cast them out, let us not torment him before his time. Besides, this excellent woman his wife; these charming girls his daughters. They love him, no doubt, and therefore, to us, at least, he ought to be sacred, because surrounded by their affections."

The next morning while breakfast was preparing, the churl renewed his hostilities, by telling us, with a malignant pleasure in his face, that he and his neighbors were making ready to go to South Carolina for negroes.

"For negroes!" replied Marion; "pray sir, what do you mean by that?"

"Why, sir," returned he, "South Carolina is now all one as conquered by the British, and why may we not go and pick up what negroes we can? They would help me in my corn-field yonder."

Marion asked him whether, if he were to find his negroes, he would think it right to take them?

"To be sure I would," answered he. "You great men who choose to fight against your king, are all now running away. And why may I not go and catch your negroes as well as any body else?"

"My God!" replied Marion, with a deep sigh, "what will this world come to?" and turned the conversation.

Soon as breakfast was over, we took leave of this most unequally yoked couple and their lovely daughters, and continued our journey. We had not got far from the house when Marion's servant rode up, and, with a very smirking face, told his master that he believed the gentlewoman where we stayed last night must be a monstrous fine lady! Marion asked him why he thought so. "Why, sir," replied he, "she not only made me almost burst myself with eating and drinking, and all of the very best, but she has gone and filled my portmanteau too, filled it up chock full, sir! A fine ham of bacon, sir, and a pair of roasted fowls, with two bottles of brandy, and a matter of a peck of biscuit."

"God bless the dear lady!" we both exclaimed at the same moment. And I trust God did bless her. For indeed to us she was a kind angel, who not only refreshed our bodies, but still more, feasted our souls.

And though eight and twenty long years have rolled away since that time, I can still see that angel smile which brightened on her face towards us, and the memory of which springs a joy in my heart beyond what the memory of his money bags ever gave to the miser.

On the evening of the same day that we left this charming family, (I mean the fairer part of it) we reached the house of colonel Thatcher, one of the noblest whigs in North Carolina. His eyes seemed as though they would never tire in gazing on our regimentals. We soon gave him the history of our travels through his native state, and of the very uncivil manner in which his countrymen had treated us. He smiled, and bid us be thankful, for that it was entirely of God's mercy that we had come off so well. "Those people," continued he, "are mere Hottentots; a set of unenlightened miserable tories, who know nothing of the grounds of the war; nothing of the rights and blessings we are contending for; nor of the corruptions and cruelties of the British ministry; and are therefore just as ready to fall into their destructive jaws, as young cat-birds are to run into the mouth of a rattle-snake."

CHAPTER XI

Glorious news—a brave army of continentals coming up—
Marion and the author hasten to meet them at Roanoke—
fortunately get introduced to the baron de Kalb—polite
reception by that amiable officer—curious and interesting
conversation.

After spending two days of very welcome repose with the elegant
colonel Thatcher, we took leave and set out for Hillsborough, where we
met general Huger and colonel W. White, of the horse, who told us the
glorious news, that "Washington had sent on a gallant detachment of
continentals, who were now in full march to aid South Carolina."

Our hearts leaped for joy at the news. So great was our impatience to
see what our hearts had so long and so fondly dwelt on, an army of friends,
that we could not wait until they came up, but hurried off instantly to
meet them at Roanoke, where it was said they were crossing. On reaching
the river, we found that they had all got over, and had just formed their
line of march. Oh! how lovely is the sight of friends in the day of our
danger! We have had many military corps, but none had ever interested us

like this. In shining regimentals and glittering arms, they moved before the eye of the glowing fancy like a host of heroes.

Thrice happy for man, that a veil, dark as the grave, is thrown over future events! For how could we, who had seen one fine army butchered at Savannah, and another captured at Charleston, have borne up under the dreadful prospect of having this gallant armament also destroyed in a few days!

Soon as our first paroxysm of joy had a little subsided, we moved toward head quarters, where we had the good fortune to fall in with our old friend Col. Semp, who appeared overjoyed to see us, and immediately offered to introduce us to the general. His excellency Horatio Gates was the commander in chief, but as he had not yet arrived, the command rested on that brave old German general, the baron de Kalb.

It was to this officer that colonel Semp introduced us, and, as was usual with him, in very flattering terms; styling us "continental colonels, and two of the wealthiest and most distinguished patriots of South Carolina!"

I shall never forget what I felt when introduced to this gentleman. He appeared to be rather elderly. But though the snow of winter was on his locks, his cheeks were still reddened over with the bloom of spring. His person was large and manly, above the common size, with great nerve and activity; while his fine blue eyes expressed the mild radiance of intelligence and goodness.

He received us very politely, saying he was glad to see us, "especially as we were the first Carolinians that he had seen; which had not a little surprised him."

Observing, I suppose, that we labored under rather too much of our national weakness, I mean modesty, he kindly redoubled his attentions to us, and soon succeeded in curing us of our reserve.

"I thought," said he, "that British tyranny would have sent great numbers of the South Carolinians to join our arms. But, so far from it, they are all, as we have been told, running to take British protections. Surely they are not tired already of fighting for liberty."

We told him the reason was very plain to us, who were inhabitants of that country, and knew very well the state of things there.

"Aye," replied he, "well, what can the reason be?"

"Why, sir," answered Marion, "the people of Carolina form but two classes, the rich and the poor. The poor are generally very poor, because, not being necessary to the rich, who have slaves to do all their work, they get no employment from them. Being thus unsupported by the rich, they continue poor and low spirited. They seldom get money; and indeed, what little they do get, is laid out in brandy to raise their spirits, and not on books and newspapers to get information. Hence they know nothing of the comparative blessings of their own country, nor of the great dangers which threaten it, and therefore care nothing about it. As to the other class, the rich, they are generally very rich, and consequently afraid to stir, unless a fair chance offer, lest the British should burn their houses and furniture, and carry off their negroes and stock. But permit me to assure you, sir, that though thus kept under by fear, they still mortally hate the British, and will, I am confident, the moment they see an army of friends at their door, fly to their standard, like a generous pack to the sound of the horn that calls them to the chase of a hated wolf."

The baron de Kalb smiled, and said he hoped it would be found so.

"No doubt of it at all sir," replied Marion.

The baron then invited us to dine with him, but added, smiling, that he hoped we had good military stomachs that could relish and digest plain fare, which was all he could promise us, and perhaps hardly enough of that.

On sitting down to table, we found that his prediction about the bill of fare, was most unwelcomely true. Our dinner was just half a side of a miserably poor hog, as miserably cooked; and in such small quantity, that before we were done there was nothing of it left but a rasher, for good manners' sake. And as to bread, there was not even a hoe-cake! It is true, that, by way of substitute, we had a trencher or two of sweet potatoes paraded. Our drink was admirably suited to the dinner; apple brandy with river water.

God forbid that I should be unmindful of his favors! For well do I know that the least of them is much better than the best of us deserve. On the contrary, I mention it rather as a compliment to his heavenly bounty, which is wont to spread our tables with so many dainties, as to cause even roast pigs and sweet potatoes to pass for a sorry meal.

Soon as dinner was over, all of us who could parade a cigar or a pipe, began to comfort our olfactories with a puff, not forgetting our brandy the while, so that by the time we had got well entrenched in clouds of fragrant kite-foot, we were in admirable cue for a dish of chat. De Kalb led the way; and, as nearly as I can recollect, in the following words.

"Colonel Marion," said he, pressing the tobacco in his pipe at the same time, "can you answer me one question?"

"Most gladly, general, and a thousand if I can!"

"Thank you, colonel, but one will do."

"Be pleased then, sir, to say on."

"Well, colonel, can you tell me how old I am?"

"That's a tough question, general."

"Tough, colonel! pray how do you make that out?"

"Why, sir, there is a strange January and May sort of contrast between your locks and your looks that quite confuses me. By your locks you seem to be in the winter, by your looks in the summer of your days."

"Well but, colonel, striking the balance between the two, whereabouts do you take me to be?"

"Why, sir, in the spring and prime of life; about forty."

"Good heavens, forty!"

"Yes, sir, that's the mark; there or thereabouts."

"What! no more?"

"No, sir, not a day more; not an hour."

"Upon honor?"

"Yes, sir, upon honor; upon a soldier's honor."

"Ha!—ha!—ha!—Well, colonel, I would not for a thousand guineas that your riflemen shot as wide off the mark as you guess. The British would not dread them as they do. Forty years old, indeed! why what will you say, colonel, when I tell you that I have been two and forty years a soldier."

Here we all exclaimed, "Impossible, general! impossible."

"I ask your pardon, gentlemen," replied he, "it is not at all impossible, but very certain. Very certain that I have been two and forty years a soldier in the service of the king of France!"

"O wonderful! two and forty years! Well then, at that rate, and pray how old, general, may you take yourself to be?"

"Why, gentlemen," replied he, "man and boy, I am now about sixty-three."

"Good heaven! sixty-three! and yet such bloom, such flesh and blood!"

"If you are so surprised, gentlemen, at my looks at sixty-three, what would you have thought had you seen my father at eighty-seven."

"Your father, general! he cannot be alive yet, sure."

"Alive! yes, thank God, and alive like to be, I hope, for many a good year to come yet. Now, gentlemen, let me tell you a little story of my father. The very Christmas before I sailed for America, I went to see him. It was three hundred miles, at least, from Paris. On arriving at the house I found my dear old mother at her wheel, in her eighty-third year, mind gentlemen!! spinning very gaily, while one of her great-granddaughters carded the wool and sung a hymn for her. Soon as the first transport of meeting was over, I eagerly asked for my father. 'Do not be uneasy, my son,' said she, 'your father is only gone to the woods with his three little great-grandchildren, to cut some fuel for the fire, and they will all be here presently, I'll be bound!' And so it proved; for in a very short time I heard them coming along. My father was the foremost, with his axe under his arm, and a stout billet on his shoulder; and the children, each with his little load, staggering along, and prattling to my father with all their might. Be assured, gentlemen, that this was a most delicious moment to me. Thus after a long absence, to meet a beloved father, not only alive, but in health and dear domestic happiness above the lot of kings: also to see the two extremes of human life, youth and age, thus sweetly meeting and mingling in that cordial love, which turns the cottage into a paradise."

In telling this little story of his aged father and his young relatives, the general's fine countenance caught an animation which perfectly charmed us all.

The eyes of Marion sparkled with pleasure. "General," said he, "the picture which you have given us of your father, and his little great-grandchildren, though short, is extremely interesting and delightful. It confirms me in an opinion which I have long entertained, which is, that there is more happiness in low life than in high life; in a cottage than in a castle. Pray give us, general, your opinion of that matter."

"Why," replied De Kalb, "this opinion of yours, colonel, is not a novel one by any means. It was the opinion of Rousseau, Fenelon, and of many other great men, and elegant writers. But notwithstanding such high authority, I must still beg leave to be a dissenter. I have seen so many people happy and also unhappy, both in cottages and castles, that I cannot but conclude, that happiness does not belong, peculiarly, to either condition, but depends on something very different from, and infinitely superior to both."

We eagerly asked what he alluded to.

"Why, gentlemen," replied he, "since you have been so polite as to ask my opinion, I will as frankly give it, though I am afraid it will seem very odd, especially coming from a soldier. However, be that as it may, my opinion you have asked, and my opinion you shall have; which is, that religion is the only thing to make a man happy in cottages or courts."

The young officers began to stare. Gathering from their looks, that some of the company did not relish this kind of philosophy, he quickly thus resumed his speech.

"Pardon! gentlemen, I beg pardon! I must not be misunderstood. By 'religion,' I don't mean 'priest-craft.' I don't mean that superstitious grimace; that rolling up of white eyes, and spreading of sanctified palms; with 'disfigured faces and long prayers,' and all the rest of that holy trumpery, which, so far from making people cheerful, tends but to throw them into the dumps. But I mean, by 'religion,' that divine effort of the soul, which rises and embraces the great author of its being with filial ardor, and walks and converses with him, as a dutiful child with his revered father. Now gentlemen, I would ask, all prejudice apart, what is there can so exalt the mind and gladden the heart, as this high friendship with heaven, and those immortal hopes that spring from religion?"

Here one of the company, half blushing, as palpably convicted by the truth of the general's argument smartly called out—"Well but, general, don't you think we can do pretty well here in camp, without religion?"

"What!" replied De Kalb, "would you give it all up to the priests?"

"Yes, to be sure I would," said the young officer, "for I am for every man's following his own trade, general. They are priests, and we are soldiers. So let them do all the praying, and we will do all the fighting."

"Why, as to the fighting part," rejoined De Kalb, "I have no objection to doing all that for the priests, especially as their profession does not allow them to fight for themselves. But as to giving them up all the devotion, I confess I am not so liberal. No! no! gentlemen, charity begins at home; and I am not for parting with pleasure so easily."

"Pleasure!" replied the young officer with a sneer.

"Yes, sir, pleasure," returned De Kalb. "According to my creed, sir, piety and pleasure are synonymous terms; and I should just as soon think of living physically, without bread, as of living pleasantly, without religion. For what is religion, as I said before, but habitual friendship with god? And what can the heart conceive so delightful? Or what can so gratify it in all its best and strongest desires. For example, gentlemen, we are all fond of honor. I, for my part, am fond of the friendship of the king of France. You glory in the friendship of the great Washington. Then what must be the glory of him who is in friendship with God? Again, gentlemen, we are all born to love, to admire, to adore. If a man have no love, he is gloomy. If he love a worthless object, he is mortified. But if he love a truly worthy object, his face shines, his eyes sparkle, his voice becomes sweet, and his whole air expressive of cheerfulness. And as this happy feeling must, in the nature of things, keep pace with the excellence of the object that is beloved, then what must be the cheerfulness of him who loves the greatest, best, and loveliest of all beings, whose eternal perfections and goodness can for ever make him happier than heart can ask or think?

"In a word, gentlemen, though I am a soldier, and soldiers you know are seldom enthusiasts in this way, yet I verily believe, as I said before, that a man of enlightened and fervent piety must be infinitely happier in a cottage, than an irreligious emperor in his palace."

In the height of this extraordinary conversation, an officer stepped in and announced the arrival of general Gates.

And here, as I have in this chapter given the reader what the jockies call a 'pretty long heat,' I beg leave to order a halt and allow him a little time to breathe.

CHAPTER XII

Gen. Gates—bon mot of British general Lee—how an army ought not to march—De Kalb prophecies—chickens counted before they are hatched, alias, Marion and the author sent by Gen. Gates to prevent the escape of Cornwallis, before he had run—the British and American armies meet—Gates and his militia-men leave De Kalb in the lurch—his gallant behavior, and glorious death.

W hen a poor fellow is going down hill, it is but too common, they say, for every body to give him a kick.

> *"Let dogs delight to bark and bite,*
> *For heaven hath made them so."*

But, if I know myself aright, I can truly say, that nothing of this vile spirit suggests a syllable of what I now write of the unfortunate general Gates. On the contrary, I feel an ardent wish to speak handsomely of him; and in one view of him I can so speak. As a gentleman, few camps or courts ever produced his superior. But though a perfect Chesterfield at court, in

camp he was certainly but a Paris. 'Tis true, at Saratoga he got his temples
stuck round with laurels as thick as a May-day queen with gaudy flowers.
And though the greater part of this was certainly the gallant workmanship
of Arnold and Morgan, yet did it so hoist general Gates in the opinion of
the nation, that many of his dear friends, with a prudent regard, no doubt,
to their own dearer selves, had the courage to bring him forward on the
military turf and run him for the generalissimoship against the great
Washington. But though they were not able to prosper him in this mad
attempt, yet they so far succeeded as to get him the command of the army
of Carolina, where his short and calamitous career soon caused every good
patriot to thank God for continuing to his servant Washington, the
command of the American armies.

On his way from the northern states, general Gates passed through
Fredericksburg, where he fell in with general Charles Lee, who, in his frank
manner, asked him where he was going.

"Why, to take Cornwallis."

"I am afraid," quoth Lee, "you will find him a tough piece of English
beef."

"Tough, sir," replied Gates; "tough! then begad I'll tender him. I'll
make 'piloo' of him, sir, in three hours after I set eyes upon him."

"Aye! will you indeed?" returned Lee. "Well then send for me, and I
will go and help you to eat him."

Gates smiled; and bidding him adieu, rode off. Lee bawled after him,
"Take care, Gates! take care! or your northern laurels will degenerate into
southern willows."

The truth is, though general Lee was extremely splenetic, other than
which, such a miserable old bachelor and infidel could hardly be, yet he
certainly had a knack of telling people's fortunes. By virtue of this faculty
he presently discovered that general Gates was no Fabius; but on the
contrary, too much inclined to the fatal rashness of his unfortunate
colleague.

And so it turned out. For, from the moment he joined the army, he appeared to act like one who thought of nothing but to have it proclaimed of him in all the newspapers on the continent, that in so many days, hours, minutes, and seconds, he flew from Philadelphia to South Carolina, 'saw, fought, and conquered' Cornwallis; and flew back again with the trophies of a second British army vanquished. Instead of moving on as old De Kalb had done, with a prudent regard to the health and refreshment of the troops, he, Jehu like, drove them on without regard to either. He would not take the lower road, as De Kalb earnestly advised, through a rich and plentiful country. Oh no; that was too round about; would too long have delayed his promised glory.

Like an eagle shaking his bold pinions in the clouds of his pride, he must dash down at once upon his prey; and so, for a near cut, take us through a pine barren, sufficient to have starved a forlorn hope of caterpillars. I shall make no attempt to describe the sufferings of the army. For, admitting that I should not lack words, my reader would, I am sure, lack faith. Indeed, at this season, when the old crop was gone and the new not quite come in, what had we to expect, especially in such a miserable country, where many a family goes without dinner, unless the father can knock down a squirrel in the woods, or his pale sickly boy pick up a terrapin in the swamps? We did, indeed, sometimes fall in with a little corn; but then, the poor, skinny, sun-burnt women, with long uncombed tresses, and shrivelled breasts hanging down, would run screaming to us, with tears in their eyes, declaring that if we took away their corn, they and their children must perish. Such times I never saw, and I pray God, I may never see nor hear of again; for, to this day, the bare thought of it depresses my spirits. But perhaps I ought to think of it, and often too, that I may be the more thankful to him who never, but in that one instance, permitted me to suffer, except in thinking of it.

There was one case in particular which I shall never forget. Almost spent with fatigue and fasting, we halted one evening near the house of a man, whose plantation bespoke him a tolerably good liver. He met us with a countenance strongly marked with terror, and begged for God's sake we would not ruin him, for that he had a large family of children to maintain. We told him that we were soldiers fighting for the country, and that it would never do for us to starve. Understanding from this that we meant to forage upon him that night, he heaved a deep sigh, and turning about, went off without saying another word. I must confess I could not help feeling very sensibly for him, especially when we saw his little white-headed children, in melancholy groups, peeping at us around the corners of the house.

His young corn, which seemed to cover about fifty acres, was just in the prime, roasting ear state, and he had also a couple of beautiful orchards of peach and apple trees, loaded with young fruit. Scarcely were our tents pitched, before the whole army, foot and horse, turned in to destroy. The trees were all threshed in a trice; after which the soldiers fell, like a herd of wild boars, upon the roasting ears, and the horses upon the blades and stalks, so that by morning light there was no sign or symptom left that corn had ever grown there since the creation of the world. What became of the poor man and his children God only knows, for by sunrise we were all under marching orders again, bending for the south. I said all, but I only meant all that were able. For numbers were knocked up every night by agues, fluxes, and other maladies, brought on by excessive fatigue and lack of food.

I once before observed how highly the baron de Kalb had been pleased to think of Marion and myself travelling so far to meet him. His liking for us grew so fast, that we had not been with him more than two days, before he appointed us his supernumerary aids. We were, of course, much in his company, and entrusted, I believe, with every thought of his bosom that related to the good of the army. He made no scruple to tell us how utterly unmilitary those proceedings were; and frequently foretold the ruin that would ensue.

"Here," said he, "we are hurrying to attack an enemy, who, if they but knew our condition, would long for nothing so much as our arrival. We, two-thirds at least, raw militia; they, all regulars. We, fatigued; they, fresh.

We, feeble and faint through long fasting; they, from high keeping, as strong and fierce as game cocks or butchers' bull dogs. It does not signify, gentlemen; it is all over with us; our army is lost as sure as ever it comes into contact with the British. I have hinted these things more than once to general Gates, but he is an officer who will take no counsel but his own."

The truth is, general Gates was one of that crazy-brained quality, to whom it is a misfortune to be fortunate. The least dram of success would intoxicate and make him fool hardy. He could never bring himself to believe, as he used to say, that "lord Cornwallis would dare to look him in the face."

So confident, indeed, was he of victory, that on the morning before the fatal action, he ordered Marion and myself to hasten on to Santee river, and destroy every scow, boat or canoe, that could assist an Englishman in his flight to Charleston!

Immediately on receiving orders, we waited on the good old De Kalb to take leave; and also to assure him of our deep regret at parting with him.

"It is with equal regret, my dear sirs," said he, "that I part with you, because I feel a presentiment that we part to meet no more."

We told him we hoped better things.

"Oh no!" replied he, "it is impossible. War is a kind of game, and has its fixed rules, whereby, when we are well acquainted with them, we can pretty correctly tell how the trial will go. To-morrow, it seems, the die is to be cast, and in my judgment, without the least chance on our side. The militia will, I suppose, as usual, play the back-game, that is, get out of the scrape as fast as their legs can carry them. But that, you know, won't do for me. I am an old soldier, and cannot run: and I believe I have with me some brave fellows that will stand by me to the last. So that, when you hear of our battle, you will probably hear that your old friend De Kalb is at rest."

I do not know that I was ever more affected in my life. I looked at Marion and saw that his eyes were watery. De Kalb saw it too, and taking us by the hand, with a firm tone, and animated look, said, "No! no! gentlemen; no emotions for me but those of congratulation. I am happy.

To die is the irreversible decree of him who made us. Then what joy to be able to meet his decree without dismay! This, thank God, is my case. The happiness of man is my wish, that happiness I deem inconsistent with slavery.—And to avert so great an evil from an innocent people, I will gladly meet the British to-morrow, at any odds whatever."

As he spoke this, I saw a something in his eyes which at once demonstrated the divinity of virtue and the immortality of the soul.

With sorrowful hearts we then left him, and with feelings which I shall never forget, while memory maintains her place in this my aged brain.

"Oh my God!" said Marion, as we rode off, "what a difference does education make between man and man! Enlightened by her sacred ray, see here is the native of a distant country, come to fight for our liberty and happiness, while many of our own people, for lack of education, are actually aiding the British to heap chains and curses upon themselves and children."

It was on the morning of August the 15th, 1780, that we left the army in a good position near Rugeley's mills, twelve miles from Camden, where the enemy lay. About ten o'clock that night orders were given to march to surprise the enemy, who had at the same time commenced their march, to surprise the Americans. To their mutual astonishment, the advance of the two armies met about two o'clock, and began to fire on each other. The firing, however, was soon discontinued by both parties, who appeared very willing to leave the matter to be decided by daylight.

A council of war was called: in which De Kalb advised that the army should fall back to Rugeley's mills, and there, in a good position, wait to be attacked.—

But Gates not only rejected this excellent counsel, but threw out suspicions that it originated from fear. Upon this, the brave old De Kalb called to his servant to take his horse, and leaping on the ground, placed himself at the head of his command, on foot. To this indecent expression of general Gates, he also retorted with considerable warmth, "Well, sir, a few hours perhaps will let us see who are the brave."

It should be recorded for the benefit of our officers, many of whose laurels have been blasted by the fumes of brandy, that general Gates was rather too fond of his nocturnal glass.

"I wonder where we shall dine to-morrow?" said one of his officers, as, in the dark, they sat on their sleepy horses waiting for the day.

"Dine, sir!" replied the confident Gates, "why at Camden, sir, to be sure. Begad! I would not give a pinch of snuff, sir, to be insured a beef-steak to-morrow in Camden, and lord Cornwallis at my table."

Presently day appeared; and, as the dawning light increased, the frighted militia began to discover the woods reddening over like crimson with the long extended lines of the British army, which soon, with rattling drums and thundering cannon, came rushing on to the charge. The militia, scarcely waiting to give them a distant fire, broke and fled in the utmost precipitation. Whereupon Gates clapped spurs to his horse, and pushed hard after them, as he said, "to bring the rascals back." But he took care never to bring himself back, nor indeed to stop until he had fairly reached Charlotte, eighty miles from the field of battle. I remember it was common to talk in those days, that he killed three horses in his flight.

Gates and the militia, composing two-thirds of the army, having thus shamefully taken themselves off, the brave old De Kalb, and his handful of continentals were left alone to try the fortune of the day. And never did men display a more determined valor! For though outnumbered more than two to one, they sustained the shock of the enemy's whole force, for upwards of an hour. With equal fury the ranks-sweeping cannon and muskets were employed by both sides, until the contending legions were nearly mixed. Then quitting this slower mode of slaughter, with rage-blackened faces and fiery eyeballs, they plunge forward on each other, to the swifter vengeance of the bayonet. Far and wide the woods resound with the clang of steel, while the red reeking weapons, like stings of infernal serpents, are seen piercing the bodies of the combatants. Some, on receiving the fatal stab, let drop their useless arms, and with dying fingers clasped the hostile steel that's cold in their bowels. Others, faintly crying out, "O God I am slain!" sank pale, quivering to the ground, while the vital current gushed in hissing streams from their bursted bosoms. Officers, as well as men, now mingle in the uproaring strife, and snatching the weapons of the slain, swell the horrid carnage. Glorying in his continentals, the brave De Kalb towers before them, like a pillar of fire. His burning face is like a red star, guiding their destructive course; his voice, as the horn that kindles the young pack in the chase of blood. A British grenadier, of giant size, rushes on him with a fixed bayonet. De Kalb parries the furious blow, and plunges his sword in the Briton's breast; then, seizing his falling arms, he deals death around him on the crowding foe. Loud rise the shouts of the Americans; but louder still the shouts of the more numerous enemy. The battle burns anew along all the fierce conflicting line. There, the distant Cornwallis pushes on his fresh regiments, like red clouds, bursting in thunder on the Americans; and here, condensing his diminished legions, the brave De Kalb still maintains the unequal contest. But, alas! what can valor do against equal valor, aided by such fearful odds? The sons of freedom bleed on every side. With grief their gallant leader marks the fall of his heroes; soon himself to fall. For, as with a face all inflamed in the fight, he bends forward animating his men, he receives eleven wounds! Fainting with loss of blood, he falls to the ground. Several brave men, Britons and Americans, were killed over him, as they furiously strove to destroy or to defend. In the midst of the clashing bayonets, his only surviving aid, Monsieur du Buyson, ran to him, and stretching his arms over the fallen hero, called out, "Save the baron de Kalb! Save the baron de Kalb!" The British officers interposed, and prevented his immediate destruction.

It has been said that lord Cornwallis was so struck with the bravery of De Kalb, that he generously superintended while his wounds were dressed, by his own surgeons. It has also been said, that he appointed him to be buried with the honors of war. British officers have been often known to do such noble deeds, but that lord Cornwallis was capable of acting so honorably, is doubtful.

De Kalb died as he had lived, the unconquered friend of liberty. For, being kindly condoled with by a British officer for his misfortune, he replied,

"I thank you, sir, for your generous sympathy; but I die the death I always prayed for; the death of a soldier fighting for the rights of man."

His last moments were spent in dictating a letter to a friend concerning his continentals, of whom he said, he "had no words that could sufficiently express his love, and his admiration of their valor." He survived the action but a few hours, and was buried in the plains of Camden, near which his last battle was fought.

When the great Washington, many years afterwards, came on a visit to Camden he eagerly inquired for the grave of De Kalb. It was shown to him. After looking on it a while, with a countenance marked with thought, he breathed a deep sigh, and exclaimed—"So, there lies the brave De Kalb; the generous stranger, who came from a distant land, to fight our battles, and to water, with his blood, the tree of our liberty. Would to God he had lived to share with us its fruits!"

Congress ordered him a monument. But the friend of St. Tammany still sleeps "without his fame." I have seen the place of his rest. It was the lowest spot of the plain. No sculptured warrior mourned at his low-laid head; no cypress decked his heel. But the tall corn stood in darkening ranks around him, and seemed to shake their green leaves with joy over his narrow dwelling.

But the roar of his battle is not yet quite passed away, nor his ghastly wounds forgotten. The citizens of Camden have lately enclosed his grave, and placed on it handsome marble, with an epitaph gratefully descriptive of his virtues and services, that the people of future days may, like Washington, heave the sigh when they read of "the generous stranger who came from a distant land to fight their battles, and to water, with his blood, the tree of their liberties."

Fair Camden's plains his glorious dust inhume,
Where annual Ceres shades her hero's tomb.

CHAPTER XIII

Marion and the author very busy in destroying the rice-makers'
boats on Santee—first got the news of the defeat of our army,
and death of the brave De Kalb—Marion addresses his
followers—their gallant reply.

Marion and myself, as yet ignorant of the fate of the army, were on
the waters of the Santee, very busily executing our boat-burning orders.
Not content with destroying the common scows and flats of the ferries, we
went on to sweep the river of every skiff and canoe that we could lay hands
on; nay, had the harmless wonkopkins been able to ferry an Englishman
over the river, we should certainly have declared war and hurled our
firebrands among them.

The reader may be sure we gained no good will by our zeal in this
affair; for it was a serious thing to the planters: and their wrath waxed
exceedingly hot against us. Among that fleet of boats and flats that perished
by our firebrands or hatchets, there were two that belonged to my excellent
old uncle, colonel E. Horry. The old gentleman could hardly believe his
negroes, when they told him that we were destroying his boats. However,

to be satisfied of the matter, he mounted his horse, and galloped down to the river to see. We had completely done for his scow, and were just giving the finishing blows to his boat as he hove in sight; whereupon, clapping whip and spur to his horse, he came on as hard as he could drive. Soon as he was within hailing distance of an ordinary speaking trumpet, he began to bawl—"Hold! hold! for God's sake hold!"

Then dashing up, with cheeks red as fire coals, and his mouth all in a lather, he roared out, "Why, what? what? what are you about here?"

"We are only trying to kidnap the British, uncle," said I.

"Kidnap the d—l," he replied.

Then looking around, and seeing how completely we had shivered his fine new boat and scow, he ripped out again—"Well! here is a pretty spot of work! a pretty spot of work! A brand new scow and boat, that cost me, only last spring, three hundred dollars! every farthing of it! and here now all cut to smash! ruined! not worth a chew of tobacco! why! did mortal flesh ever see the like of this? Breaking up our boats! why, how are we to harvest our rice?"

"Uncle," said I, "you had better think less of harvesting your rice, and more of catching the muskrats," meaning the British.

Here, darting at me an eye of inexpressible astonishment and rage, he exclaimed—"Why, certainly the d—l is in the young man! catch the British? Why, have you not heard that the British are carrying every thing before them; have broke up our army; cut the regulars to pieces; scattered the militia; and chased general Gates to Jericho, and to the d—l for what I care?"

"God forbid!" said Marion.

"Nay, that is past praying for," replied my uncle, "and if you had any interest in heaven, you ought to have made it sooner. It is too late now."

"Great God!" returned Marion; "and so our army is lost!"

"Yes," continued my uncle; "lost, as sure as a gun: and that is not all; for De Kalb is killed; Sumter surprised and cut to pieces; and Charleston illuminated every night for joy."

We could neither of us utter a word.

Presently my uncle, casting a searching eye around on our men, about thirty in number, asked where our troops were. I told him those were all the troops we had. I thought the good old gentleman would have gone into fits. He rolled up his eyes to heaven; smacked his hands together, and bringing them by a sudden jerk to his breast, with a shrill whistle exclaimed, "Mad!—mad!—the young fellow is as mad as a March hare—Well, I'll tell you what, nephew of mine, you may go about on the river, chopping the planters' boats at this rate, but I would not be in your coat, my lad, for your jacket, though it was stiff with gold."

I asked him what he meant by that?

"Why, I mean," replied he, "that if you are not, all of you, knocked on the head in three hours, it will be a wonder."

"Aye! what makes you think so, uncle," said I.

He answered: "You know my old waiting man, Tom, don't you?"

"To be sure I do," said I; "I have known Tom ever since I was a boy, and should be confounded sorry to hear Tom prophesy any harm of me; for I have always taken him to be a very true man of his word."

"Yes, I'll warrant him," said my uncle; "for though Tom is a negro, and as black as old Nick, yet I would as soon take Tom's word as that of any white man in Carolina. Well, Tom, you know, has a wife at Mr. ——'s, as rank a tory as we have hereabouts. On coming home this morning, he shook his head and said he was mighty 'fraid you and Col. Marion were in a bad box; for, that he got it from one of the black waiters in the house, who overheard the talk, that there are three companies of tories now moulding their bullets, and making ready to cut you off."

I looked at Marion and saw battle in his face.

My uncle was about to invite us to the house; but Marion interrupted him by saying, "This is no time to think of visiting;" and turning to his trumpeter, ordered him to wind his horn, which was instantly done. Then placing himself at our head, he dashed off at a charging lope; with equal speed we followed and soon lost sight of my uncle Horry.

On reaching the woods, Marion ordered the troop to halt and form; when, with his usual modesty, he thus addressed us:

"Well, gentlemen, you see our situation! widely different from what it once was. Yes, once we were a happy people! Liberty shone upon our land, bright as the sun that gilds yon fields; while we and our fathers rejoiced in its lovely beams, gay as the birds that enliven our forests. But, alas! those golden days are gone, and the cloud of war now hangs dark and lowering over our heads. Our once peaceful land is now filled with uproar and death. Foreign ruffians, braving us up to our very firesides and altars, leave us no alternative but slavery or death. Two gallant armies have been marched to our assistance; but, for lack of competent commanders, both have been lost. That under general Lincoln, after having been duped and butchered at Savannah, was at last completely trapped at Charleston. And that under general Gates, after having been imprudently overmarched, is now cut up at Camden. Thus are all our hopes from the north entirely at an end; and poor Carolina is left to shift for herself. A sad shift indeed, when not one in a thousand of her own children will rise to take her part; but, on the contrary, are madly taking part with the enemy against her. And now, my countrymen, I want to know your minds. As to my own, that has long been made up. I consider my life as but a moment. But I also consider, that to fill that moment with duty, is my all. To guard my innocent country against the evils of slavery, seems now my greatest duty; and, therefore, I am determined, that while I live, she shall never be enslaved. She may come to that wretched state for what I know, but MY eyes shall never behold it. Never shall she clank her chains in my ears, and pointing to the ignominious badge, exclaim, "it was your cowardice that brought me to this."

In answer to this, we unanimously assured him, that those sentiments and resolutions were exactly our own: and that we were steadfastly determined to die with him, or conquer for our country.

"Well then, my brave friends," said he, "draw your swords! Now for a circle, emblematical of our eternal union! and pointing your blades to heaven, the bright throne of Him who made us free, swear you will never be slaves of Britain."

Which was all most devoutly done.

Soon as this patriotic rite was performed, we all dismounted, and taking our seats on the trunks of two fallen pines that lay conveniently parallel, we made our simple dinner of cold roots; and for our beverage drank of the lucid stream that softly murmured by.

The reader will please to keep in mind, that our troops consisted of but thirty mounted militia; chiefly gentlemen volunteers, armed with muskets and swords, but almost without powder and ball. How Marion came to be at the head of this little party, it may be amusing to the reader to hear.

Some short time before this date, 1779-80, when the war began to rage in South Carolina, a British captain by the name of Ardeisoff came up to Georgetown in an armed vessel, and filled the country with printed proclamations from lord Cornwallis, calling on the good people of South Carolina to submit and take royal protections!! Numbers of the ignorant and pusillanimous sort closed with the offer. But the nobler ones of the district, (Williamsburgh,) having no notion of selling their liberties for a 'pig in a poke,' called a caucus of their own, from whom they selected captain John James, and sent him down to master captain Ardeisoff, to know what he would be at. This captain James, by birth an Irishman, had rendered himself so popular in the district, that he was made a militia captain under the royal government. But in '75, soon as he found that the ministry were determined to tax the Americans, without allowing them the common British right of representation, he bravely threw up his commission, declaring that he would never serve a tyrant. Such was the gentleman chosen by the aforesaid liberty caucus, to go on the embassy before mentioned. In the garb of a plain planter, James presented himself before the haughty captain Ardeisoff, and politely asked "on what terms himself and friends must submit?"

"What terms, sir!" replied the angry Briton, "what terms! why, no other terms, you may be sure, than unconditional submission."

"Well but sir," answered James, very calmly, "are we not to be allowed to stay at home in peace and quiet?"

"In peace and quiet, indeed!" replied Ardeisoff, with a sarcastic grin; "a pretty story, truly! Stay at home in peace and quiet, heh? No, no, sir, you have all rebelled against your king; and if treated as you deserve, would now be dancing like dogs at the arms of the gallows. But his majesty is merciful, sir; and now that he has graciously pardoned you, he expects you will immediately take up arms and turn out in support of his cause."

"You are very candid, sir," said James; "and now I hope you will not be displeased with me for being equally plain. Permit me, then, sir, to tell you that such terms will never go down with the gentlemen whom I have the honor to represent."

"The gentlemen you have the honor to represent, you d—n-d rebel!"

Vesuvius! Aetna! and Strumbolo! what are your fires and flames, compared with those that raged in the bosom of James, when he heard himself called a d—n-d rebel!

Instantly springing up, with eyes of lightning, he snatched up his chair, and, regardless of consequences, laid the audacious Ardeisoff sprawling on the floor; then flying to his horse, he mounted and made his escape. Learning from him, at his return, what they had to understand by 'British protections,' his gallant constituents came at once to the resolution to arm and fight till death, rather than hold life on such ignominious terms. Immediately the whole force of the district, about two hundred, able to bear arms, were mustered and placed under captains William M'Coltery, John M'Cawley, Henry Mowizon, and our brave captain James, who was appointed major and captain general of the whole. Feeling that distrust in themselves which is common with raw troops, and learning that the northern army was just entering South Carolina, they despatched a messenger to general Gates, to request that he would send them an officer who had seen service. Governor Rutledge, who happened at that time to be in camp, advised general Gates by all means to send Marion. Marion was accordingly sent; but with orders, as we have seen, to destroy, on his route, all the boats on the Santee river, lest lord Cornwallis should make his escape. At the time of leaving general Gates, Marion had but ten men with him; but on reaching Santee, we were joined by major John James, with about twenty gallant gentlemen volunteers, making his whole force about thirty.

A slender force, to be sure, to oppose to the tremendous powers which Marion had to encounter! But, "the Lord is king, the victory is his!" and when he pleases to give it to an oppressed people, he can make the few and feeble overcome the many and mighty.

As the brave major James may perhaps be mentioned no more in this history, I must gratify the reader by informing him, that the noble major lost nothing by his attachment to duty and the rights of man. He lived to see Cornwallis, Tarleton, and Rawdon, laid as low as the insolent Ardeisoff; and after enjoying many years of sweet repose, under the pleasant shade of peace and plenty, he sunk gently to rest. But though now fallen asleep, he still lives in his country's gratitude, and in the virtues of his son, who fills one of the highest places in the judiciary of his native state.

CHAPTER XIV

Carolina apparently lost—Marion almost alone keeps the field—begins to figure—surprises a strong British party at Nelson's old field—scourges the tories at Black Mingo—again smites them hip and thigh on Pedee.

T he history of the American Revolution is a history of miracles, all bearing, like sunbeams, on this heavenly fiat: "America shall be free!"

Some of our chimney-corner philosophers can hardly believe, when they read of Samson making such a smash among the Philistines with the jawbone of an ass. Then how will they believe what I am going to tell them of Marion? How will they believe that, at a time when the British had completely overrun South Carolina; their headquarters at Charleston, a victorious army at Camden; strong garrisons at Georgetown and Jacksonborough, with swarms of thievish and bloody minded tories, filling up all between; and the spirits of the poor whigs so completely cowed, that they were fairly knocked under to the civil and military yoke of the British, who, I ask again, will believe, that in this desperate state of things, one little, swarthy, French-phizzed Carolinian, with only thirty of his ragged countrymen, issuing out of the swamps, should have dared to turn his horse's head towards this all conquering foe?

Well, Marion was that man. He it was, who, with his feeble force, dared to dash up at once to Nelson's ferry, on the great war path between the British armies at Charleston and Camden.

"Now, my gallant friends," said he, at sight of the road, and with a face burning for battle, "now look sharp! here are the British wagon tracks, with the sand still falling in! and here are the steps of their troops passing and repassing. We shall not long be idle here!"

And so it turned out. For scarcely had we reached our hiding place in the swamp, before in came our scouts at half speed, stating that a British guard, with a world of American prisoners, were on their march for Charleston.

"How many prisoners do you suppose there were?" said Marion.

"Near two hundred," replied the scouts.

"And what do you imagine was the number of the British guard?"

"Why, sir, we counted about ninety."

"Ninety!" said Marion with a smile; "ninety! Well, that will do. And now, gentlemen, if you will only stand by me, I've a good hope that we thirty will have those ninety by to-morrow's sunrise."

We told him to lead on, for that we were resolved to die by his side.

Soon as the dusky night came on, we went down to the ferry, and passing for a party of good loyalists, we easily got set over. The enemy, with their prisoners, having just effected the passage of the river as the sun went down, halted at the first tavern, generally called "the Blue House," where the officers ordered supper. In front of the building, was a large arbor, wherein the topers were wont to sit, and spend the jocund night away in songs and gleeful draughts of apple brandy grog. In this arbor, flushed with their late success, sat the British guard; and tickler after tickler swilling, roared it away to the tune of "Britannia strike home:" till overcome with fatigue, and the opiate juice, down they sunk, deliciously beastified, to the ground.

Just as the cock had winded his last horn for day we approached the house in perfect concealment, behind a string of fence, within a few yards of it. But in spite of all our address, we could not effect a complete surprisal of them. Their sentinels took the alarm, and firing their pieces, fled into the yard. Swift as lightning we entered with them, and seizing their muskets, which were all stacked near the gate, we made prisoners of the whole party, without having been obliged to kill more than three of them.

Had Washington and his whole army been upon the survivors, they could hardly have roared out louder for quarter. After securing their arms, Marion called for their captain; but he was not to be found, high nor low, among the living or dead. However, after a hot search, he was found up the chimney! He begged very hard that we would not let his men know where he had concealed himself. Nothing could equal the mortification of the British, when they came to see what a handful of militia-men had taken them, and recovered all their prisoners.

Marion was at first in high hopes, that the American regulars whom he had so gallantly rescued, would, to a man, have joined his arms, and fought hard to avenge their late defeat. But equally to HIS surprise and their own disgrace, not one of them could be prevailed on to shoulder a musket! "Where is the use," said they, "of fighting now, when all is lost?"

This was the general impression. And indeed except these unconquerable spirits, Marion and Sumter, with a few others of the same heroic stamp, who kept the field, Carolina was no better than a British province.

In our late attack on the enemy, we had but four rounds of powder and ball; and not a single sword that deserved the name. But Marion soon remedied that defect. He bought up all the old saw blades from the mills, and gave them to the smiths, who presently manufactured for us a parcel of substantial broadswords, sufficient, as I have often seen, to kill a man at a single blow.

From our prisoners in the late action, we got completely armed; a couple of English muskets, with bayonets and cartouch-boxes, to each of us, with which we retreated into Britton's Neck.

We had not been there above twenty-four hours before news was brought us by a trusty friend, that the tories, on Pedee, were mustering, in force, under a captain Barfield. This, as we learnt afterwards, was one of the companies that my uncle's old coachman had been so troubled about. We were quickly on horseback; and after a brisk ride of forty miles, came upon their encampment, at three o'clock in the morning. Their surprise was so complete, that they did not fire a single shot! Of forty-nine men, who composed their company, we killed and took about thirty. The arms, ammunition, and horses of the whole party, fell into our hands, with which we returned to Britton's Neck, without the loss of a man.

The rumor of these two exploits soon reached the British and their friends the tories, who presently despatched three stout companies to attack us. Two of the parties were British; one of them commanded by major Weymies, of house-burning memory. The third party were altogether tories. We fled before them towards North Carolina. Supposing they had entirely scouted us, they gave over the chase, and retreated for their respective stations; the British to Georgetown, and the tories to Black Mingo. Learning this, from the swift mounted scouts whom he always kept close hanging upon their march, Marion ordered us to face about, and dog them to their encampment, which we attacked with great fury. Our fire commenced on them at but a short distance, and with great effect; but outnumbering us, at least two to one, they stood their ground and fought desperately. But losing their commander, and being hard pressed, they at length gave way, and fled in the utmost precipitation, leaving upwards of two-thirds of their number, killed and wounded, on the ground.—The surprise and destruction of the tories would have been complete, had it not been for the alarm given by our horses' feet in passing Black Mingo bridge, near which they were encamped. Marion never afterwards suffered us to cross a bridge in the night, until we had first spread our blankets on it, to prevent noise.

This third exploit of Marion rendered his name very dear to the poor whigs, but utterly abominable to the enemy, particularly the tories, who were so terrified at this last handling, that, on their retreat, they would not halt a moment at Georgetown, though twenty miles from the field of battle; but continued their flight, not thinking themselves safe, until they had got Santee river between him and them.

These three spirited charges, having cost us a great deal of rapid marching and fatigue, Marion said he would give us "a little rest." So he led us down into Waccamaw, where he knew we had some excellent friends; among whom were the Hugers and Trapiers, and Alstons; fine fellows! rich as Jews, and hearty as we could wish: indeed the wealthy captain, now colonel William Alston, was one of Marion's aids. These great people all received us as though we had been their brothers, threw open the gates of their elegant yards for our cavalry, hurried us up their princely steps; and, notwithstanding our dirt and rags, ushered us into their grand saloons and dining rooms, where the famous mahogany sideboards were quickly covered with pitchers of old amber colored brandy, and sugar dishes of double refined, with honey, for drams and juleps. Our horses were up to the eyes in corn and sweet-scented fodder; while, as to ourselves, nothing that air, land, or water could furnish, was good enough for us. Fish, flesh, and fowl, all of the fattest and finest, and sweetly graced with the smiles of the great ladies, were spread before us, as though we had been kings: while Congress and Washington went round in sparkling bumpers, from old demijohns that had not left the garret for many a year.

This was feasting indeed! It was a feasting of the soul as well as of the sense. To have drawn the sword for liberty and dear country's sake, was, of itself, no mean reward to honest republicans; but, beside that, to be so honored and caressed, by the great ones of the land, was like throwing the zone of Venus over the waist of Minerva, or like crowning profit with pleasure, and duty with delight.

In consequence of the three fortunate blows which he had lately struck, Marion, as before observed, was getting the enviable honor to be looked up to as the rallying point of the poor whigs; insomuch, that although afraid as mice to stir themselves, yet, if they found out that the tories and British were any where forming encampments about the country, they would mount their boys and push them off to Marion to let him know. Here I must give the reader an instance on the spot.

We had just got ourselves well braced up again, by rest and high feeding, among the noble whigs of Waccamaw, when a likely young fellow at half speed drove up one morning to the house, and asked for general Marion.

Marion went to the door.

"Well, my son, what do you want with me?"

"Why, sir general," replied the youth, "daddy sent me down to let you know, as how there is to be a mighty gathering of the tories, in our parts, to-morrow night."

"Aye indeed! and pray whereabouts, my son, may your parts be?"

"Heigh, sir general! don't you know where our parts is? I thought everybody knowed where daddy lives."

"No, my son, I don't; but, I've a notion he lives somewhere on Pedee; perhaps a good way up."

"Yes, by jing, does he live a good way up! a matter of seventy miles; clean away up there, up on Little Pedee."

"Very well, my son, I thank your daddy, and you too, for letting me know it. And, I believe, I must try to meet the tories there."

"O la, sir general, try to meet 'em indeed! yes, to be sure! dear me, sirs, hearts alive, that you must, sir general! for daddy says, as how, he is quite sartin, if you'll be there to-morrow night, you may make a proper smash among the tories; for they'll be there thick and threefold. They have heard, so they say, of your doings, and are going to hold this great meeting, on purpose to come all the way down here after you."

"After me?"

"Yes, indeed are they, sir general! and you had better keep a sharp look out, I tell you now; for they have just been down to the British, there at Georgetown, and brought up a matter of two wagon loads of guns; great big English muskets! I can turn my thumb in them easy enough! And, besides them plaguy guns, they have got a tarnal nation sight of pistols!

and bagonets! and swords! and saddles! and bridles! and the dear knows what else besides! so they are in a mighty good fix, you may depend, sir general."

"Well, perhaps you and I may have some of them fine things to-morrow night. What say you to it, my son?"

"By jing, I should like it proper well! But, to be sure, now, sir general, you look like a mighty small man to fight them great big tories there, on Pedee. But daddy says as how the heart is all: and he says, too, that though you are but a little man, you have a monstrous great heart."

Marion smiled, and went out among his men, to whom he related the boy's errand; and desired them to question him, so that there might be no trick in the matter. But every scruple of that sort was quickly removed; for several of our party were well acquainted with the lad's father, and knew him to be an excellent whig.

Having put our firearms in prime order for an attack, we mounted; and giving our friends three cheers, dashed off, just as the broad-faced moon arose; and by daybreak next morning, had gained a very convenient swamp, within ten miles of the grand tory rendezvous. To avoid giving alarm, we struck into the swamp, and there, man and horse, lay snug all day. About eleven o'clock, Marion sent out a couple of nimble-footed young men, to conceal themselves near the main road, and take good heed to what was going on. In the evening they returned, and brought word, that the road had been constantly alive with horsemen, tories they supposed, armed with new guns, and all moving on very gaily towards the place the lad had told us of. Soon as it was dark, we mounted, and took the track at a sweeping gallop, which, by early supper time, brought us in sight of their fires. Then leaving our horses under a small guard, we advanced quite near them, in the dark without being discovered; for so little thought had they of Marion, that they had not placed a single sentinel, but were, all hands, gathered about the fire: some cooking, some fiddling and dancing, and some playing cards, as we could hear them every now and then bawling out, "Huzza, at him again, damme! aye, that's the dandy! My trick, begad!"

Poor wretches, little did they think how near the fates were grinning around them.

Observing that they had three large fires, Marion divided our little party of sixty men into three companies, each opposite to a fire, then bidding us to take aim, with his pistol he gave the signal for a general discharge. In a moment the woods were all in a blaze, as by a flash of lightning, accompanied by a tremendous clap of thunder. Down tumbled the dead; off bolted the living; loud screamed the wounded; while far and wide, all over the woods, nothing was to be heard but the running of tories, and the snorting of wild bounding horses, snapping the saplings. Such a tragi-comedy was hardly ever seen. On running up to their fires, we found we had killed twenty-three, and badly wounded as many more; thirteen we made prisoners; poor fellows who had not been grazed by a bullet, but were so frightened that they could not budge a peg. We got eighty-four stand of arms, chiefly English muskets and bayonets, one hundred horses, with new saddles and bridles, all English too, with a good deal of ammunition and baggage. The consternation of the tories was so great that they never dreamt of carrying off anything. Even their fiddles and fiddle bows, and playing cards, were all left strewed around their fires. One of the gamblers, (it is a serious truth) though shot dead, still held the cards hard gripped in his hands. Led by curiosity to inspect this strange sight, a dead gambler, we found that the cards which he held were ace, deuce, and jack. Clubs were trumps. Holding high, low, jack, and the game, in his own hand, he seemed to be in a fair way to do well; but Marion came down upon him with a trump that spoiled his sport, and non-suited him for ever.

But the most comfortable sight of all, was the fine supper which the tories had cooked! three fat roasted pigs and six turkeys, with piles of nice journey cakes. 'Tis true, the dead bodies lay very thick round the fires: but having rode seventy miles, and eating nothing since the night before, we were too keen set to think of standing on trifles; so fell upon the poor tories' provisions, and made the heartiest supper in the world. And, to crown all, we found among the spoil, upwards of half a barrel of fine old peach brandy.

"Ah, this brandy!" said Marion, "was the worst foe these poor rogues ever had. But I'll take care it shall be no foe to us." So, after ordering half a pint to each man, he had the balance put under guard. And I must observe, by way of justice to my honored friend, that success never seemed to elate him; nor did ever he lose sight of safety in the blaze of victory. For instantly after the defeat, our guns were all loaded and our sentinels set, as if an enemy had been in force in the neighborhood.

CHAPTER XV

The whigs in high spirits on account of our success—an express
from Governor Rutledge—promotions—British and tories in
great wrath—sketch of their treatment of the patriots.

*T*he news of this fourth overthrow of the enemy, was soon spread
far and wide among both our friends and foes; producing everywhere the
liveliest emotions of joy or sorrow, according as the hearers happened to
be well or ill affected towards us. The impression which it made on our
honored executive, was sweeter to our thoughts than honey or the
honeycomb. For on the fifth day after our last flaggellation of the tories, in
came an express from governor Rutledge, with a commission of brigadier
general for Marion, and a full colonel's commission for me. Having always
looked up to my country as to a beloved mother, whose liberty and
prosperity were inseparably connected with my own, it is no wonder that
I should have been so delighted at hearing her say, by her favorite son,
governor Rutledge, that, 'reposing especial trust in my courage, conduct,
and attention to her interests, she had appointed me a colonel in her armies,'
&c. &c.

Scarcely had I perused my commission, before Marion reached me HIS; and with a smile, desired me to read it. Soon as I came to his new title, "brigadier general", I snatched his hand and exclaimed, "Huzza! God save my friend! my noble General Marion! general! general! Aye that will do! that will do! that sounds somewhat in unison with your deserts."

"Well, but what do you think of the style," replied he, "and of the prerogative—is it not prodigiously in the pompous?"

"Not at all," said I.

"No," continued he; "why now to my notion, it is very much in the turgid, in the Asiatic. It gives me dominions from river to river, and from the mountains to the great sea, like Tamerlane or Ghengis Khan; or like George III. 'by the grace of God, king of Great Britain, France,' &c. &c. whereas, poor George dares not set a foot there, even to pick up a periwinkle!"

"Well, but general," said I, "as the English gave France to George because they wish him to have it, so I suppose the good governor gives you this vast district for the same reason."

"Perhaps so," replied Marion.

The truth is, governor Rutledge was a most ardent lover of his country; and, therefore, almost adored such an unconquerable patriot as Marion.

Hence, when he found, that notwithstanding the many follies and failures of northern generals and armies; notwithstanding the victories, and proclamations, and threats of Cornwallis and Tarleton, Marion still stood his ground, and fought and conquered for Carolina; his whole soul was so filled with love of him, that I verily believe he would have given him "all the kingdoms of the earth and the glory thereof," had they been in his gift. Indeed what he did give him was sketched out with a prodigiously bold hand. He gave him all that territory, comprehended within a line drawn from Charleston along the sea, to Georgetown; thence westerly to Camden; and thence to Charleston again; making a domain of extent, population, and wealth, immense; but over which the excellent governor had no more power to grant military jurisdiction, than to give kingdoms in the moon;

for the whole of it was in the hands of the British, and their friends the tories; so that the governor had not a foot to give Marion; nor did Marion hold a foot of it but by his own vigilance and valor; which were so extraordinary, that his enemies, with all their men, money, and malice, could never drive him out of it.

But while governor Rutledge, with all the good whigs of the state, were thus heartily rejoicing with Marion for his victories, the British and tories were as madly gnashing their teeth upon him for the same. To be struck four such severe blows, in so short a time, and all rising one over another in such cursed climax of bad to worse; to be losing, in this manner, their dear allies, with all their subsidies of arms, ammunition, and money; to have their best friends thus cooled; their worst enemies thus heated; and rank rebellion again breaking up, out of a soil where they had promised themselves nothing but the richest fruits of passive obedience: and all this by a little, ugly spawn of a Frenchman! It was too much! they could not stand it. Revenge they must and would have; that was certain: and since, with all their efforts, they could not get at Marion, the hated trunk and root of all, they were determined to burn and sweat his branches, the poor whigs, i.e. to carry the curses of fire and sword through all their families and habitations.

Now, had this savage spirit appeared among a few poor British cadets, or piney wood tories, it would not have been so lamentable. Their ignorance of those divine truths, which exalt the soul above such hellish passions, would have furnished some plea for them. But, that a British general, and that general a nobleman! a lord! with an archbishop for his brother, and hot-pressed bibles, and morocco prayer books, and all such excellent helps, to teach him that "God is love," and "mercy his delight;" that such a one, I say, should have originated the infernal warfare, of plundering, burning, and hanging the American patriots, is most horrible. And yet, if possible, more true than horrible. Yes, sure as the day of doom, when that fearful day shall come, and lord Cornwallis, stript of his "brief authority," shall stand, a trembling ghost before that equal bar: then shall the evil spirit, from the black budget of his crimes, snatch the following bloody order, and grinning an insulting smile, flash it before his lordship's terrified optics.

> August 18, 1780,
>
> To lieutenant colonel Cruger, commandant at the British garrison at Ninety-Six.
>
> Sir,
>
> I have given orders that all the inhabitants of this province, who had submitted, and who have taken a part in this revolt, shall be punished with the greatest rigour; that they shall be imprisoned, and their whole property taken from them or destroyed. I have likewise directed, that compensation should be made out of their effects, to persons who have been plundered and oppressed by them. I have ordered, in the most positive manner, that every militia-man who had borne arms with us, and had afterwards joined the enemy, should be immediately hanged. I have now sir, only to desire that you will take the most vigorous measures to extinguish the rebellion in the district which you command, and that you will obey, in the strictest manner, the directions I have given in this letter, relative to the treatment of this country.

This order of lord Cornwallis proved to South Carolina like the opening of Pandora's box. Instantly there broke forth a torrent of cruelties and crimes never before heard of in our simple forests. Lord Rawdon acted, as we shall see, a shameful part in these bloody tragedies, and so did colonel Tarleton. But the officer who figured most in executing the detestable orders of Cornwallis, was a major Weymies. This man was, by birth, a Scotsman; but, in principle and practice, a Mohawk. So totally destitute was he of that amiable sympathy which belongs to his nation, that, in sailing up Winyaw bay, and Waccamaw and Pedee rivers, he landed, and pillaged, and burnt every house he durst approach! Such was the style of his entry upon our afflicted state, and such the spirit of his doings throughout: for wherever he went, an unsparing destruction awaited upon his footsteps.

Unhappily, our country had but too many pupils that fitted exactly such a preceptor. The lazy, dram-drinking, plunder-loving tories, all gloried in major Weymies: and were ever ready, at the winding of his horn, to rush forth with him, like hungry bloodhounds, on his predatory excursions. The dogs of hell were all now completely uncoupled, and every devilish passion in man had its proper game to fly at. Here was a fine time for malice to feed her ancient grudges; for avarice to cram her maw with plunder; and revenge to pay off her old scores, with bloody interest.

A thievish tory, who had been publicly whipped by a whig magistrate, or had long coveted his silver tankard, or his handsome rifle, or his elegant horse, had but to point out his house to major Weymies, and say, "There lives a d——d rebel." The amiable major and his myrmidons, would surround the noble building in a trice; and after gutting it of all its rich furniture, would reduce it to ashes. It was in vain that the poor delicate mother and her children, on bended knees, with wringing hands and tear-swimming eyes implored him to pity, and not to burn their house over their heads. Such eloquence, which has often moved the breasts of savages, was all lost on major Weymies and his banditti. They no more regarded the sacred cries of angel-watched children than the Indians do the cries of the young beavers, whose houses they are breaking up.

But, oh, joy eternal! "the Lord is king." His law is love, and they who sin against this law, soon or late, shall find that they have sinned against their own souls.

A planter, in his fields, accidentally turning towards his house, suddenly discovers a vast column of smoke bursting forth, and ascending in black curling volumes to heaven. "Oh my God! my house!" he exclaims, "my poor wife and children!" Then, half bereft of his senses, he sets off and runs towards his house.—Still, as he cuts the air, he groans out, "Oh, my poor wife and children!" Presently he hears their cries: he sees them at a distance with outstretched arms flying towards him. Oh, pa! pa! pa! his children tremblingly exclaim; while his wife, all pale and out of breath, falls on his bosom, and, feebly crying out, "The British! oh the British," sinks into a swoon.

Who can tell the feelings of the father and the husband! His wife convulsed in his arms! his little beggared children screaming around him! and his property all sinking to ruin, by merciless enemies! Presently his wife, after a strong fit, with a deep sigh, comes to herself; he wipes her tears; he embraces and hushes his children. By and bye, supposing the British to be gone, arm in arm the mournful group return. But ah, shocking sight! their once stately mansion which shone so beauteous on the plain, the pride and pleasure of their eyes, is now the prey of devouring flames. Their slaves have all disappeared; their stock, part is taken away, part lies bleeding in the yard, stabbed by bayonets; their elegant furniture, tables, glasses, clocks, beds, all is swallowed up. An army of passing demons could have done no worse. But while with tearful eye they are looking round on the wide-spread ruin, undermined by the fire, down comes the tall building with thundering crash to the ground. The frightened mourners start aghast from the hideous squelch, and weep afresh to see all the hopes and glories of their state thus suddenly ended in smoke and ashes.

It was in this way exactly that the British treated my brother, major Hugh Horry, as brave a soldier as ever fought in America. They laid in ashes all his dwelling houses, his barns of clean rice, and even his rice stacks! Destroyed his cattle; carried off eighty negroes, which were all he had, not leaving him one to bake him a cake. Thus, in one hour, as the wild Arabs served Job, did the British serve my poor brother, breaking him up root and branch; and, from a state of affluence, reduced him to a dunghill.

These savage examples, first set by the British, and followed by the tories, soon produced the effect which Marion had all along predicted. They filled the hearts of the sufferers with the deadliest hate of the British; and brought them, in crowds, to join his standard, with muskets in their hands, and vows of revenge eternal in their mouths.

Hence it was that nothing so pleased Marion as to hear of British cruelty to his countrymen.

" 'Tis a harsh medicine," he used to say, "but it is necessary; for there is nothing else that will work them. And unless they are well worked and scoured of their mother milk, or beastling partiality to the English, they are lost. Our country is like a man who has swallowed a mortal poison. Give him an anodyne to keep him easy, and he's a dead man. But if you can only knock him about, and so put the poison in motion as to make him deadly sick at the stomach, and heave like a dog with a bone in his throat, he is safe. Cornwallis has all this time been lulling them by his proclamations, and protections, and lies. But, thank God, that time is pretty well over now; for these unfeeling monsters, these children of the devil, have let out the cloven foot, and the thing is now beginning to work as I expected. Our long deluded people are opening their eyes, and beginning to see and smell the blood and burnings of that 'Tophet', that political hell of slavery and ruin, to which the British army is now endeavoring, by murder and rapine, to reduce them."

This was truly the case: for, every day the whigs were coming into Marion's camp. Those who were too old to fight themselves, would call upon their sturdy boys to "turn out and join general Marion."

It was diverting to see how they would come staving upon their tackies; belted round with their powderhorns and shotbags, with rifles in hand, and their humble homespun streaming in the air. The finely curling smile brightened in the face of Marion; and his eye beamed that laughing joy, with which a father meets his thoughtless boy, returning dirty and beaten by blackguards, from whose dangerous company he had sought in vain a thousand times to wean him.

"Well, my son!" Marion would say, "and what good news do you bring us?"

"Why, why, why, sir general," replies the youth, half cocked with rage, and stammering for words, "as I was overlooking my father's negroes in the rice grounds, the British and tories came and took them and carried them all away; and I only am left alone to tell you."

Presently another comes and says: "As I was driving the horses and cattle down to the pasture, the British and tories fell upon them, and carried them all away; and I alone am left to tell you."

While he was yet speaking, another comes and says: "The British and tories came with fire and burnt our houses and goods, and have driven my mother and the children into the woods; and I only am left alone to tell you."

Next comes another, who says: "My father and myself were ploughing together in the field, and the British and tories came upon us and shot my father! and I only am left alone to tell you."

Another comes and tells, that "lord Rawdon is taking the whig prisoners every week, out of the jail in Camden, and hanging them up by half dozens, near the windows, like dead crows in a corn-field, to frighten the rest, and make good tories of them." Another states, that "colonel Charles Pinckney, prisoner in Charleston, for striking a couple of insolent negroes, was cursed by the British officers as a d——d rebel, and driven with kicks and blows into the house, for daring to strike his 'Britannic Majesty's subjects'!"

Here Marion snapped his fingers for joy, and shouted, "Huzza! that's right! that's right! O my noble Britons, lay on! lay on the spaniels stoutly! they want British protections, do they? O the rogues! show them no quarter, but give it to them handsomely! break their backs like dogs! cut them over the face and eyes like cats! bang them like asses! thank ye! thank ye, Cornwallis and Rawdon! most noble lords, I thank ye! you have at last brought the wry face upon my countrymen, the cold sweat, the sardonic grin. Thank God! the potion begins to work! huzza, my sons! heave! heave! aye, there comes the bile; the atrabiliary; the black vomiting which portends death to the enemy. Now Britons, look to your ships, for Carolina will soon be too hot to hold you."

CHAPTER XVI

Colonel Tynes, the famous tory partisan, attempts to surprise Marion—is himself surprised and taken, with nearly all his party—the author, with thirty choice cavaliers, sent by Marion to reconnoitre—defeat of a British party of horse—anecdote of Scotch Macdonald—surprise and slaughter of the tories—captain Lewis is killed—anecdote of an extraordinary lad.

Soon after this last victory on Pedee, Marion moved down into the neighborhood of Black river; where he instantly got notice, that a large body of tories under the celebrated Col. Tynes, were making great preparations to attack him. This Tynes was a man of valor and address worthy of a better cause. In several contests with the whigs, he had handled them very roughly; and was become such a terror to the friends of liberty in that part of the world, that they were greatly alarmed on finding that he was mustering all his forces to attack Marion. We were scarcely encamped, before three expresses arrived from the whig settlements on Black river, stating colonel Tynes' movements; and advising to keep a good look out, for that he was a very artful and dangerous fellow. According to their conjectures, colonel Tynes must have had no less than one hundred and fifty men: our number did not quite reach ninety, but they were all volunteers, and exceedingly chafed and desperate in their minds, by the barbarous usage of the British and tories. Having, by this day's march of fifty miles, got within twenty miles of the enemy, who supposed that we were still on Pedee, Marion instantly resolved to attack him that night. No sooner was this made known to the troops, than the fatigues of the day appeared to be entirely forgotten. All hands fell to work, currying, rubbing and feeding their horses, like young men preparing for a ball or barbecue. Then after a hearty supper and a few hours' sleep, we all sprung upon our chargers again, and dashed off about one o'clock, to try our fortune with colonel Tynes. Just before day, we came upon the enemy, whom we found buried in sleep. The roar of our guns first broke their slumbers; and by the time the frightened wretches had got upon their legs, man and horse, we were among them hewing down. Three and thirty fell under our swords; forty-six were taken; the rest, about sixty, made their escape. Colonel Tynes himself, with upwards of one hundred horses, and all the baggage, fell into our hands.

A day or two after this victory, the general ordered me to take captain Baxter, lieutenant Postell, and sergeant Macdonald, with thirty privates, and see if I could not gain some advantage over the enemy near the lines of Georgetown. About midnight we crossed Black river; and, pushing on in great silence through the dark woods, arrived at dawn of day near the enemy's sentries, where we lay in ambush close on the road. Just after the usual hour of breakfast, a chair, with a couple of young ladies, 'squired by a brace of British officers elegantly mounted, came along at a sweeping rate from Georgetown.

They had not passed us more than fifty steps, before they stopped short. I was confoundedly afraid at first that they had, somehow or other, smelt a rat; but it turned out, as we afterwards learned, that this was only a little courting party, going into the country to dine. On getting into the gloomy woods, the girls were taken with a quaking fit for their sweethearts, lest that vile "swamp fox," as they called Marion, should come across them.

Whereupon the halt aforesaid was ordered, and a consultation held; the result of which was, that the girls should go on to their friend's house, and the officers back to town for a party of dragoons. Accordingly the chair proceeded, and the officers galloped back by us, undisturbed; for we did not think it worth while to risk an alarm for the sake of a couple of officers. Presently beginning to feel very hungry, for we had travelled all night and eaten nothing, we agreed to retire to the house of a neighboring planter, who was known to be a good whig. As we entered the yard, what should we see but the identical chair that had passed us a little before!—and on stepping into the house behold the very same young ladies! They were richly dressed, and well formed, and would no doubt have appeared handsome, but for the hostile passions which glared from their eyes, and gave their whole physiognomy a fury-like expression. They asked us, with great pertness, "what business we had there? The gentleman of the house," continued they, "is not at home, and there are no provisions here for you, and to be sure, you are too much of gentlemen to think of frightening a family of poor helpless women!"

Happily I made no reply; for while these young viragoes were catechising us at this rate, I discovered with much pleasure, that the lady of the house did not utter a word, but walked the room backward and forward with a smiling countenance. Presently she went out; and showing herself at an opposite window, beckoned me to come to her; when she said, in a low voice, "Go back into the house, I'll be there directly. On my stepping in you must demand provisions; I will deny that I have any. You must then get into a violent passion, and swear you will have them, or set the house on fire. I will then throw down the keys, and you can take just what you want; for thank God, there is enough, both for you and your horses."

Such was the farce, which the whigs in those days, both ladies and gentlemen, were obliged to play, when they had any of their tory acquaintance about them. We now played it, and with the desired success; for the troughs in the yard were all presently filled with corn and fodder for our cavalry; while for ourselves the good-natured cook wenches soon served up a most welcome repast of fried bacon and eggs, with nice hearth cakes and butter and milk. "God be praised," said we; and down we sat, and made a breakfast, of which even kings, without exercise and keen appetites, can form no idea.

Just as we had got completely refreshed, and braced up again, what should we hear but the firing of our sentinels. "To horse! to horse! my brave fellows!" was the cry of one and all. Quick as thought, we were all mounted and formed, when in came our sentinels, with the British dragoons hard after them, smack up to the fence. Charge boys, charge! was the word. In a moment the yard was bright with the shining of our swords. The tory girls shrieked out for their sweethearts—"Oh the British! the British! murder! murder! Oh!" Then off we went, all at once, in solid column. The enemy took to their heels, and we pursued. Over the fence we bounded like stags. Down the hill went the British. Down the hill went we; helter-skelter, man and horse, we flew; roaring through the woods like the sound of distant thunder.

We were all excellently mounted; but there was no horse that could hold the way with Selim. He was the hindmost of all when the chase began; and I wondered at first what had become of Selim; but presently I saw him and Macdonald coming up on my right like a thundergust. Indeed, with his wide-spread nostrils, and long extended neck, and glaring eyeballs, he seemed as a flying dragon in chase of his prey. He soon had his master up with the enemy. I saw when Macdonald drew his claymore. The shining of his steel was terrible, as, rising on his stirrups, with high-lifted arm, he waved it three times in fiery circles over his head, as if to call up all his strength. Then, with a voice of thunder, he poured his charging shout, dreadful as the roar of the lion when, close up to his game, with hideous paws unclenched, he makes his last spring on the fat buffaloes of his chase.

Though their mortal enemy, I could not but pity the poor fugitives, for I saw that their death was at hand. One of the British officers fired a pistol at him, but without effect: before he could try another, he was cut down by Macdonald. After this, at a blow a piece, he sealed the eyes of three dragoons in lasting sleep. Two fell beneath the steel of the strong-handed Snipes; nor did my sword return bloodless to its scabbard. In short, of the whole party, consisting of twenty-five, not a man escaped, except one officer, who, in the heat of the chase and carnage, cunningly shot off, at right angles, for a swamp, which he luckily gained, and so cleared himself.

The name of this officer was Meriot, and as finished a gentleman he was too, as I ever saw. I got acquainted with him after the war, at New York. Soon as the ceremony of introduction was over, he smiled, and asked if I were not in the skirmish just related? On being answered in the affirmative, he again inquired, if I did not recollect how handsomely one of the British officers gave me the slip that day? I told him I did. "Well," continued he, "I was that officer; and of all the frights I ever had in my life, that was the most complete. Will you believe me, sir, when I assure you, that I went out that morning, with my locks of as bright an auburn as ever curled upon the forehead of youth; and by the time I had crawled out of the swamp, into Georgetown, that night, they were as gray as a badger! I was well nigh taking an oath never to forgive you, during breath, for frightening me so confoundedly. But, away with all malice! let it go to the devil, where it belongs. So come, you must go dine with me, and I'll show you a lovelier woman than either of those that rode in the chair that day."

I went with him, and was introduced to his wife, a lovely woman indeed! to whom, with great glee, he related the whole history of the chase, and his own narrow escape, and then laughed very heartily. But not so his gentle partner. For, as he told of the shrill whizzing of our swords close behind him, and of the groans of his dragoons as they fell, cut down from their horses, her face turned pale, and pensive; then, looking at him with great tenderness, she heaved a deep sigh, to think how near her husband had been to death.

Meriot looked with pleasure on the troubled countenance of his lovely wife, because he well knew the fond source of her troubles. Then, snatching up a goblet of sangree, richly mantled over with nutmeg, he presented it to her ruby lips, saying, "Come, my dear, drink, and forget the past!" Then, taking my hand with great cordiality, he exclaimed, "Well, colonel Horry, we have been foes, but thank God, we are good friends again. And now let me drink to you a sentiment of my heart, 'Here's friendship in marble, enmity in dust.'"

The behavior of this noble Englishman, has often served to deepen my abhorrence of war, which too frequently sets those to cutting each other's throats, who were born to be brothers.

But to return to our story. "Meriot," you'll say, "and his brother officer, brought 'their pigs to a bad market'." Yes, indeed: but not a jot worse than some of their friends came to the very day afterwards. On the morning of that day, Marion, now concealed in the swamps, near Georgetown, was pleased to order me out on a second excursion. "Take captain Snipes," said he, "with thirty men, and proceed down the Sandpit road, in quest of the enemy. The moment you discover them, whether British or tories, charge with spirit, and I'll warrant your success."

As we approached the bridge, still moving on very circumspectly, in the woods, we discovered at a short distance, a body of horsemen, perhaps a hundred, apparently in great confusion, and very anxious to form. Instantly we took the road, and clapping spurs to our horses, dashed upon them at full speed, at the same time shouting as we rushed on. The enemy broke and fled in all directions. We pursued. Then you might have seen the woods all covered with armed men; some flying, others pursuing; and with muskets, and pistols, and swords, shooting and cutting down as fast as they could.

From the unevenness of the ground, and rapidity of the charge, my men were all soon out of sight, leaving with me but a lad of fourteen, named Gwinn, who carried a musket. At that instant, a party of nine or ten men were seen advancing, whom I took for whigs, and challenged as such, asking if they were not friends?

"Friends! O yes!" replied their captain, (one Lewis) "friends to be sure; friends to king George!"

Quick as thought, off went Gwinn's musket, close by my side, and down tumbled captain Lewis from his horse, with a heavy squelch, to the ground. But in the very instant of receiving his death, his musket, which was raised to kill me, took fire and shot my horse dead on the spot. Seeing my horse drop, Gwinn dismounted, and led his horse up to me in a moment.

Happily for us both, captain Snipes heard the report of our pieces, and thinking that we might be in danger, dashed on to our aid, with several of my troops whooping and huzzaing as they came on. The tory party then fired at us, but without effect, and fled leaving four of Marion's men, whom they had just taken, and beaten very barbarously with the butts of their muskets.

This was a fatal day to the tories, who must have lost more than half their number. For I had with me not only Macdonald and Snipes, but several other very strong and brave men, whose families had suffered very severely, by British and tory cruelty; and, I am afraid, they did not forget this, when their swords were hanging over the heads of the fugitives. At any rate, they took but few prisoners.

In the course of this day's fighting, there happened an affair which served to amuse us not a little on our return to our camp that night. The tories, who, from time to time had fallen into our hands, were often easing their vexation, by saying, that it was true, "Marion had proved too cunning for colonel Tynes and captain Barfield, and other British and loyal officers, whom he had attacked; but that there was still one left behind, who, they were sure, if he could come forward, would soon show us quite a different sort of play; and that was colonel Gainey, from the head waters of Pedee." We answered, that it was all very well; and that we should be glad to see colonel Gainey. Now, as God was pleased to have it, who should it be, that with one-third of his number, we had been chasing so to-day, but colonel Gainey; a stout officer-looking fellow he was too, and most nobly mounted. Macdonald made a dash at him, in full confidence of getting a gallant charger. But the good book tells us, that "the race is not always to the swift;" and owing partly to the fleetness of his horse, and partly to a most extraordinary sort of accident, colonel Gainey made his escape from our Scotsman. The chase was towards Georgetown, distant little more than two miles. Never on earth did two horses or horsemen make greater exertions. Fear impelling the one, fury urging the other. Macdonald declared, that in the chase he had passed several tories whom he could easily have cut down, but like the lion in pursuit of a favorite buffalo, he took no notice of them. His eye was fixed on colonel Gainey. Just as they turned Richmond corner, Selim had brought his master near enough to his prey to make a stroke at him with his bayonet. By a sudden jerk, it is supposed, the weapon turned; so that when Macdonald drew back the carbine, he left the bayonet up to the hilt in his back. In this way colonel Gainey rode into town, prodigiously to his own and the mortification of his friends the British and tories.

CHAPTER XVII

Spirit of the tories—assassination of lieutenant Marion—the murderer murdered—Marion's reflections on the death of his nephew—his manner of rewarding extraordinary courage among his men—sketch of the brave boy Gwinn.

"If mortal hands thy peace destroy,
  Or friendship's gifts bestow,
Wilt thou to man ascribe the joy—
  To man impute the woe?

'Tis GOD, whose thoughts for wisest ends
  The human lots dispose;
Around thee plants assisting friends,
  Or heaps chastising foes.

Not from the BOW the deaths proceed,
  But from the ARCHER'S skill,
He lends the winged shaft its speed
  And gives it power to kill."

And here I must relate a tragical affair that befell us that day, and which filled us all with grief, because of our beloved general. I mean the barbarous murder of his nephew. Of all men who ever drew the sword, Marion was one of the most humane. He not only prevented all cruelty, in his own presence, but strictly forbade it in his absence. I have known him to talk for a quarter of an hour together, with one of his men, for striking over the head, a horse that had started, and to punish another for taking away from a negro, his ragged chicken. To reason then like men, one would suppose that he was the last person on whom such a cruel blow as the murder of a favorite nephew should have fallen. But thanks to God, for that most comfortable doctrine, that not even a sparrow can die until his death-warrant has been signed in heaven; and, since this young man did die at that time, there can be no doubt but that was the right time.

The manner of his death was this. We have told the reader, that, in the course of this day's fighting, we retook from the tories four of Marion's Men, whom they had very barbarously beaten with the butts of their guns. On being asked how they came to fall into such bad company, they said, that immediately after sending me off, in the morning, Marion got information that a party of tories were encamped not far distant, on a plantation of colonel Alston's, called "The Penns." Captain M—— was despatched to surprise them; but he played his cards so badly, that, instead of surprising them, they surprised him, killed several of his men, and took the others. Among the prisoners was the general's nephew, lieutenant Gabriel Marion, of the continentals, who, happening at that time on a visit to his uncle, turned out a volunteer, and was taken. The tories murdered several of their unfortunate prisoners in cold blood, by first beating them over the head with the butts of their muskets, and then shooting them. They said that lieutenant Marion, at sight of such horrid scenes, appeared much shocked: and seeing among them a man who had often been entertained at his uncle's table, he flew to him for protection, and threw himself into his arms. The man seemed greatly distressed, and tried hard to save him; but the others roared out, that "he was one of the breed of that d——d old rebel," and that they would have his heart's blood. They, moreover, swore, with the most horrid oaths, that if the man did not instantly push young Marion from him, they would blow him through also. The unfortunate youth being then thrust from the side of his friend, was immediately destroyed.

I hope the tender mercies of God are so great as not to let our unworthiness prevent him from always doing what is exactly right and good for us. We ought not, therefore, to breathe a wish different from the will and order of Providence. But still, to us, it seems a great pity we did not get notice of captain M——'s advancing. We could have made a handsome joint attack of it, and thereby not only have prevented the horrid murders above related, but have scourged those barbarians, as they deserved. For we heard the firing, but thought it was colonel Alston's people killing beeves.

Among the very few prisoners that we made in our last action, was a mulatto fellow, who was suspected to be one of those who had murdered the general's nephew. Whether the suspicion was well or ill founded, I cannot say: but, certain it is, that the indignation excited against him, on that account, soon proved his destruction. For, as we were crossing the swamps of Black river that night, an officer rode up to him, while marching in the line of prisoners under guard, and with a pistol, shot him dead on the spot. The captain of the guard was instantly sent for, and severely reprimanded by the general, for not having killed the author of that savage deed.

It was said the officer had offered a bottle of rum to have the mulatto shot, but, finding none that would do it, he did it himself. I do not give this as a fact, but, I know it was the talk in camp, though carefully kept from the general, as everybody knew it would have given him great pain. He often said, "he truly lamented the untimely death of his nephew; and that he had been told, that this poor man was his murderer. But that, as a prisoner, his life ought to have been held most sacred; especially as the charge against him was without evidence, and, perhaps, no better than conjecture. As to my nephew," continued he, "I believe he was cruelly murdered: but living virtuously, as he did, and then dying fighting for the rights of man, he is, no doubt, happy: and this is my comfort."

The next day Marion ordered the troops under arms, and formed them into a large circle, all fronting the centre. While we were wondering what could be the meaning of this strange manoeuvre, a sergeant was seen leading into the circle an elegant horse, under saddle and bridle, with portmanteau, sword, pistols, and musket. This was the horse, furniture, and arms of captain Lewis, whom the lad Gwinn, so fortunately for me, had killed in the action three days before. Marion then called Gwinn from the ranks.

The boy approached him with his hat off.

The general, placing his hand upon his head, in the presence of the whole squadron, pronounced him "a brave little man; and there," pointing to the horse and furniture, "there is the reward of your gallantry."

"Gwinn, sir," said I, "is not a good soldier, he fired without orders."

"That's very true," replied he, "but I am sure, colonel, you are the last that ought to blame me, on that account; for if I had not fired and killed captain Lewis, exactly as I did, he would have killed you; and besides, his saying he was the friend of George the Third, was enough for me; I did not think I could fire too quick on such a man as that."

But when the sergeant, at the order of Marion, led up to him the horse, richly furnitured, as aforesaid, the confusion and grimace of the lad were truly diverting. He blushed, he chuckled, he looked around and around upon his comrades, as if at a loss how to contain himself, or what to do. At length he made shift to reach out his hand to the bridle, though deeply blushing, and said, "Dear me now! well la! what will mammy think, and the children, when they come to see me, riding up here on this famous horse, and all these fine things! I know well enough how mammy will have a hearty cry, that's what she will; for she will think I stoled him. But if any of the folks up our way should go to jaw about me, at that rate, I trust as how, general, you will take my part, and set 'em straight."

Marion smiled, and commended him for a good boy, and told him to give his compliments to his mother, and also his thanks to her, for being such a true mother to her children, in bringing them up so honestly.

But the general was told the next day, that Gwinn had said, "he always hated the tories, because they would not fight for their country; and, since the general had paid him so well for killing one of them, he was determined to try if he could not kill more."

And he did kill more too, I'll warrant him, for he was with us to the end of the war, in many a hard brush. And then he was such a dead shot with a rifle! Standing, running, or flying, it was all one to Gwinn. He would make nothing, at a hundred yards, to stop you a buck, at full tilt through the woods, as hard as he could crack it; and at every clip, to bring down the squirrels from the tops of the tallest trees of the forest.

CHAPTER XVIII

Mutiny in our camp—Marion suppresses it—his address to the officers.

This war, though on our part a war of virtue, was not always so pleasant as might have been expected. Instances of human weakness often occurred to disturb our harmony, and fill good men's hearts with sorrow. For how, without grief, could we behold a man fighting by our side to-day like a hero, for the rights of bleeding humanity; to-morrow, like a headstrong child, or a headlong beast, trampling them under foot! And oh! how sad to see nature's goodliest gifts, of manly size, and strength, and courage, set off, too, in the proudest ornaments of war, the fierce cocked hat, the flaming regimentals, and golden shoulder-knots, all defeated of their power to charm, nay, all turned into pity and contempt, in consequence of our knowing the owners to be gamblers, swindlers, and villains!

Such was the truly pitiable case of some, in this our glorious war of liberty. For want of a good education, I mean the early precepts of virtue, from a parent's lips, with a few excellent books, to lift the noble kindlings of the soul, the flame could not ascend to what was heavenly and just; but with inverted point, struck downward to selfishness and vice. Men of this character, though enlisted in the war of liberty, were not her soldiers, felt not her enthusiasm, nor her consolations. They did not walk the camp, glorying in themselves, as men called to the honor of humbling the tyrant, and of establishing the golden reign of equal laws, in their own dear country, and thence, perhaps over all the earth. Alas! no! strangers to these divine views and wishes, they look no higher than sordid gain! and as there was but little of that reward to be had, they were often gloomy and low spirited. "Their life," they were wont murmuringly to say, "was wearing away; their country gave them nothing, and they must e'en try to do something for themselves."

In truth, plunder, plunder, was what they were spelling for. They were continually darting their greedy eyes upon every piece of merchandise that came in their way. They had the heart not only to plunder the tories, and to bring their unoffending children to want; but also to rob and ruin their own friends the whigs, if they could but do it with impunity.

I am led to these reflections by a most shameful affair, which happened in our camp about this time, and which threatened consequences as serious as their source was shameful.

We were encamped near the house of a rich man by the name of Cross. His wife, in sense and domestic virtues, was an Abigail; while as to her husband, his riches, though great, were his least recommendation, for he possessed all the generosity and honor of the noblest patriot. His soul delighted in Marion, whom he called the 'pillar of our cause'. Oft as he took leave of us, for battle, his bosom would heave, his visage swell, and the tear would start into his eye. And when he saw us return again, loaded with the spoils of victory, he would rush to meet us, with all a brother's transports on his face. His flocks and herds, his meat-houses and corn-fields, were all our own; while his generous looks would tell us that he still wished for more to give. Indeed, often at the most imminent risk of his life, he used to send us intelligence, and also furnish us with powder and ball. But this most amiable of men, was not permitted to see our cause triumphant; for in the midst of his sighs and tears for his struggling country, God took him to his own rest. The messenger of death came to him, in the character of a nervous fever. As the physicians did not like to visit him on his plantation, he was carried into Georgetown to be near them.

Marion went to see him the morning he set out; and immediately after his departure, fixed a guard at his house, that nothing might be disturbed. One would indeed have supposed it unnecessary to place a guard over such a house as his. But alas! what will not a base heart-hardening avarice do! And I blush while I relate, that, the very day after our generous friend was carried off, pale and hollow-eyed, to Georgetown, whence he never more returned, two of our officers, one of them a major, went to his house to pillage it!

The guard, of course, opposed: but they damned him for an "impertinent rascal," and swore that if he opened his mouth again, they would spit him on the spot. Then bursting the door, they went in, and after forcing the desks, drawers, and trunks, they rifled them of whatever they wanted.

This most unsoldierly and detestable transaction was communicated to me by Mrs. Cross herself; whose servant came to me next morning with her compliments, and requested that I would go down to her, where she was sitting in her carriage at the road. I waited on her at once; and greatly to my grief, found her in tears. I entreated to know the cause.

"Oh, sir," replied she, "we are ruined! we are ruined! Poor Mr. Cross is, I fear, on his deathbed. And then what will become of me and my poor children, when he is gone, and every thing is taken from us!" She then reminded me of her husband's love to general Marion and his people, from whom he withheld nothing, but gladly imparted of all he had, though often at the risk of his utter destruction from the British and tories. "And yet, after all," said she, "soon as my poor sick husband's back is turned, your people can go and break him up!"

"Madam," I replied, "I hope 'tis no offence to ask your pardon; for I really cannot admit a suspicion so disgraceful to our troop: and to my certain knowledge, general Marion placed a guard over your house the moment Mr. Cross left it."

"Yes, sir," said she, "that's very true. And it was like general Marion. But some of our officers have forced the guard and broken open the house, and this instant I saw one of them with Mr. Cross's sword by his side."

I never felt more mortified in my life. Then, after entreating her to be perfectly easy about her house and furniture in future, I took leave of this excellent lady, and flew to the guard to see if what I had heard were true.

He told me it was too true; mentioned the names of the officers; and even went so far as to show me one of them strutting about with the sword by his side!

It was well for the wretch, that I did not possess the eyes of a basilisk, for I should certainly have blasted him on the spot. Pausing, however, one salutary moment, to confirm myself in the love of virtue, by noting how abominable a villain looks, I hasted to the general with the hateful tale; which excited in his honest bosom the indignation which I had expected. Then calling one of his aids, he said, "Go to major ——, and desire him to send me Mr. Cross's sword immediately."

The aid was presently back, but without the sword. On being asked by the general, why he had not brought it, he replied; "The major says, sir, that the sword does not belong to Mr. Cross. He says, moreover, that if you want the sword, you must go for it yourself."

"Well, go back," said the general, "and desire those two officers to come to me."

It was not for such an affair as this to be kept secret. It took wind in a moment; and by the time the two officers were arrived, almost all the field officers had come together to the general's quarters, to see how he would act on this extraordinary occasion.

Inferring from the looks of the two culprits, that they meant to test his firmness; and, willing that the company should fully understand the merits of the case, he thus addressed us:

"You well know, gentlemen," said he, "how like a brother the proprietor of this plantation has always treated us. We never gained a victory, but it caused him tears of joy; and however starved by others, by him we have ever been feasted. You also know, that he is now gone, sick, to Georgetown—there, perhaps, to die. Soon as he left us, I placed a guard over his house; but, at the same time, blushed for the reflection cast on my men; all of whom, as I thought, would, instead of robbing, have defended it with their lives. But, equally to my astonishment and grief, I find I was mistaken. Yes, gentlemen, our friend has been robbed, not by the poor untutored privates in the ranks, but by my officers! by those who ought to have abhorred such an act! Yes, gentlemen, two of our brethren in arms— two of our officers—forgetting what they owed to you, what they owed to me, and, most of all, to their country and to themselves, have done this odious deed! And one of them (here he pointed to the major) now wears by his side the sword of our sick and injured friend.

"Well knowing that all men, even the best, have too often 'done those things which they ought not to have done,' I felt it my duty to be as tender with this gentleman as possible; and therefore, sent him a polite request that he would return the sword: to which he was pleased to reply, that 'if I wanted it, I must come and take it myself.' Still wishing to settle the affair in a way as much to his credit as possible, I sent for him to come to me. And now, sir, (addressing the major) I entreat of you, for the last time, to give me up that sword."

With great rudeness he swore he would not. Instantly every face was dark: and, biting his lip with rage, each officer laid his hand upon his sword and looked to the general. One word, nay, one assenting look, and the brute would have been hewed into mincemeat in a moment. For my own part, whether I felt more, or governed myself less than the rest, I cannot say: but looking to the general, I broke out with an oath, that if I commanded as he did, I would have that fellow hung in five minutes.

"This is no business of yours, sir," replied he, rather sternly; "they are now before me."

Then looking at the major, still with great benignity, he said—"And do you really mean, sir, not to give me up that sword?"

"Sir, I will not!" replied the major.

"Sergeant of the guard!" said the general, "bring me instantly a file of soldiers!"

Upon this, the major's colleague, who stood by, was seen to touch him.

Seeing the guard coming up with their naked weapons, and much anger in their looks, the major lost his courage, turned pale, and, in a sadly altered tone, whined out, "General, you needed not to have called in the guard. I will deliver up the sword. Here it is."

"No, sir, I will not accept it at your hands. Give it to the sergeant."

To this humiliating order, with much shame and blushing, the poor major was constrained to comply. Thus, happily, were extinguished the first sparks of a mutiny, which, it was once thought, would have broken out into a dangerous flame. The cool, dispassionate address which effected this, did not fail to produce a proper impression on us all. This the general easily perceived in our looks; and thereupon, as was common with him, when any such occasion served, he arose and addressed us, in, as nearly as I can recollect, the following words:

"When, gentlemen, shall we catch the spirit of our profession; the spirit of men fighting for a republic, a commonwealth of brothers! that government most glorious, where God alone is king! that government most pleasant, where men make and obey their own laws! and that government most prosperous, where men, reaping as they sow, feel the utmost stimulus to every virtue that can exalt the human character and condition! This government, the glory of the earth, has ever been the desire of the wise and good of all nations. For this, the Platos of Greece, the Catos of Rome, the Tells of Switzerland, the Sidneys of England, and the Washingtons of America, have sighed and reasoned, have fought and died. In this grand army, gentlemen, we are now enlisted; and are combatting under the same banners with those excellent men of the earth. Then let self-gratulation gladden our every heart, and swell each high-toned nerve. With such worthies by our sides, with such a CAUSE before our eyes, let us move on with joy to the battle and charge like the honored champions of God and of human rights. But, in the moment of victory, let the supplicating enemy find us as lovely in mercy, as we are terrible in valor. Our enemies are blind. They neither understand nor desire the happiness of mankind. Ignorant, therefore, as children, they claim our pity for themselves. And as to their widows and little ones, the very thought of them should fill our souls with tenderness. The crib that contains their corn, the cow that gives them milk, the cabin that shelters their feeble heads from the storm, should be sacred in our eyes. Weak and helpless, as they are, still they are the nurslings of heaven—our best intercessors with the Almighty. Let them but give us their blessings, and I care not how much the British curse. Let their prayers ascend up before God in our behalf, and Cornwallis and Tarleton shall yet flee before us, like frightened wolves before the well armed shepherds!"

Such were the words of Marion, in the day when he saw in our looks, that our hearts were prepared for instruction. And such was the epilogue to the mutiny. The satisfaction which it gave to the officers was so general and sincere, that I often heard them say afterwards, that since the mutiny was suppressed, they were glad it happened; for it had given them an opportunity to hear a lecture, which they hoped would make them better men and braver soldiers too, as long as they lived.

About this time we received a flag from the enemy in Georgetown; the object of which was, to make some arrangements about the exchange of prisoners. The flag, after the usual ceremony of blindfolding, was conducted into Marion's encampment. Having heard great talk about general Marion, his fancy had, naturally enough, sketched out for him some stout figure of a warrior, such as O'Hara or Cornwallis himself, of martial aspect and flaming regimentals. But what was his surprise, when, led into Marion's presence, and the bandage taken from his eyes, he beheld in our hero, a swarthy, smoke-dried little man, with scarce enough of threadbare homespun to cover his nakedness! and in place of tall ranks, of gaily dressed soldiers, a handful of sunburnt yellow-legged militia-men; some roasting potatoes and some asleep, with their black firelocks and powder-horns lying by them on the logs! Having recovered a little from his surprise, he presented his letter to general Marion; who perused it, and soon settled everything to his satisfaction.

The officer took up his hat to retire.

"Oh no!" said Marion; "it is now about our time of dining; and I hope, sir, you will give us the pleasure of your company to dinner."

At mention of the word 'dinner', the British officer looked around him; but to his great mortification, could see no sign of a pot, pan, Dutch-oven, or any other cooking utensil that could raise the spirits of a hungry man.

"Well, Tom," said the general to one of his men, "come, give us our dinner."

The dinner to which he alluded, was no other than a heap of sweet potatoes, that were very snugly roasting under the embers, and which Tom, with his pine stick poker, soon liberated from their ashy confinement; pinching them, every now and then, with his fingers, especially the big ones, to see whether they were well done or not. Then having cleansed them of the ashes, partly by blowing them with his breath, and partly by brushing them with the sleeve of his old cotton shirt, he piled some of the best on a large piece of bark, and placed them between the British officer and Marion, on the trunk of the fallen pine on which they sat.

"I fear, sir," said the general, "our dinner will not prove so palatable to you as I could wish; but it is the best we have."

The officer, who was a well bred man, took up one of the potatoes and affected to feed, as if he had found a great dainty; but it was very plain, that he ate more from good manners than good appetite.

Presently he broke out into a hearty laugh. Marion looked surprised. "I beg pardon, general," said he: "but one cannot, you know, always command his conceits. I was thinking how drolly some of my brother officers would look, if our government were to give them such a bill of fare as this."

"I suppose," replied Marion, "it is not equal to their style of dining."

"No, indeed," quoth the officer; "and this, I imagine, is one of your accidental lent dinners; a sort of a 'ban yan'. In general, no doubt, you live a great deal better."

"Rather worse," answered the general: "for often we don't get enough of this."

"Heavens!" rejoined the officer. "But probably, what you lose in meal you make up in malt; though stinted in provisions, you draw noble pay?"

"Not a cent, sir," said Marion, "not a cent."

"Heavens and earth! then you must be in a bad box. I don't see, general, how you can stand it."

"Why, sir," replied Marion, with a smile of self-approbation, "these things depend on feeling."

The Englishman said, he "did not believe that it would be an easy matter to reconcile his feelings to a soldier's life on general Marion's terms; all fighting and no pay! and no provisions but potatoes!"

"Why, sir," answered the general, "the heart is all; and, when that is much interested, a man can do any thing. Many a youth would think it hard to indent himself a slave for fourteen years. But let him be over head and ears in love, and with such a beauteous sweetheart as Rachael, and he will think no more of fourteen years' servitude than young Jacob did. Well, now, this is exactly my case. I am in love; and my sweetheart is liberty. Be that heavenly nymph my companion, and these wilds and woods shall have charms beyond London and Paris in slavery. To have no proud monarch driving over me with his gilt coaches; nor his host of excise-men and tax-gatherers insulting and robbing me; but to be my own master, my own prince and sovereign, gloriously preserving my national dignity, and pursuing my true happiness; planting my vineyards, and eating their luscious fruits; and sowing my fields, and reaping the golden grain: and seeing millions of brothers all around me, equally free and happy as myself. This, sir, is what I long for."

The officer replied, that both as a man and a Briton, he must certainly subscribe to this as a happy state of things.

"Happy!" quoth Marion; "yes, happy indeed! and I had rather fight for such blessings for my country, and feed on roots, than keep aloof, though wallowing in all the luxuries of Solomon. For now, sir, I walk the soil that gave me birth, and exult in the thought that I am not unworthy of it. I look upon these venerable trees around me, and feel that I do not dishonor them. I think of my own sacred rights, and rejoice that I have not basely deserted them. And when I look forward to the long ages of posterity, I glory in the thought that I am fighting their battles. The children of distant generations may never hear my name; but still it gladdens my heart to think that I am now contending for their freedom, and all its countless blessings."

I looked at Marion as he uttered these sentiments, and fancied I felt as when I heard the last words of the brave De Kalb. The Englishman hung his honest head, and looked, I thought, as if he had seen the upbraiding ghosts of his illustrious countrymen, Sidney and Hampden.

On his return to Georgetown, he was asked by colonel Watson, why he looked so serious?

"I have cause, sir," said he, "to look serious."

"What! has general Marion refused to treat?"

"No, sir." "Well, then, has old Washington defeated sir Henry Clinton, and broke up our army?"

"No, sir, not that neither; but worse."

"Ah! what can be worse?" "Why, sir, I have seen an American general and his officers, without pay, and almost without clothes, living on roots and drinking water; and all for liberty! What chance have we against such men!"

It is said colonel Watson was not much obliged to him for this speech. But the young officer was so struck with Marion's sentiments, that he never rested until he threw up his commission, and retired from the service.

CHAPTER XIX

"Ah brandy! brandy! bane of life,
Spring of tumult—source of strife:
Could I but half thy curses tell,
The wise would wish thee safe at hell."

Curious and Instructive Anecdotes.

*T*hat great poet, John Milton, who seems to have known him well, assures us that the devil was the inventor of gunpowder. But, for my own part, were I in the humor to ascribe any particular invention to the author of all evil, it should be that of distilling apple-brandy. We have scripture for it, that he began his capers with the apple; then, why not go on with the brandy, which is but the fiery juice of the apple?

At any rate, I am pretty sure I shall hardly ever be able to think of it again with tolerable patience, as long as I live. For, it was that vile filthy poison that cut me out of one of the finest plumes that I ever expected to feather my cap with.

The case stands briefly thus. I have told the reader, that Marion surprised and captured the celebrated tory partisan, colonel Tynes, after killing the major part of his men. For safe keeping, he was sent into North Carolina; whence he made his escape—got back into the forests of Black river, and collected a stout force to try his fortune a second time with Marion.

But, getting knowledge of the thing, Marion made one of his forced marches, fell upon him, unawares, and broke him up worse than before; killing and taking his whole party. Tynes was sent again to North Carolina; whence he contrived again to make his escape; and, returning to his old haunts, soon rallied a formidable force, for a third trial. This news was soon brought to general Marion, who thereupon, desired me to take forty of our best cavaliers, and see if we could not scourge colonel Tynes once more.

About sunset we mounted, and travelled hard all that night and until the middle of next day, when we halted, for refreshment, at the house of one who was truly a "publican and sinner," for he was a great Tory.

Not knowing what secret intelligence the man might convey to the enemy, who were but fifteen miles off, I had him taken up and put under guard. We then got dinner, for which we honorably paid the poor woman his wife. And now comes my woeful story. While, after dinner, I was busily employed in catechising my prisoner, how should the devil be employed, but in tempting my men with the distilled juice of the apple? Having, by some ill luck, found out that there was a barrel of it in the house, they hastened to the poor landlady, who not only gave them a full dose for the present, but filled their bottles and canteens.

As we pushed on, after dinner, in high spirits, for the enemy, I could not but remark how constantly the men were turning up their canteens.

"What the plague have you got there, boys," said I, "that you are so eternally drinking."

"Water! sir, water! nothing but water!" The rogues were drinking brandy all the time; but, by way of whipping the devil round the stump, they called it 'water!' that is, 'apple water.'

Presently, finding, from their gaiety and frolicksomeness, what they had been after, I ordered a halt, and set myself to harangue them for such unsoldierly conduct. But I might as well have talked to a troop of drunken Yahoos. For, some of them grinned in my face like monkeys; others looked as stupid as asses; while the greater part chattered like magpies; each boasted what a clever fellow he was, and what mighty things he could do, yet reeling all the time, and scarcely able to sit his horse. Indeed our guide, a fat jolter-headed fellow, fetching one of his heavy lee lurches, got so far beyond his perpendicular, that he could not right again; but fell off, and came to the ground as helpless as a miller's bag. In short, among my whole corps there was but one sober man, and that was captain Neilson.

It is not for language to express one thousandth part of my mortification and rage. To have made such an extraordinary march, and at the head of such choice fellows too; to have come almost within sight of the enemy; an enemy that I was eager to humble, and which would have yielded me so complete and glorious a victory; and yet to have lost all so shamefully: and thus like a fool to be sent back to my general, with my finger in my mouth, was, indeed, almost beyond endurance. But I was obliged to endure it. For, to have led my men into action, in that condition, would have been no better than murdering them. And to have kept them there until they could have cooled off, was utterly out of the question. For there was not a family in that whole district that would, with their good will, have given us an hour's repose, or a morsel of bread. I therefore instantly ordered a retreat, which was made with all the noise and irregularity that might have been expected from a troop of drunkards, each of whom mistaking himself for commander in chief, gave orders according to his own mad humor; and whooped and halloed at such a rate, that I verily believed, no bull-drivers ever made half the racket.

That we should have obtained a most complete victory, is very certain. For in a few days after this, we laid hands upon some of those very same tories, who stated, that in consequence of the noise which we made that night, colonel Tynes despatched some of his cavalry up the road next morning, to see what was the matter. On coming to the spot, where I had vainly endeavored to form my drunken dogs, they found on the ground some of our plumes, which colonel Tynes no sooner saw than he bawled out, "Marion! Marion!" then, leaping on their horses, off they went, whip and spur.

"Well, where is colonel Tynes?" said the general, as I entered his presence. This was the question which I had expected, and, indeed, blushed for the answer. But after hearing my doleful story, he replied with his usual philosophy: "Well, you did right to retreat; but pray keep a careful eye on the apple water next time."

But to give the devil his due, I must confess there was one instance, in which I thought some good was done by brandy. This was in the case of captain Snipes and his command, which by way of farce to my own tragedy, I beg leave to relate.

Hearing of a tory camp-meeting not far distant, Marion despatched the brave captain Snipes with a party to chastise them. They had scarcely got upon the tory cruising-ground, before, at a short turn in the road, they came full butt upon a large body of horsemen. Supposing them to be tories, Snipes instantly gave the word to charge; himself leading the way with his usual impetuosity. The supposed tories, wheeling about, took to the sands, and went off, as hard as their horses could stave; and thus, crack and crack, they had it for about two miles.

Finding that Snipes was gaining upon them, the runagates began to lighten themselves of every thing they could spare, and the road was presently strewed with blankets and knapsacks. One of them, it seems, carried a five gallon keg of brandy, which he could not think of parting with; and being well mounted, he stood a good pull for the two first miles. But, finding he was dropping astern very fast, he slyly cut the straps of his mail pillion, and so let his keg, brandy and all go by the run, over his horse's rump. Captain Snipes, who led the chase, found no difficulty in passing the keg: but his men coming up instantly, broached to, all standing; for they could no more pass by a keg of brandy, than young monkeys could pass a basket of apples.

Snipes cursed and raved like a madman, but all in vain: for they swore they must have a dram. While they were devising ways and means how to get into the keg, the supposed tories, now a good distance ahead, came to a halt, and their captain fortunately reflecting that their pursuers might not be enemies, sent back a flag. The result was, the very joyful discovery, that the owners of the keg were good whigs coming to join general Marion. Thus, to a moral certainty, this keg of brandy was made, of kind heaven, the happy means of preventing much bloodshed that day.

Having given two cases of brandy, the one good, the other bad, I will now give a third, which the reader, if he pleases, may call indifferent, and which runs as follows.

General Marion, still encamped in the neighborhood of Georgetown, ordered captain Withers to take sergeant Macdonald, with four volunteers, and go on the enemy's lines to see what they were doing. On approaching the town, they met an old tory; one of your half-witted fellows, whom neither side regarded any more than a Jew does a pig, and therefore suffered him to stroll when and where he pleased. The old man knew captain Withers very well; and as soon as he had got near enough to recollect him, he bawled out, "God's mercy, master Withers! why, where are you going this course?"

"Going, old daddy! why to the devil, perhaps," replied Withers.

"Well faith! that's like enough, captain," said the old man, "especially if you keep on this tack much longer. But before you go any further, suppose you take a pull with me of this," holding up a stout tickler of brandy, "mayhap you may not get such good liquor where you are going."

"With all my heart, daddy," answered Withers, and twigg'd the tickler to the tune of a deep dram: and passed it on to Macdonald, who also twigg'd it, "and Tom twigg'd it, and Dick twigg'd it, and Harry twigg'd it, and so they all twigg'd it." In the mean time the chat went round very briskly, and dram after dram, the brandy, until the tickler was drained to the bottom. And then the subtle spirit of the brandy, ascending into their noddles, worked such wonders, that they all began to feel themselves as big as field officers. Macdonald, for his part, with a face as red as a comet, reined up Selim, and drawing his claymore, began to pitch and prance about, cutting and slashing the empty air, as if he had a score of enemies before him, and ever and anon, roaring out—"Huzza, boys! damme, let's charge!"

"Charge, boys! charge!" cried all the rest, reining up their horses, and flourishing their swords.

"Where the plague are you going to charge?" asked the old tory.

"Why, into Georgetown, right off," replied they.

"Well, you had better have a care, boys, how you charge there, for I'll be blamed if you do not get yourselves into business pretty quick: for the town is chock full of red coats."

"Red coats!" one and all they roared out, "red coats! egad, that's just what we want. Charge, boys! charge! huzza for the red coats, damme!"

Then, clapping spurs to their steeds, off went these six young madcaps, huzzaing and flourishing their swords, and charging at full tilt, into a British garrison town of three hundred men!!

The enemy supposing that this was only our advance, and that general Marion, with his whole force, would presently be upon them, flew with all speed to their redoubt, and there lay, as snug as fleas in a sheep-skin. But all of them were not quite so lucky, for several were overtaken and cut down in the streets, among whom was a sergeant major, a stout greasy fellow, who strove hard to waddle away with his bacon; but Selim was too quick for him: and Macdonald, with a back-handed stroke of his claymore, sent his frightened ghost to join the majority.

Having thus cleared the streets, our young troopers then called at the houses of their friends; asked the news; and drank their grog with great unconcern.

The British, after having for some time vainly looked for Marion, began to smell the trick, and in great wrath sallied forth for vengeance. Our adventurers then, in turn, were fain to scamper off as fast as they had made the others before, but with better success; for though hundreds of muskets were fired after them, they got clear without receiving a scratch.

But nothing ever so mortified the British, as did this mad frolic. "That half a dozen d—n-d young rebels," they said, "should thus dash in among us in open daylight, and fall to cutting and slashing the king's troops at this rate. And after all, to gallop away without the least harm in hair or hide. 'Tis high time to turn our bayonets into pitch forks, and go to foddering the cows."

CHAPTER XX

History of captain Snipes—wanton destruction of his property by the tories—his own miraculous escape—admirable fidelity of his negro driver Cudjo.

Captain Snipes, who made such a figure in the wars of Marion, was a Carolinian, of uncommon strength and courage; both of which he exerted with great good will, against the British and tories; from principle partly, and partly from revenge. But though a choice soldier, he was no philosopher. He did not consider that to fight for duty, people must love it; that to love it, they must understand it; that to understand it, they must possess letters and religion: that the British and tories, poor fellows! possessing neither of these, were not to have been expected to act any other than the savage and thievish part they did act; and therefore, no more to be hated for it than the cats are for teasing the canary birds.

But captain Snipes had no turn for investigations of this sort. Knowledge, by intuition, was all that he cared for; and having it, by instinct, that an "Englishman ought never to fight against liberty," nor an "American against his own country," he looked on them, to use his own phrase, as a "pack of d—n-d rascals, whom it was doing God service to kill wherever he could find them."

But Snipes was not the aggressor. He kept in, very decently, till the enemy began to let out, as they did, in plundering, burning, and hanging the poor whigs; and then, indeed, like a consuming fire, his smothered hate broke forth:

> "That hate which hurled to Pluto's gloomy reign
> The souls of royal slaves untimely slain."

Afraid, in fair fight, to meet that sword which had so often shivered their friends, they determined to take him as the Philistines did Samson, by surprise; and having learned from their spies, that he was at home, they came upon him in force about midnight. His complete destruction, both of life and property, was their horrid aim. Happily, his driver, or black overseer, overheard their approach; and flying to his master with terror-struck looks, cries out "Run! run! massa, run! de enemy 'pon you."

Snipes, stark naked, save his shirt, darted out as swift as his legs could carry him. "But where shall I run, Cudjo? into the barn?"

"Oh no, massa! dey burn de barn, dat sure ting!"

"Well, where shall I run then?"

"Take de bush massa! take de briar bush."

Within fifty yards of the house was a clump of briers, so thick set, that one would have thought a frightened cat would scarcely have squeezed herself into it from the hot pursuing dogs. But what will not fear enable a man to do? Captain Snipes, big as he was, slipped into it with the facility of a weasel through the chinks of a chicken-coop; but lost every thread and thrumb of his shirt; and moreover, got his hide so scratched and torn by the briers, that the blood trickled from him fast as gravy from a fat green goose.

Scarcely had he gained his hiding-place, before the tories, with horrid oaths, burst into his house, with their guns cocked, ready to shoot him. But oh! death to their hopes! he was gone: the nest was there, and warm, but the bird was flown!

Then seizing poor Cudjo by the throat, they bawled out: "You d——d rascal, where's your master?"

He told them he did not know.

"You lie! you black son of a b-t-h! you lie."

But he still asserted he knew nothing of his master.

Suspecting that he must be in some one or other of his buildings, they set fire to them all; to his dwelling house, his kitchen, his stables, and even his negro cabins, watching all the while, with their muskets ready to shoot him as he ran out. From their nearness to his lurking place, the heat of his burning houses was so intense as to parch his skin into blisters. But it was death to stir, for he would certainly have been seen.

Not having made the discovery they so much wished, they again seized Cudjo; and, with their cocked pieces at his breast, swore if he did not instantly tell them where his master was, they would put him to death.

He still declared he did not know where he was.

Then they clapped a halter round his neck, and told him to "down on his knees, and say his prayers at once, for he had but two minutes to live!"

He replied, that he "did not want to say his prayers now, for that he was no thief, and had always been a true slave to his master."

This fine sentiment of the poor black was entirely lost on our malignant whites; who, throwing the end of the halter over the limb of an oak, tucked him up as though he had been a mad dog. He hung till he was nearly dead; when one of them called out, "D—n him, cut him down, I'll be bound he'll tell us now." Cudjo was accordingly cut down; and, as soon as a little recovered, questioned again about his master. But he still declared he knew nothing of him. He was then hoisted a second time; and a second time, when nearly dead, cut down and questioned as before: but still asserted his ignorance. The same inhuman part was acted on him a third time, but with no better success; for the brave fellow still continued faithful to his master, who squatted and trembled in his place of torment, his brier bush, and saw and heard all that was passing.

Persuaded now that Cudjo really knew nothing of his master, they gave up the shameful contest, and went off, leaving him half dead on the ground, but covered with glory.

It is not easy to conceive a situation more severely torturing than this of captain Snipes. His house, with all his furniture, his kitchen, his barn and rice-stacks, his stables, with several fine horses, and his negro houses, all wrapped in flames; himself scorched and blistered with the furious heat, yet not daring to stir; his retreat well known to a poor slave; and that slave alone, in the hands of an enraged banditti, with their muskets at his breast, imprecating the most horrid curses on themselves, if they did not instantly murder him unless he disclosed the secret! What had he to expect of this poor slave, but that he would sink under the dreadful trial, and to save himself would sacrifice his master. But Snipes was safe. To discover his hiding-place, death stared his slave in the face, but, happily, his slave possessed for him that "love which is stronger than death."

Captain Snipes and his man Cudjo had been brought up from childhood together; and the father of our hero being a professor of Christianity, a Baptist preacher, whose main excellence is "to teach little children to love one another," had taken great pains to inspire his son with love towards his little slave. Nor did that love pass unrequited. For Cudjo used every day to follow his young master to school, carrying his basket for him, prattling as he went; and smiling, would remind him of the coming Saturday, and what fine fishing and hunting they would have that day. Many a time had they wrestled, and slept side by side on the green; and thence springing up again with renovated strength, set out in full march for some favorite fruit tree, or some cooling pond, there to swim and gambol in the refreshing flood. And when the time of dinner came, Cudjo was not scornfully left to sigh and to gnaw his nails alone, but would play and sing about the door till his young master was done, and then he was sure to receive a good plate full for himself. Love, thus early ingrafted on his heart, grew up with daily increasing strength to manhood; when Snipes, by the death of his father, became master of the estate, made Cudjo his driver or overseer, and thus rivetted on his honest bosom that sacred friendship which, as we have seen, enabled him to triumph in one of the severest trials that human nature was ever put to.

The above is a solemn fact, and the wise will lay it to heart.

CHAPTER XXI

Marion pursues major Muckleworth—fine anecdote of the major—Marion's generosity to him.

*L*earning that a detachment of the British were marching up Black river towards Statesburgh and Camden, general Marion gave orders to chase; which was conducted, as usual, with such rapidity, that about sunset of the second day we came up with them. Our advance, composed of choice fellows, instantly began to skirmish with the enemy, of whom they killed eight or nine. A few on both sides, rather badly wounded, were made prisoners. Marion, coming up, gave orders to call off the troops, meaning to give the enemy a serious brush in the morning.—But of this gratification they entirely disappointed us, by striking their tents and pushing off in silence before day.

Soon as light returned, and the retreat of the British was announced, we renewed the pursuit; and by late breakfast-time, reached the house at which the enemy had refreshed themselves. This house belonged to a poor, but excellent old lady, well known to Marion.

The general was hardly alighted from his horse, before the old lady had him by the hand, declaring how happy she had always been to see him, "but now," continued she, "if I an't right down sorry to see you, then I'll be hanged."

Marion, with a look of surprise, asked her why she was sorry to see him now.

"Oh! don't I know you too well, general? don't I know that old Scratch himself can't keep you from fighting? And now you are hurrying along here, with all your men, only to fight the British. An't it so now, general?"

Marion told her, that that was indeed his business.

"Well, dear me now! and did I not tell you so? But pray now, my dear general Marion, let me beg of you, don't you do any harm to that dear good man, that major Muckleworth, who went from here a little while ago: for O! he's the sweetest-spoken, mildest-looking, noblest-spirited Englishman I ever saw in all my born days. As to that Rawdon and Tarleton, God's curse upon the thieves and blackguards! I would not care if you could kill a thousand of them. But that good major Muckleworth! indeed, indeed now general, you must not hurt a hair of his head, for it would be such a crying sin."

Marion asked her in what respects was he better than other British officers.

"Better than other British officers!" replied the old lady.—"Lord bless your dear soul, general Marion! Well, come along, come along with me, and I'll let you see."

We followed the old lady, who, tripping along nimble as a girl, conducted us into a clean looking cabin, wherein sat a middle-aged man very genteelly dressed, and several wounded persons lying before him, on pallets on the floor. Marion saluted the stranger, who informed us that he was "a surgeon in the service of his Britannic majesty, and left by major Muckleworth to take care of the wounded; of whom, sir, I believe that nearly one half are your own men."

Here the old lady's face brightened up towards Marion; and giving him a very significant look, she said, "Ah ha, general! didn't I tell you so?"

Then diving her withered hand in her pocket, she scooped up a shining parcel of English guineas, and exultingly cried out, "See there, general! see there's a sight for you? and every penny of it given me by that dear good gentleman, major Muckleworth; every penny of it, sir. Yes, and if you will but believe me, general, when I and my daughters were getting breakfast for him and his people, if he didn't come here himself with his sergeants, and had this place swept out all so sweet and clean for them poor sick people; and, with his own dear hands too, helped that gentleman there to dress and doctor the poor things, that he did.

"And then besides all that, general, he was such a sweet spoken gentleman! for when I asked him how his men came to be hurt so, he did not, like that beast Tarleton, turn black and blue in the face, and fall to cursing the d——d rebels. Oh no! not he indeed. But he said with a smile, We got them wounded last night, madam, in a little brush with your brave countryman, general Marion.

"Now only think of that, general! And besides, when he was going away, what do you think he did? Why, sir, he sent for me and said,—Well, my good madam, and what shall I pay you for all the trouble we have given you, and also for taking care of the doctor I am going to leave with you, and the sick people, who may be on your hands for a fortnight yet?

"I told him it was no business of mine to fix a price.

"He seemed surprised, and asked me what I meant by that.

"I answered that I was now all one as his prisoner, and prisoners had nothing they could call their own.

"My king, madam, said he, does not make war against widows.

"I told him I wished to God all his countrymen had remembered that! it would have saved the hunger and nakedness, and cries and tears of many a poor widow and orphan. At this he seemed mightily hurt.

"I then told him that many of the British officers, after eating and drinking all that they wanted, for themselves and people, and horses, instead of turning round to pay, as he had done, had turned in to plunder, and then set fire to the houses, not leaving the widows and children a cover

over their heads, nor a bit of bread for their mouths, nor a stitch of clothes for their backs.

"My God! said he, and is this the way that my countrymen have come here to carry on war! Well madam, (so he went on) my king does not know any thing of this, nor does the English nation, I am sure. If they did, they would certainly call those officers to account. Such men will ruin our cause. For the word of God assures us, that his ear is always open to the cry of the widow and orphan; and believe me, madam, I dread their cry more than I do the shouts of an enemy's army. However, madam, (continued he,) I have not a moment to lose, for I am sure general Marion is pursuing me as hard as he can, so let me know what I owe you.

"I told him again, I made no charge; but since he was so good as to insist on giving me something, I begged to leave the matter entirely to himself. Upon which, after a moment's study, he looked at me and said, Well, madam, suppose we say sixpence sterling a-piece man and horse, all around, will that do? I replied that was too much, a great deal too much, for such a poor breakfast as I had given him and his men. Not a penny too much, madam, said he, live and let live is the royal law, madam, and here's your money. With that he put all these guineas here, into my hand! and said moreover, that if the doctor and sick people should be longer with me, and give me more trouble and cost than we had counted on, then I must send a note to him, at such a house in Charleston, and he would send me the money. And now, general, would it not be a burning shame to go kill such a dear good gentleman as that?"

Marion listened with delight to the old lady's history of this amiable officer; but on her leaving him to hasten our breakfast, he looked very pensive, and at a loss what to do. However, as soon as the troops were refreshed, he ordered my brother, colonel H. Horry, who led the advance, to remount, and push after the enemy with all speed. We followed close in the rear. For an hour the general did not open his mouth, but rode on like one absorbed in thought. At length heaving a deep sigh, he said, "Well, I suppose I feel now very much as I should feel, were I in pursuit of a brother to kill him."

About three o'clock our advance came up with the enemy, near the wealthy and hospitable captain John Singleton's mills, where the firing instantly commenced, and was as spiritedly returned by the British, still retreating. Our marksmen presently stopped one of Muckleworth's captains, and several of his men, who lay dead on the ground at the very spot where we happened to join the advance. The sight of these poor fellows lying in their blood, gave the general's wavering mind the casting vote in favor of generosity; for he immediately cried out, "Call off the troops! call off the troops!" Then turning to his aid he said, "I cannot stand it any longer; we owe yon Englishmen to our injured country; but there is an angel that guards them. Ten righteous Lots would have saved Sodom. One generous Muckleworth shall save this handful. Let us turn and fight other enemies."

The general's orders were quickly passed on to the troops to cease firing. And to their credit be it spoken, they never, I believe, obeyed his orders with more alacrity than on this occasion. Indeed I heard many of them say, afterwards, that major Muckleworth's generosity to their wounded comrades and to the poor widow, had so won their hearts to him, that they had none left wherewith to fight against him; and they said also, that, for their parts, they had rather kill a thousand such savages as Rawdon and Tarleton, than hurt a hair of major Muckleworth's head.

From the effect produced on our troops, by this amiable officer's conduct, I have often been led to think favorably of a saying common with Marion, viz., had the British officers but acted as became a wise and magnanimous enemy, they might easily have recovered the revolted colonies.

Never did the pulse of love towards a parent state beat stronger in human bosoms, than in those of the Carolinians towards Britain. We looked on her as indeed our mother, and on her children as our brothers. And ah! had their government but treated us with correspondent kindness, Carolina would have been with them to a man. Had they said to the people, as they might easily have done (for there was a time, and a long time too, when the whole state was entirely at their feet,) had they then said to us, "We are far richer, far stronger, than you; we can easily burn your houses, take your provisions, carry off your cattle, and sweep your country with the besom of destruction; but we abhor the idea. Your houses, your women, your children, are all sacred in our eyes; and even of your goods we will touch nothing without giving you a reasonable price." Had they but said this, Carolina would, to a certainty, have been divorced from Congress, and re-wedded to Britain.

We may lay what emphasis we please on the term countrymen, countrymen! but after all, as Christ says, "he is our countryman who showeth mercy unto us."

A British officer, a major Muckleworth, for example, calls at my plantation, and takes my fine horses and fat beeves, my pigs, my poultry and grain; but at parting, launches out for me a fist full of yellow boys! On the other hand, an American officer calls and sweeps me of everything, and then lugs out a bundle of continental proc! such trash, that hardly a cow would give a corn shock for a horse load of it.

The Englishman leaves me richer than he found me, and abler to educate and provide for my children: the American leaves me and my family half ruined. Now I wish to know where, in such a selfish world as this, where is there a man in a million, but would take part with the generous Englishman, and fight for him?

This was the theory of Marion; and it was the practice of Muckleworth, whom it certainly saved to the British; and would, if universal, have saved Carolina and Georgia to them too; and perhaps, all America. But so little idea had they of this mode of conciliating to conquer, that when the good major Muckleworth returned to Charleston, he was hooted at by the British officers, who said he might do well enough for a chaplain, or a methodist preacher, for what they knew, but they'd be d—n-d if he were fit to be a British major.

The truth is, such divine philosophy was too refined for such coarse and vulgar characters, as Cornwallis, Rawdon, Tarleton, Balfour, and Weymies; monsters who disgraced the brave and generous nation they represented, and completely damned the cause they were sent to save. But what better was to have been expected of those, who, from early life, if tradition say true, discovered a total dislike to the ennobling pleasures of literature and devotion, but a boundless passion for the brutalizing sports of the bear-garden and cock-pit? Bull-baiters, cock-fighters, and dog worriers, turned officers, had no idea of conquering the Americans, but by "cutting their throats or knocking out their brains;" or as the tender-hearted Cornwallis commanded, by "hanging them, and taking away, or destroying their goods."

Now Satan himself could have counselled my lord better than that; as any man may see, who will but open his bible and turn to the book of Job, chap. the 1st, verse 6th, and so on. There Moses informs, that when Satan, whose effrontery is up to any thing, presented himself at the grand levee, the Almighty very civilly asked him, (now mind that, 'saints,' in your speech to poor sinners)—the Almighty, I say, very civilly asked him "where he had been of late."

To this, his royal highness, the brimstone king, replied, that he had been only taking a turn or two "up and down the earth."

The divine voice again interrogated: "Hast thou considered my servant Job? an excellent man, is he not; one who feareth God and escheweth evil?"

"Job's well enough," replied Satan, rather pertly, but where's the wonder of all that? You have done great things for the fellow; you have planted a hedge around him, and around all that he hath on every side. You have blessed the works of his hands, and his substance is increased in the land; and if, after all this, he cannot afford you a little gratitude, he must be a poor devil indeed. But put forth thy hand now, and touch all that he hath, and he'll curse thee to thy face."

This was the devil's logic as to Job: but the British general had not the wit to reason in that style towards the Americans. For my Lord Cornwallis said unto my lord Rawdon; and my lord Rawdon said unto my would-be lord, colonel Tarleton; and colonel Tarleton said unto major Weymies; and major Weymies said unto Will Cunningham, and unto the British soldiers with their tory negro allies; "Put forth your hands, boys, and burn, and plunder the d—n-d rebels; and instead of cursing you to your face, they will fall down and kiss your feet."

"Experience," says Doctor Franklin, "is a dear school; but fools will learn in no other, and hardly in that." And what right had lord North to expect success in America, when for officers he sent such fools as would take no lesson either from God or devil.

CHAPTER XXII

Colonel Watson attempts to surprise Marion—is out-generaled, and after much loss driven back to Georgetown.

In consequence of his incessant attacks on the British and tories, Marion was, I believe, heartily hated by them, as ever Samson was by the Philistines, or George Whitefield by the devil. Numerous were the attempts made by their best officers to surprise him; but such was his own vigilance and the fidelity of his whig friends, that he seldom failed to get the first blow at them, and to take their unwary feet in the same evil net which they had spread for him.

His method to anticipate the meditated malice of his enemies, is well worthy of notice. He always had in his service a parcel of active young men, generally selected from the best whig families, and of tried courage and fidelity. These, mounted on the swiftest horses, he would station in the neighborhood of those places where the British and tories were embodied in force, as Camden, Georgetown, &c. with instructions to leave no stratagem untried to find out the intended movements of the enemy. Instantly as this information was obtained, (whether by climbing tall trees that overlooked the garrisons; or from friends acting as market people) they were to mount and push off at full speed to the nearest of a chain of posts established at short and convenient distances, with fleet horses ready saddled and bridled, to bear the intelligence with equal speed, the first to the second, the second to the third, and so on. In this expeditious method, as by a telegraph, Marion was presently notified of the designs of the enemy. Of the exceeding importance of such a plan, we had a very striking proof at this time. Exasperated against Marion, for the infinite harm he did the royal cause in Carolina, the British general, in Camden, determined to surprise him at his old place of retreat, Snow's Island; and thus destroy or break him up completely. To this end he despatched a couple of favorite officers, colonels Watson and Doyle, with a heavy force, both cavalry and infantry, to seize the lower bridge on Black river and thereby effectually prevent our escape. But the vigilance and activity of his scouts frustrated this well-concerted plan entirely. Getting early notice of this manoeuvre by captain, now general Canty, Marion instantly started his troops, composed chiefly of mounted riflemen and light dragoons and pushed hard for the same point. By taking a nearer cut, we had the good fortune to gain the bridge before the enemy, and having destroyed it as soon as we crossed, we concealed ourselves in the dark swamp, anxiously waiting their arrival. In a short time, they came in full view on the opposite hill, and there encamped.—Presently, unapprehensive of danger, for they saw nothing of us, two of their men came down for water to the river. Unable to resist such a temptation, two of our noted marksmen instantly drew their sights and let fly. The two Englishmen fell; one of them was killed dead; the other badly wounded, and so frightened, that he bellowed like a bull-calf for help. Several of his gallant countrymen ran to his assistance, but they were shot down as fast as they got to him.

The next morning colonel Watson sent a flag over to Marion, whom he charged with carrying on war in a manner entirely different from all civilized nations. "Why sir," said he to Marion, "you must certainly command a horde of savages, who delight in nothing but murder. I can't cross a swamp or a bridge, but I am waylaid and shot at as if I were a mad dog. Even my sentries are fired at and killed on their posts. Why, my God, sir! this is not the way that Christians ought to fight!"

To this Marion replied, that "he was sorry to be obliged to say, that from what he had known of them, the British officers were the last men on earth who had any right to preach about honor and humanity. That for men to come three thousand miles to plunder and hang an innocent people, and then to tell that people how they ought to fight, betrayed an ignorance and impudence which he fain would hope had no parallel in the history of man. That for his part, he always believed, and still did believe that he should be doing God and his country good service to surprise and kill such men, while they continued this diabolical warfare, as he would the wolves and panthers of the forest."

Thus ended the correspondence for that time.

While things remained in this state between the hostile parties, Macdonald, as usual, was employing himself in a close and bold reconnoitre of the enemy's camp. Having found out the situation of their sentries, and the times of relieving them, he climbed up into a bushy tree, and thence, with a musket loaded with pistol bullets, cracked away at their guard as they passed by; of whom he killed one man, and badly wounded the lieutenant, whose name was Torquano; then sliding down the tree, he mounted his swift-footed Selim, and made his escape.

The next morning colonel Watson sent another flag to Marion, requesting that he would grant a passport to his lieutenant Torquano, who was badly wounded, and wished to be carried to Charleston. On receiving the flag, which happened while I was by him, Marion turned to me, and with a smile said, "Well, this note of colonel Watson looks a little as if he were coming to his senses. But who is lieutenant Torquano?"

I replied that he was a young Englishman, who had been quartered in Charleston, at the house of that good whig lady, Mrs. Brainford and her daughters, whom he had treated very politely, and often protected from insults.

"Well," said he, "if that be lieutenant Torquano, he must be a very clever fellow; and shall certainly have a passport to Charleston, or even to Paradise, if I had the keys of St. Peter."

On repassing Black river in haste, Macdonald had left his clothes behind him at a poor woman's house, where the enemy seized them. By the return of the flag just mentioned, he sent word to colonel Watson, that if he did not immediately send back his clothes, he would kill eight of his men to pay for them.

Several of Watson's officers who were present when the message was delivered, advised him by all means to return his clothes, for that they knew him to be a most desperate fellow, one who would stop at nothing he set his head upon; witness his late daring act of climbing like a cougar, into a tree, to kill his passing enemies. Watson sent him back his wallet of clothes.

Soon after this, the enemy decamped silently in the night, and took the road towards Santee. On the return of day announcing their flight, Marion ordered me to take the mounted riflemen, thirty in number, with fifty horse, and pursue and harass the enemy as much as possible, till he could come up with the infantry.

About night I approached their encampment, and halted in a neighboring swamp; whence I continued to send out small parties, frequently relieved, with orders to pop away at their sentinels, and keep them alarmed and under arms all night. At daybreak they pushed hard for the sandpit bridge. We followed close in the rear, constantly firing on them from every thicket and swamp; and often, in spite of their field pieces, making false charges. Never did I see a body of infantry ply their legs so briskly. The rogues were constantly in a dog trot, except when they occasionally halted to give us a blast, which they did from their whole line. But though their bullets made a confounded whizzing and clatter among the branches over our heads, yet thank God they did no harm, save that of scratching some three or four of us.

On coming within a few miles of it, we made a rapid push for the bridge, which we quickly rendered impassable, by throwing off the plank and sleepers. Then having posted my riflemen in the thick woods, within fifty yards of the ford, under command of lieutenant Scott, I drew up my cavalry close in the rear, and waited impatiently for the enemy, hoping to give a handsome Bunker's Hill account of them.

The enemy were presently in sight, and formed in close column, began to push through the fording place, though full waist deep. My heart now throbbed with anxiety; looking every moment for a stream of fire to burst upon the British, spreading destruction through their ranks.

But, to my infinite mortification, no lightnings bursted forth; no thunders roared; no enemy fell. As, half choked with grief and rage, I looked around for the cause, behold! my brave lieutenant Scott, at the head of his riflemen, came stooping along with his gun in his hand, and the black marks of shame and cowardice on his sheepish face. "Infamous poltroon," said I, shaking my sword over his head, "where is that hetacomb of robbers and murderers due to the vengeance of your injured country?"

He began to stammer out some apology, which I quickly suppressed, by ordering him out of my sight. It is worthy of remark, that his men, instead of apologising for him, called him a coward to his face, and declared that it was he who had restrained them by telling them they were flanked by the enemy, who would assuredly cut them to pieces if they fired a shot.

As the advance of the British were thus undisturbedly passing on, a heavy firing was suddenly heard in the rear. It was Marion; who, having come up with the enemy, had attacked him with great fury. The British did not halt, but continued a running fight through the woods till they gained the open fields; where, by means of their artillery, they kept us at a distance. In this rencontre, Watson had his horse killed under him, and left about twenty of his men dead on the ground. His wounded filled several wagons.

He did not halt a moment, but pushed hard for Georgetown; and late at night encamped on the plantation of Mr. Trapier, to whom he told a dreadful story about Marion and his damned rebels, who would not, as he said, sleep and fight like gentlemen, but, like savages, were eternally firing and whooping around him by night; and by day, waylaying and popping at him from behind every tree he went by.

As it was too late to pursue the enemy, Marion encamped for the night near the field of battle, and next morning marched for his old post, Snow's Island, where he allowed us a few days of welcome repose.

CHAPTER XXIII

Patriotism of Mrs. Jenkins—colonel Watson, colonel Doyle, and the tories, make alarming advances upon general Marion— his men begin to desert him—Horry turns orator, and harangues the troops—they repeat their assurances of patriotism and attachment to Marion—he dashes out again upon the enemy— prospects brighten—and the good old cause begins to look up again.

It was not for the British and Marion to lie long at rest in the same neighborhood. After a short repose, Colonel Watson, with a stout force of regulars and tories, made an inroad upon Pedee; which was no sooner known in our camp, than Marion pushed after him. We presently struck their trail; and after a handsome day's run, pitched our tents near the house of the excellent widow Jenkins, and on the very spot which the British had left in the morning. Colonel Watson, it seems, had taken his quarters that night in her house; and learning that she had three sons with Marion, all active young men, he sent for her after supper, and desired her to sit down and take a glass of wine with him. To this request, a good old lady of taste and manners could have no objection: so waiting upon the colonel, and taking a chair which he handed her, she sat down and emptied her glass to his health. He then commenced the following conversation with her:

"So, madam, they tell me you have several sons in general Marion's camp; I hope it is not true."

She said it was very true, and was only sorry that it was not a thousand times truer.

"A thousand times truer, madam!" replied he with great surprise, "pray what can be your meaning in that?"

"Why, sir, I am only sorry that in place of three, I have not three thousand sons with general Marion."

"Aye indeed! well then, madam, begging your pardon, you had better send for them immediately to come in and join his majesty's troops under my command: for as they are rebels now in arms against their king, should they be taken they will be hung as sure as ever they were born."

"Why, sir," said the old lady, "you are very considerate of my sons; for which at any rate I thank you. But, as you have begged my pardon for giving me this advice, I must beg yours for not taking it. My sons, sir, are of age, and must and will act for themselves. And as to their being in a state of rebellion against their king, I must take the liberty, sir, to deny that."

"What, madam!" replied he, "not in rebellion against their king? shooting at and killing his majesty's subjects like wolves! don't you call that rebellion against their king, madam?"

"No, sir," answered she: "they are only doing their duty, as God and nature commanded them, sir."

"The d—l they are, madam!"

"Yes, sir," continued she, "and what you and every man in England would glory to do against the king, were he to dare to tax you contrary to your own consent and the constitution of the realm. 'Tis the king, sir, who is in rebellion against my sons, and not they against him. And could right prevail against might, he would as certainly lose his head, as ever king Charles the First did." Colonel Watson could hardly keep his chair under the smart of this speech: but thinking it would never do for a British colonel to be rude to a lady, he filled her glass, and saying, "he'd be d—n-d if she were not a very plain-spoken woman at any rate," insisted she would drink a toast with him for all.

She replied she had no objection.

Then filling the glasses round, he looked at her with a constrained smile, and said, "Well, madam, here's George the Third."

"With all my heart, sir!" and turned off her bumper with a good grace.

After a decent interval of sprightly conversation, he called on the widow for a toast; who very smartly retorted, "Well, sir, here's George Washington!" At which he darkened a little, but drank it off with an officer-like politeness.

The next morning early, we left the good Mrs. Jenkins; and burning with impatience to give Watson another race, we drove on Jehu-like.

We encamped that night almost within sight of the enemy's fires: but found them too much on the alert for surprise. We kept, however, a good look out, and learning next morning, that a roosting party were out, Marion detached my brother colonel Horry, with some choice cavaliers, to attack them; which he did with such spirit, that at the first onset he killed nine, and made the balance, sixteen, all prisoners. The rogues were so overloaded with plunder, that for their lives they could not regain their camp, though in full view of it when they were charged. This brilliant stroke of my brother, threw the enemy's camp into the utmost hurry and uproar; and their dragoons were quickly mounted, dashing out to rescue their comrades; but in vain, for my brother brought them all off in safety to our camp.

Our strength at this time was far inferior to that of the enemy. But it soon became alarmingly reduced. For learning that, besides this heavy force under Watson, there was another from Camden under colonel Doyle, and also of mounted tories from Pedee, all in full march against us, our men took a panic and began to desert, and those who stayed behind looked very serious, and talked as if certain ruin both to themselves and families would follow from their continuing to fight in so hopeless a cause.

In answer to these desponding gentlemen, I replied, that I was ashamed and grieved too, to hear them talk at that rate.

"Our prospects," said I, "gentlemen, are to be sure dark, very dark; yet thank God, they are not desperate. We have often before now seen as heavy clouds hanging over us; and yet with heaven's blessing on our arms, those clouds have been dispersed, and golden days restored. And who knows but we may shortly see it so again? I am sure we have good reason to expect it; and also to hope that God will assist us, who are only fighting to make ourselves free and happy, according to his own most blessed will. And will it not be a most sweet cordial to your spirits as long as you live, to think that, in such trying times as these, you stood up for your country, and fought and won for yourselves and children all the blessings of liberty.

"And, besides," said I, "do not the tories, who are more than half the authors of your misfortunes, possess large estates? And have you not arms in your hands, wherewith to pay yourselves out of their ill-saved treasures?"

This speech seemed to raise their spirits a good deal.

I then went to see the general, who with his hands behind him, was walking backwards and forwards in front of his tent, meditating, no doubt, on the desertion of his men; whose numbers, from more than two hundred, were now reduced to less than seventy.

"General Marion," said I, "I am sorry to tell you that our men are now so few; especially since, according to report, we shall soon want so many."

"Why," replied he, "that is the very thing I have been grieving at; but it will signify nothing for us to stand here sighing and croaking; so pray go and order a muster of the men, that I may say a few words to them before they all run off and leave me."

Soon as the troops were all paraded around the door of his tent, he stepped upon the trunk of a fallen pine, and in his plain but impressive manner, addressed us nearly as follows:—

"Gentlemen and fellow-soldiers.

"It is not for words to express what I feel when I look around upon your diminished numbers. Yesterday I commanded 200 men; men whom I gloried in, and who I fondly thought, would have followed me through my dangers for their country. And, now, when their country most needs their services, they are nearly all gone! And even those of you who remain, are, if report be true, quite out of heart; and talk, that you and your families must be ruined if you resist any longer! But, my friends, if we shall be ruined for bravely resisting our tyrants, what will be done to us if we tamely lie down and submit to them? In that event, what can we expect but to see our own eternal disgrace, and the wide-spread ruin of our country; when our bravest and best citizens shall be hung up like dogs, and their property confiscated to enrich those villains who deserted their country, and joined her enemies; when Cornwallis, Rawdon and Tarleton, after so long plundering and murdering your friends, shall, in reward of such services, be set over you as your governors and lord lieutenants, with princely salaries out of your labors; when foreign bishops and hireling clergy shall be poured upon you like hosts of consecrated locusts, consuming the tithes and fat of the land; when British princes, and nobles, and judges, shall swarm over your devoted country, thick as eagles over a new-fallen carcass; when an insatiate king, looking on your country as his plantation, and on your children as his slaves, shall take away your substance, every year, for his pomps and pleasures; and to keep you under for ever, shall fill your land with armies; and when those armies, viewing you with malignant eyes, shall constantly be insulting you as conquered rebels; and under pretence of discovering among you the seeds of another rebellion, shall be perpetually harassing and giving up to military execution the best and worthiest of your fellow-citizens?

"Now my brave brethren in arms, is there a man among you, who can bear the thought of living to see his dear country and friends in so degraded and wretched a state as this? If there be, then let that man leave me and retire to his home. I ask not his aid. But, thanks to God, I have now no fears about you: judging by your looks, I feel that there is no such man among us. For my own part I look upon such a state of things as a thousand times worse than death. And God is my judge this day, that if I could die a thousand deaths, most gladly would I die them all, rather than live to see my dear country in such a state of degradation and wretchedness."

In reply to this speech of our honored general, we told him, in brief, it was on account of his noble sentiments we had always so highly esteemed him; that it was on account of these we had already suffered so much, and were ready to suffer more; and that rather than see our country in that wretched state which he had so feelingly described, and which, with him, we firmly believed would be the case if the British were to get the upper hand, we had made up our minds to fight by his side to a glorious death.

I never saw such a change on the face of a human being, as then took place on that of Marion. His eyes sparkled with pleasure, while in transport he exclaimed—"Well, now colonel Doyle, look sharp, for you shall presently feel the edge of our swords."

Soon as night came on we mounted, and took the swamps of Lynch's creek, though swimming deep, and after a long time spent in plunging and splashing through the dark floods, we got over, at least about two-thirds of us. The rest, driven down by the force of the current, were cast ashore on hills and high banks, which by the freshet were converted into islands; and there they continued whooping and hallooing to each other all night. When the welcome light returned, they plunged again into the furious stream, and though swept down a good way by the force of the current, arrived safely on our side where we had prepared some large fires to dry their clothes and muskets, and plenty of roasted roots and Indian cakes for breakfast.

As God was pleased to have it, none of us lost our lives, though many did their great coats, blankets, and saddles, and some few their pieces. As to myself, I must needs say, I was never so near the other world in my life. For, as we were borne along down the stream in the dark, my horse and I were carried under the limb of a tree hung thick with wild vines, which soon caught me by the head like Absalom, and there held me fast, dangling in the furious flood, while my horse was swept from under me. I hallooed for some time like a lusty fellow, without getting any answer, which made me begin to think my chance was bad. And, God forgive me for it! I could not help thinking it a sad thing, that after so many fierce frays and hard knocks with the British and tories, I should come at last to be choked like a blind puppy, in this dirty swamp: but God be praised for his good angel, who had brought me through six dangers, and now took me out of the seventh. For, as I was near giving out, a bold young fellow of the company overheard me bawling, and having the advantage of a stout horse, dashed in and took me safely off.

I was afraid at first that my horse was drowned—but sagaciously following the rest of the horses, he made his way good, but lost my saddle, great coat, and clothes. But what grieved me most of all was the loss of my holsters, with a pair of elegant silver mounted pistols, a present from Macdonald, and which he had taken from a British officer whom he killed near Georgetown.

Soon as our firearms were dried, and ourselves and horses were refreshed, we mounted and rode hard all that day, to surprise colonel Doyle. About midnight we had approached the house of a good whig, who told us that Doyle had been there, but that warned by an express from Camden, he had started in great haste, and was certainly by that time far beyond our reach. We were much puzzled in our minds for the meaning of this precipitate retreat of colonel Doyle; however, after one day of welcome rest and high cheer, we faced about, fully determined, notwithstanding our inferiority of force, once more to try our fortune with colonel Watson. But in reaching the ground where we had left him encamped, we got advice that he too, with all his troops, were gone off, at a tangent, as hard as he could drive. While we were wondering what could have possessed the British to scamper thus in every direction, captain Conyers, of Lee's legion, hove in sight, with the welcome news that the brave colonel Lee was at hand, coming up full tilt to join us; and also that general Green, with a choice detachment from the great Washington, was bending towards Camden, to recover the laurels which the incautious Gates had lost. These glorious tidings at once explained the cause of the enemy's flight, and inspired us with a joy which the reader can better conceive than I express.

CHAPTER XXIV

Marion's method of managing the militia—sends the author on another expedition against the tories—anecdote of Mr. F. Kinloch—curious dream of black Jonathan, and fortunate escape of Mr. Kinloch—the author's party surprised by the British, but come off with flying colors.

*T*he world, perhaps, never contained a partisan officer who better understood the management of militia than did general Marion. He was never for 'dragooning' a man into the service. "God loves a cheerful giver, and so do I," said he, "a willing soldier. To have him such you must convince him that it is his interest, for interest is every man's pole star. Every man wishes to be happy, and thereto wishes a happy wife and children, a happy country and friends. Convince him that all these invaluable blessings cannot be had without sweet liberty, and you shall have a soldier as brave as Washington.—For no man, worthy of the name, could ever yet bear to see his wife, children and friends, enslaved and miserable." Such was Marion's method of making soldiers. And what with this, and the cruelty of the

British and tories, he had with him, perhaps, some of as brave and desperate men as ever fought.

"Never ride a free horse to death," he used to say to his officers; "push, while he is fresh, but soon as he begins to lag, then lie by and feed high is your play."

For this purpose he always kept a snug hiding-place in reserve for us; which was Snow's Island, a most romantic spot, and admirably fitted to our use. Nature had guarded it, nearly all around, with deep waters and inaccessible marshes; and the neighboring gentlemen were all rich, and hearty whigs, who acted by us the double part of generous stewards and faithful spies, so that, while there, we lived at once in safety and plenty.

We had reposed ourselves but two days in the pleasant wilds of Snow's Island, before Marion, learning that a part of the enemy were in the neighborhood, desired me to take captains Clarke and Irwin, with fifty men, and try if I could not bring him a good account of them.

We encamped the first night on the plantation of Mr. John Withers, where hearing that Mr. F. Kinloch, our member of Congress, was at a neighboring house, I sent him the following note.

> Honorable Sir,
>   If in these dangerous times you can think yourself safe among a handful of militia-men, I shall be very glad to see you at our camp. As to supper, thank God we can give you a trencher of fat pork and potatoes, but for bed and furniture, we can promise you nothing better than earth and sky. I shall place a sentinel on the road to conduct you to,
>   Honorable Sir, your friend,
>   Peter Horry.

Mr. Kinloch, who was one of the cleverest men in the world, instantly set out to come to us, but unluckily missed our sentinel, and went several miles below us to Mr. Alexander Rose's plantation, managed by a mulatto driver named Jonathan. The day being nearly spent, Jonathan very politely urged Mr. Kinloch to alight and spend the night there, promising him a warm supper and a good bed. Mr. Kinloch accepted Jonathan's offer very cheerfully, and after taking part of a nice fowl and a cup of coffee, went to bed. He had not slept long before Jonathan waked him up, and, with great terror in his looks, told him, "he was mighty 'fraid there was harm a-brewing."

"Aye, Jonathan! why so, my good lad."

"Oh, sir," replied Jonathan, "such a dream as I have had, sir! a marvellous bad dream about the enemy's coming upon you to-night, sir!"

"Poh!" quoth Mr. Kinloch, turning himself over for another nap: "I have dreamed nothing about it, Jonathan. And I'm sure such a dream ought to have come to me, and not to you: so we'll even go to sleep again, and trust to heaven."

Accordingly he fell asleep a second time; but had not long enjoyed that sweetest of opiates, before Jonathan comes again, and awakes him with the old story of his dream.

"Well, Jonathan," said Mr. Kinloch, very good-naturedly, "if you are determined to turn me out of doors, I suppose I must go. But where can I get to this time of night?"

"Why, sir," quoth Jonathan, "I'll get your horse and go with you to the main road, sir, and from there, you can't miss your way back to the house you came from this afternoon."

On Jonathan's return from the short distance he had conducted Mr. Kinloch, he found the yard filled with the British light horse!

These dreams are droll things; but they sometimes come so well attested, that there is no doubting them. He who made our frame, can certainly speak to us as well asleep as awake; and the wise will feel the importance of making a friend of Him, who can cause an airy dream to defend us as effectually as a legion of angels.

The next night, just as we were about to encamp, we lighted on a negro fellow, belonging to Mr. Joseph Alston, whom I quickly had by the heels, lest he should give intelligence to the enemy. But, as the devil would have it, just before day, the sergeant of the guard, overcome by the negro's importunities, loosened him and let him go. And, mark now, young officers, what comes from disobeying orders. This villain of a blackamoor had not gone above three miles before he fell in with the British, to whom, Judas-like, he betrayed us off hand! and they as quickly took horse, and pushed on to surprise us.

By sunrise I had all my men mounted; captain Clarke leading the advance, myself and captain Irvin bringing up the rest of the corps.

The British first discovered captain Clarke, which they did in the way of a glimpse, through an opening in the woods; then sounding their bugles, they rushed on to the charge. Unfortunately, Clarke had not yet seen the enemy, and mistaking their bugles for the huntsmen's horns, ordered a halt to see the deer go by. But instead of a herd of flying deer, behold! a column of British cavalry all at once bursting into the road, and shouting and rushing on with drawn swords to the charge. In a moment, as if themselves metamorphosed into deer, Clarke and his advance wheeled about, and giving their horses "the timber",* flew back upon our main body, roaring out as they came in sight—"The British! the British!"—

Quick as thought my men caught the panic, and facing about, took to their heels, and went off as if the d—l had been behind them. I bawled after them as loud as I could roar, "Halt! Halt!" but I might as well have bawled to the whirlwinds, for it appeared to me the louder I bawled, the swifter the rascals flew. Whereupon I clapped spurs to my young Janus, and went off after them at full stretch, hoping to gain their front and so bring them to. Being mounted on a young full-blooded charger, fresh and strong from the stable, I bid fair to gain my point too, for I was coming up with them hand over hand.—But, in that very juncture of time, as the Lord was pleased to order it, my girth gave way, my saddle turned, and my charger fetching a ground start, threw me, saddle, holsters, and all, full ten feet

---

* This is a Carolina phrase for slashing. If a husband should so far forget himself as to beat his wife! which, thank God, is very rare, his neighbors, with great scorn, say of him as he pokes his hated face along, Aye, that's the jockey that gives his wife the timber.

over his head, and then ran off. I received no harm, God be praised for it, but recovering my legs in an instant, bawled out again to my men to halt and form.

Happily for me, at the very moment of my disaster, the enemy, suspecting our flight to be only a finesse, had halted, while only sixteen dragoons under colonel Camp, continued the chase.

Scorning to fly from such a handful, some of my more resolute fellows, thirteen in number, faced about, and very deliberately taking their aim at the enemy as they came up, gave them a 'spanker', which killed upwards of half their number. The rest took to flight, leaving their colonel, whose horse was slain, to shift for himself, which he quickly did by running into the woods.

The British were so near us when they received the fire of my men, that one of them, a stout fellow, as he wheeled to go off, came so close to me, where I stood on the ground, that he was lifting his broadsword for a back-handed stroke, which would probably have saved me the trouble of writing this history, had I not, with one of my pistols, which I took from the saddle when my horse left me, anticipated his kindness, by driving a bullet through his shoulder, which brought him to the ground. Then mounting his horse, while my men caught the horses of those that were killed, we galloped off, very well satisfied that the affair had turned out no worse.

On returning to Marion, I could not help complaining to him of my men, whose behavior, I said, in this last affair, had been so very dastardly, that I was much afraid, I should never again put confidence in them, nor gain any credit by commanding them. "Pshaw!" said he, with a smile, "it is because you do not understand the management of them: you command militia; it will not do to expect too much from that sort of soldiers. If on turning out against the enemy, you find your men in high spirits, with burning eyes all kindling around you, that's your time, then in close columns, with sounding bugles and shining swords, dash on, and I'll warrant your men will follow you, eager as the lion's whelps bounding with their sire to the chase of the buffaloes. But on the other hand, if by any un-looked-for providence they get dismayed, and begin to run, you are not to fly in a passion with them, and show yourself as mad as they are cowardly. No! you must learn to run too: and as fast as they; nay faster, that you may get into the front and encourage them to rally.

"And as to the credit that you are to get by commanding them, I find, my dear fellow, that you are entirely in the wrong there also. Our country cannot expect us to cope with British regulars. War is an art, the deepest of all arts, because the greatest of all earthly consequences depend on it. And none can expect to be masters of that terrible art, but such as serve a long apprenticeship to it. But as we have served no apprenticeship, we can know but little about it in comparison with our enemies, who in discipline and experience have greatly the advantage of us. But, thank God, we have our advantages too.—We are far better riders, better woodsmen, and better marksmen than they. These are noble advantages. Let us but improve them by redoubled activity and vigilance, and kindness to our men, and especially by often conversing with them on the grounds of the war, the merits of our cause, and the vast consequences depending. Let us, I say, in this way, make them soldiers in principle, and fond of their officers, and all will be well yet. By cutting off the enemy's foraging parties, drawing them into ambuscades and falling upon them by surprise, we shall, I hope, so harass and consume them, as to make them glad to get out of our country. And then, the performance of such a noble act will bring us credit, and credit enough too, in the eyes of good men; while as to ourselves, the remembrance of having done so much to vindicate the rights of man, and make posterity the happier for us, will afford us a pleasure that may outlive this momentary being."

CHAPTER XXV

Colonel Harry Lee joins general Marion—Georgetown surprised—colonel Campbell made prisoner—major Irwin killed—adjutant Crookshanks miraculously saved by his sweetheart—force of female affection—American generosity contrasted with British barbarism—interesting anecdotes of Mr. Cusac, young Gales and Dinkins, colonel Lee's little bugler, John Wiley, Peter Yarnal, young M'Coy, major Brown, colonel Haynes, and lord Rawdon.

T he next day, colonel Lee with his legion came up, to the inexpressible joy of us all; partly on account of his cavalry, which to be sure, was the handsomest we had ever seen; but much more on account of himself, of whom we had heard that, in deep art and undaunted courage, he was a second Marion.—This, our high opinion of him, was greatly exalted by his own gallant conduct, for he had been with us but a few days before he proposed the surprise of Georgetown, which was very cordially concurred with by general Marion.

The infantry and cavalry employed on the occasion, were to approach the town at different points, after midnight, and at a signal from the latter, to commence the attack. Unfortunately, the cavalry did not get up in time, owing to some fault of their guide. The infantry arrived at the appointed moment, and dreading the dangers of delay, charged at once into the town, which they found utterly unprepared for an attack. Colonel Campbell, the commander, was made prisoner in his bed; adjutant Crookshanks, major Irwin, and other officers were sound asleep at a tavern belonging to a genteel family, with whom they had spent the evening with great hilarity. A detachment of our men approached the house and surrounded it. Soon as the alarm was given, the officers leaped out of bed, and not waiting to dress, flew into the piazza, flourishing their pistols and shouting to the charge. Major Irwin, with more courage than discretion, fired a pistol, and would have tried another, but just as he had cocked it, he was stopped short by the stroke of a bayonet, which ended him and his courage together. Adjutant Crookshanks, acting in the same heroic style, would have shared the same fate, had it not been for an angel of a young woman, daughter of the gentleman of the house. This charming girl was engaged to be married to Crookshanks. Waked by the firing and horrid din of battle in the piazza, she was at first almost 'reft of her senses by the fright. But the moment she heard her lover's voice, all her terrors vanished, and instead of hiding herself under the bedclothes, she rushed into the piazza amidst the mortal fray, with no armor but her love, no covering but her flowing tresses. Happily for her lover, she got to him just in time to throw her arms around his neck and scream out, "Oh save! save major Crookshanks!" Thus, with her own sweet body shielding him against the uplifted swords of her enraged countrymen!

Crookshanks yielded himself our prisoner; but we paroled him on the spot, and left him to those delicious sentiments which he must have felt in the arms of an elegant young woman, who had saved his life by an effort of love sufficient to endear her to him to all eternity.

It was told us afterwards of this charming girl, that as soon as we were gone, and, of course, the danger past and the tumult of her bosom subsided, she fell into a swoon, from which it was with difficulty that she was recovered. Her extreme fright, on being waked by the firing and horrid uproar of battle in the house, and her strong sympathy in her lover's danger, together with the alarm occasioned by finding herself in his arms, were too much for her delicate frame.

There is a beauty in generous actions which charms the souls of men! and a sweetness, which like that immortal love whence it flows, can never die. The eyes of all, even the poorest soldiers in our camp, sparkled with pleasure whenever they talked, as they often did, of this charming woman, and of our generosity to major Crookshanks; and to this day, even after a lapse of thirty years, I never think of it but with pleasure; a pleasure as exquisite, perhaps, as what I felt at the first moment of that transaction.

And it is a matter of great satisfaction to me, to think how nobly different in this respect was our conduct from that of the British. I speak not of the British nation, which I hold most magnanimous; but of their officers in Carolina, such as Cornwallis, Rawdon, Tarleton, Weymies, Brown, and Balfour, who instead of treating their prisoners as we did Crookshanks, have often been known to butcher them in cold blood; though their fathers, mothers and children, on bended knees, with wringing hands and streaming eyes, have been imploring pity for them.

There was Mr. Adam Cusac, of Williamsburg district; this brave man,

> "This buckskin Hampden; that, with dauntless breast,
> The base invaders of his rights withstood,"

was surprised in his own house by major Weymies, who tore him away from his shrieking wife and children, marched him up to Cheraw court-house, and after exposing him to the insults of a sham trial, had him condemned and hung! The only charge ever exhibited against him was, that he had shot across Black river at one of Weymies' tory captains.

There was that gallant lad of liberty, Kit Gales, with his brave companion, Sam Dinkins: these two heroic youths were dogged to the house of a whig friend, near the hills of Santee, where they were surprised in their beds by a party of tories, who hurried them away to lord Rawdon, then on his march from Charleston to Camden. Rawdon quickly had them, according to his favorite phrase, "knocked into irons," and marched on under guard with his troops. On halting for breakfast, young Gales was tucked up to a tree, and choked with as little ceremony as if he had been a mad dog. He and young Dinkins had, it seems, the day before, with their horses and rifles, ventured alone, so near the British army, as to fire several shots at them! For such heroic daring in defence of their country, in place of receiving applause from lord Rawdon, Gales, as we have seen, received his bloody death. His gallant young friend, Dinkins, was very near drawing his rations of a like doleful dish, for lord Rawdon had him mounted upon the same cart with the halter round his neck, ready for a launch into eternity, when the tories suggested to his lordship their serious apprehensions that a terrible vengeance might follow: this saved his life.

Everybody has heard the mournful story of colonel Lee's little bugler, and how he was murdered by colonel Tarleton. This "poor beardless boy," as Lee, in his pathetic account of that horrid transaction, calls him, had been mounted on a very fleet horse; but to gratify a countryman who had brought some news of the British, and was afraid of falling into their hands, Lee ordered the boy to exchange his horse, a moment, for that of the countryman, which happened to be a miserable brute. This Lee did in his simplicity, not even dreaming that any thing in the shape of civilized man could think of harming such a child. Scarcely had Lee left him, when he was overtaken by Tarleton's troopers, who dashed up to him with looks of death, brandishing their swords over his head. In vain his tender cheeks, reminding them of their own youthful brothers, sought to touch their pity; in vain, with feeble voice, and as long as he was able, he continued to cry for quarter. They struck their cruel swords into his face and arms, which they gashed with so many mortal wounds that he died the next day.

"Is your name Wiley?" said one of Tarleton's captains, whose name was Tuck, to Mr. John Wiley, sheriff of Camden, who had lately whipped and cropped a noted horse thief, named Smart. "Is your name Wiley?" said captain Tuck to the young man, at whose door he rode up and asked the question.—"Yes, sir," replied Mr. Wiley. "Well, then, sir, you are a d—n-d rascal," rejoined captain Tuck, giving him at the same time a cruel blow over the forehead with his broadsword. Young Wiley, though doomed to die, being not yet slain, raised his naked arm to screen the blow. This, though no more than a common instinct in poor human nature in the moment of terror, served but to redouble the fury of captain Tuck, who continued his blows at the bleeding, staggering youth, until death kindly placed him beyond the reach of human malice.

All this was done within a few hundred paces of lord Cornwallis, who never punished captain Tuck.

But poor Peter Yarnall's case seems still more deplorable. This hard fated man, a simple, inoffensive quaker, lived near Camden. Having urgent business with a man, who, as he understood, was with general Sumter, on the opposite side of the Catawba, he went over to him. The man happened, at that moment, to be keeping guard over some tory prisoners. A paper which Yarnall wanted to see was, it seems, in a jacket pocket in the man's tent hard by. "Hold my piece a moment, sir," said he to Yarnall, "and I'll bring the paper." Yarnall, though averse, as a quaker, from all killing of enemies with a gun, yet saw no objection to holding one a moment. The next day, a day for ever black in the American calendar, witnessed the surprisal of general Sumter and the release of the tory prisoners, one of whom immediately went his way and told colonel Tarleton that he had seen Peter Yarnall, the day before, keeping guard over the king's friends, prisoners to the rebels. The poor man's house was quickly surrounded by the British cavalry. Vain were all his own explanations, his wife's entreaties, or his children's cries. He was dragged to Camden, and thrust into prison. Every morning, his wife and daughter, a girl of about fifteen, rode into town in an old chair, to see him and to bring him milk and fruits, which must have been highly acceptable to one crammed, in the dogdays, into a small prison, with one hundred and sixty-three half-stifled wretches. On the fourth day, an amiable young lady, Miss Charlton, living near the prison, had heard of poor Yarnall's fate that morning. Soon therefore as she saw

Mrs. Yarnall and her daughter coming along as usual, with their little present to their husband and father, she burst into tears. Mrs. Yarnall alighted at the door of the jail, and begged to see her husband. "Follow me," said one of the guard, "and I'll show you your husband." As she turned the corner, "There he is, madam," said the soldier, pointing to her husband as he hung dead on a beam from the window. The daughter sunk to the ground; but her mother, as if petrified at the sight, stood silent and motionless, gazing on her dead husband with that wild keen eye of unutterable woe, which pierces all hearts. Presently, as if braced up with despair, she seemed quite recovered, and calmly begged one of the soldiers to assist her to take down the corpse and lay it in the bottom of the chair. Then taking her seat, with her daughter sobbing by her side, and her husband dead at her feet, she drove home apparently quite unmoved; and during the whole time she was preparing his coffin and performing the funeral duties, she preserved the same firm unaltered looks. But soon as the grave had shut its mouth on her husband, and divorced him for ever from her sight, the remembrance of the past rushed upon her thoughts with a weight too heavy for her feeble nature to bear. Then clasping her hands in agony, she shrieked out, "Poor me! poor me! I have no husband, no friend now!" and immediately ran raving mad, and died in that state.

There was young M'Coy: the eye of humanity must weep often, as she turns the page that tells how this amiable youth was murdered. His father was one of the most active of our militia captains. As none better understood American rights, so none more deeply resented British aggressions, than did captain M'Coy. His just views and strong feelings, were carefully instilled into his boy, who, though but fifteen, shouldered his musket, and, in spite of his mother's tears, followed his father to war. Many a gallant Englishman received his death at their hands. For, being well acquainted with the river, and bravely supported by their friends, they often fired upon the enemy's boats, killing their crews and intercepting their provisions. This so enraged colonel Brown, the British commander at Augusta, that he made several attempts to destroy captain M'Coy. Once, in particular, he despatched a captain and fifty men to surprise him. But M'Coy kept so good a look out, that he surprised and killed the captain and twenty of his men. The rest, by giving good 'leg bail,' made their escape. Young M'Coy fought by the side of his father in this and many other rencontres, in one of which he had the great good fortune to save his father's life.

At the head of some gallant friends, they fell in with a strong party of tories, near Brier creek, commanded by a British officer. As usual, an obstinate and bloody contest ensued. The combatants quickly coming to close quarters, M'Coy grappled with the officer; but not possessing strength equal to his courage, he was overpowered and thrown on the ground. The youth, who had just fired his piece into the bosom of a tory, seeing his father's danger, flew to his aid, and with the butt of his gun knocked out the brains of the officer, at the very instant he was lifting his dirk for the destruction of his father.

In a skirmish, in which his party were victorious, captain M'Coy was mortally wounded, and died exhorting his son still to fight undauntedly for the liberties of his country. After the death of his father, young M'Coy joined the brave captain Clarke. In an expedition against colonel Brown, Clarke was defeated, and young M'Coy made prisoner. Hearing of his misfortune, his mother hastened to Augusta, but arrived only in time to meet him with colonel Brown and a guard, carrying him out to the gallows. With gushing tears, she fell upon his neck, and bitterly mourned her lot, as wretched above all women, in thus losing her husband and only son.

The behavior of young M'Coy, it is said, was heroic beyond his years. Instead of melting with his disconsolate mother, he exhorted her like one who had acted on principle, and now felt its divine consolations stronger than death.

He entreated his mother not to weep for him, nor for his father. "In the course of nature, mother," said he, "we were to part. Our parting indeed, is early; but it is glorious. My father was like a lion in battle for his country. As a young lion, I fought by his side. And often, when the battle was over, did he embrace and call me his boy! his own brave boy! and said I was worthy of you both. He has just gone before, and I now follow him, leaving you the joy to remember, that your son and husband have attained the highest honor on earth; the honor of fighting and dying for the rights of man."

Anxious to save the life of so dear a son, poor Mrs. M'Coy fell on her knees to colonel Brown, and with all the widowed mother agonizing in her looks, plead for his life. But in vain. With the dark features of a soul horribly triumphant over the cries of mercy, he repulsed her suit, and ordered the executioner to do his office! He hung up the young man before the eyes of his mother! and then, with savage joy, suffered his Indians, in her presence, to strike their tomahawks into his forehead; that forehead which she had so often pressed to her bosom, and kissed with all the transports of a doting mother.

Who, without tears, can think of the hard fate of poor colonel Haynes and his family?

Soon as the will of heaven had thrown Charleston into the hands of the British, lord Cornwallis, famed for pompous proclamations, began to publish. The tenor of his gasconade was, that Carolina was now, to all intents and purposes, subjugated; that the enemies of his lord the king were all at his mercy; and that though, by the war rubrick for conquered rebels, he had a right to send fire and sword before him, with blood and tears following in his course; though he had a right to feed the birds of heaven with rebel carcasses, and to fatten his soldiers with their confiscated goods, yet he meant not to use that dreadful right. No, indeed! Far from him were all such odious thoughts. On the contrary he wished to be merciful: and as proof of his sincerity, all that he asked of the poor deluded people of his majesty's colony of South Carolina was, that they should no longer take part nor lot in the contest, but continue peaceably at their homes. And that, in reward thereof, they should be most sacredly protected in property and person.

This proclamation was accompanied with an instrument of neutrality, as an "outward and visible sign of an inward and spiritual grace," in my lord Cornwallis towards the Carolinians; and which instrument they were invited to sign, that they might have a covenant right to the aforesaid promised blessings of protection, both in property and person.

The heart of colonel Haynes was with his countrymen, and fervently did he pray that his hands could be with them too. But, these, alas! were bound up by his wife and children, whom, it is said, he loved passing well. Helpless and trembling as they were, how could they be deserted by him in this fearful season, and given up to a brutal soldiery? And why should he insure the destruction of a large estate, when all opposition seemed hopeless? In short, with thousands of others, he went and signed an instrument, which promised security to his family and fortune. But alas! from that fatal moment he never more enjoyed peace. To hate the ministerial measures as he did, and yet thus tamely to have submitted to them; to love his country as heartily as he did, and to know that she was now fighting, with her all at stake, and yet thus to have deserted her!

These keen self-condemning reflections harrowed every root of quiet from his soul. If he went to his couch, it was only to groan, sleepless and tossing, all the restless night. If he got up, it was but to sit, or walk to and fro in his family, with dark and woeful looks, like one whom trouble had overcome.

In the midst of these anguishing reflections, which appeared to be wearing him fast to the grave, a respite was afforded, and by a hand from which it was least expected. Lord Cornwallis, having by his first proclamation, obtained to the instrument of neutrality aforesaid, the signatures of many thousands of the citizens of South Carolina, then came out with a second proclamation, in which he nominates the paper above not an instrument of neutrality, but a bond of allegiance to the king, and calls upon all who had signed it, to take up arms against the rebels!— threatening to treat as deserters those who refused!

This fraud of my lord Cornwallis, excited in all honest men the deepest indignation. It completely revived colonel Haynes. To his unspeakable joy, he now saw opened a door of honorable return to duty and happiness. And since, contrary to the most solemn compact, he was compelled to fight, he very naturally determined to fight the British, rather than his own countrymen. He fled to his countrymen, who received him with joy, and gave him a command of horse. He was surprised and carried to Charleston, where lord Rawdon, then commandant, ordered him, in his favorite phrase, to be 'knocked into irons.' A mock trial, dignified with the name of 'court martial,' was held over him, and colonel Haynes was sentenced to be hung. Everybody in Charleston, Britons as well as Americans, all heard this sentence with horror, except colonel Haynes himself. On his cheek alone, all agree, it produced no change. It appeared that the deed which he had done, signing that accursed paper, had run him desperate. Though the larger part, even of his enemies, believing that it was done merely from sympathy with his wife and children, felt the generous disposition to forgive him, yet he could never forgive himself. It had inflicted on his mind a wound too ghastly to be healed.

To their own, and to the great honor of human nature, numbers of the British and loyalists, with governor Bull at their head, preferred a petition to lord Rawdon in his behalf. But the petition was not noticed. The ladies then came forward in his favor with a petition, couched in the most delicate and moving terms, and signed by all the principal females of Charleston, tories as well as whigs. But all to no purpose. It was then suggested by the friends of humanity, that if the colonel's little children, for they had no mother, she, poor woman! crushed under the double weight of grief and the small-pox, was just sunk at rest in the grave. It was suggested, I say, that if the colonel's little children, dressed in mourning, were to fall at the knees of lord Rawdon, he would pity their motherless condition, and give to their prayers their only surviving parent. They were accordingly dressed in black, and introduced into his presence: they fell down at his knees, and, with clasped hands and tear-streaming eyes, lisped their father's name, and begged his life: but in vain.

So many efforts to save him, both by friends and generous foes, could not be made, unknown to colonel Haynes. But he appeared perfectly indifferent about the result! and when told that they had all failed, he replied with the utmost unconcern—"Well, thank God, lord Rawdon cannot hurt me. He cannot be more anxious to take my life than I am to lay it down."

With his son, a youth of thirteen, who was permitted to stay with him in the prison, colonel Haynes used often to converse, in order to fortify him against the sad trial that was at hand. And indeed it was necessary, for seldom has a heavier load been laid on a tender-hearted youth. War, like a thick cloud, had darkened up the gay morning of his days: the grave had just closed her mouth on a mother who doted on him; and he now beheld his only parent, a beloved father, in the power of his enemies, loaded with irons, and condemned to die. With cheeks wet with tears, he sat continually by his father's side, and looked at him with eyes so piercing and sad, as often wrung tears of blood from his heart.

"Why," said he, "my son, will you thus break your father's heart with unavailing sorrow? Have I not often told you, that we came into this world but to prepare for a better? For that better life, my dear boy, your father is prepared. Instead then of weeping, rejoice with me, my son, that my troubles are so near an end. To-morrow, I set out for immortality. You will accompany me to the place of my execution; and when I am dead, take and bury me by the side of your mother."

The youth here fell on his father's neck, crying, "Oh my father! my father! I will die with you! I will die with you!"

Colonel Haynes would have returned the strong embrace of his son; but, alas! his hands were loaded with irons. "Live," said he, "my son, live to honor God by a good life; live to serve your country; and live to take care of your brother and little sisters!"

The next morning colonel Haynes was conducted to the place of execution. His son accompanied him. Soon as they came in sight of the gallows, the father strengthened himself and said—"Now, my son, show yourself a man. That tree is the boundary of my life, and of all my life's sorrows. Beyond that, the wicked cease from troubling and the weary are at rest. Don't lay too much to heart our separation from you; it will be but short. 'Twas but lately your dear mother died. To-day I die. And you, my son, though but young, must shortly follow us."

"Yes, my father," replied the broken-hearted youth, "I shall shortly follow you: for indeed I feel that I cannot live long." And so it happened unto him. For on seeing his father in the hands of the executioner, and then struggling in the halter, he stood like one transfixed and motionless with horror. Till then he had wept incessantly; but soon as he saw that sight, the fountain of his tears was staunched, and he never wept more. It was thought that grief, like a fever, burnt inwardly, and scorched his brain, for he became indifferent to every thing around him, and often wandered as one disordered in his mind. At times, he took lessons from a fencing master, and talked of going to England to fight the murderer of his father. But he who made him had pity on him, and sent death to his relief. He died insane, and in his last moments often called on the name of his father, in terms that brought tears from the hardest hearts.

I hope my reader will not suppose, from these odious truths which I have been telling him about the British and tories, that I look on them as worse than other men; or that I would have him bear an eternal hatred against them. No, God forbid. On the contrary, I have no doubt on my mind, that the British and tories are men of the same passions with ourselves. And I also as firmly believe, that, if placed in their circumstances, we should have acted just as they did. Upon honor this is my conviction now; but it was not always so: for I confess there was a time, when I had my prejudices against them, and prejudices, too, as strong as those of any other man, let him be who he would. But thank God those prejudices, so dishonorable to the head, and so uneasy to the heart, are done away from me now. And from this most happy deliverance, I am, through the divine goodness, principally indebted to my honored friend, general Marion, of whose noble sentiments, on these subjects, I beg leave to give the reader some little specimen in the next chapter.

CHAPTER XXVI

Short and sweet—or, a curious dialogue between general Marion
and captain Snipes, on retaliation.

> *"No radiant pearls that crested fortune wears,*
> *No gem that sparkling hangs in beauty's ears;*
> *Not the bright stars that night's blue arch adorn,*
> *Nor opening suns that gild the vernal morn,*
> *Shine with such lustre as the tear that flows*
> *Down virtue's manly cheeks, for others' woes."*

What gigantic form is that which stalks thus awfully before the
eyes of my memory; his face, rough and dark as the cloud of winter, and
his eyeballs burning like coals of fire? 'Tis the impetuous captain Snipes.
He is just returned from the quarter house near Charleston, where he and
captain M'Cauley, with Macdonald and forty men, have recently surprised
and cut to pieces a large party of the enemy. He looks as if the fury of the
battle had not yet subsided in his wrathful countenance. His steps are
towards Marion, and as he presents a packet, he exclaims in an angry tone,

"There, sir, is a Charleston paper. You'll see there how those villains are going on yet. Not satisfied with all the murders they had committed before, they have gone now and murdered colonel Haynes." Here he gave the heads of that disgraceful act, seasoning his speech every now and then, as he went along, with sundry very bitter imprecations on lord Rawdon.

"Ah shame! shame upon him!" replied the general with a sigh, and shaking his head; "shame upon lord Rawdon!"

"Shame!" answered captain Snipes, his eyes flashing fire; "shame! I hope something heavier than shame will light upon him for it soon. The American officers have sworn never again to give quarter to the British or tories."

Marion. God forbid that my countrymen should have taken such an oath as that!

Snipes. Why, general Marion, would you have the enemy go on at this rate, and we take no revenge?

M. Revenge? O yes, to be sure, sir; revenge is sweet, and by all means let us have it; but let it be of the right kind.

S. Of the right kind, sir! what do you call revenge of the right kind?

M. Why, sir, I am for taking that kind of revenge which will make our enemies ashamed of their conduct, and abandon it for ever.

S. Ashamed of their conduct! Monsters! they are not capable of shame.

M. Pshaw! don't talk so, captain Snipes! our enemies, sir, are men, and just such men as we are; and as capable of generous actions, if we will but show them the way.

S. Well then, general Marion, how do you account for that great difference between us and them in point of spirits? We have never yet killed any of their men, except in fair fight, that I have heard of; but they have often murdered ours. Yes, the cowardly rascals! they have often done it, and that in cold blood too.

M. Granted. And I am very glad that when we have had them in our power, we have always treated them so much more generously. But, I suppose the reason of such barbarity on their part, is, they have had, or which is the same thing, have thought they had greater provocations.

S. They be d—n-d, they and their provocations too! Are not we the persons who have been invaded, and plundered and murdered by them, and not they by us? How then can they have greater provocations?

M. Why, sir, sprung originally from them, and always looked on by them as their children, our turning now and fighting against them, must appear, in their sight, a very great provocation; as great perhaps as that of children fighting against their parents. And again, our shaking off what they glory in, as the wisest, and freest, and happiest government on earth, must make us seem to them as no better than the vilest traitors and rebels; which cannot otherwise than prove another very great provocation. And again, after having been first settled in this country by them, as they will have it, and afterwards, so long and liberally assisted with their best blood and treasure, in hope that some day or other we should be of service to them; that now, at the very time when, by our immense population, we were just arrived to the so long desired point, to swell their wealth and spread their commerce and arms over the world, we should separate from them, blast all their fond hopes, and throw them back to the former level; this, I say, you will certainly allow, must be a very severe provocation. Now, sir, putting all these provocations together, and also taking poor human nature into the account, is it to be wondered at, that the British should be so much more angry, and consequently more violent than we?

S. Why, certainly, general Marion, you have always a very fine knack of setting off your arguments. But still, sir, I can't see things in that light. For a man, sir, to go and trump up a pack of claims against me, and all of them because I can't credit him in the abominable extent he wishes, to fall upon me and kill and murder me, as the British and tories have done with us, and we not stop them by revenge! why, my God! sir, it will never do. For, at this rate, whom shall we have living in all this country, in a little time, but the British, and their friends the tories and negroes?

M. My brave captain let me tell you again, I am as anxious to stop them as you can possibly wish me to be; but I am for doing it in what I think the right way. I mean the way of policy and humanity.

S. Policy, sir! can there be policy in letting our best men be murdered by these savages! I'm sure general Washington did not think so. For, though I am no man of learning myself, yet I have been told by those that are, that, on its being threatened by general Gage to hang an American soldier, he instantly wrote him word, that if he dared to do such a thing, the life of a British soldier should pay for it. And, it is well known, that he kept the British army and nation too, in a fright for three months together, with the halter constantly around the neck of captain Asgil, expecting every day to be hung for the murder of captain Huddy.

M. True; general Washington did act so. And it was policy to act against a foreign enemy. But our standing with the tories is quite a different case, and requires a very different course. The tories are our countrymen, a part of our own population and strength, so that every man of them that is killed, is a man forever lost to ourselves. Now, since the British have put them up to murder us, if we go, out of revenge, to murder them again, why, in the course of a little time our population will be so cut up, as to allow the British ministry, with ease, to take our country, and make slaves of us all; which is just what lord North desires.

S. Yes, I dare say it is. But I hope he'll be disappointed yet.

M. No doubt of it, sir; if we shall be wise and magnanimous enough to follow the true policy, which is no other than humanity to these deluded people, the tories; and to this we have every inducement that generous spirits could desire. The tories and ourselves are brothers; many of us went to the same school together; and a thousand times have ate and drank in each other's houses. And as to the quarrel in which we are now unfortunately engaged, though not the most, still we are much in fault. We made no allowances for those follies of theirs which led to it. They thought—First, That we were too nearly allied to England to go to war with her; this was a weakness, but there was something amiable in it.—Secondly, They thought the British were much too warlike and powerful to be resisted by us: this was an error, but it was learned in the nursery.—Thirdly, They wished to keep in with the British, merely that they might save their property; this was altogether from fear, and therefore claimed some commiseration. But no! we could not grant one grain of indulgence to any of their mistakes. We would have it, they all proceeded from the vilest of motives. We called them traitors, and cowards, and scoundrels; and loaded them with a thousand indignities besides. Well, the consequences were, as might have been expected from human weakness and passion. Wrought to desperation, and caring not what they did, they have gone and joined our enemies, and many valuable lives have been lost on both sides. Surely 'tis high time now that we should set about doing something to end it.

S. Well! let them set about ending it themselves. They were the first to begin it.

M. But would you have the tories to lead to glory?

S. Glory! I should think it meanness to be the first to make overtures to such rascals!

M. Well, but, captain Snipes, when brethren, as we are, fall out, is it policy to go on to exasperate and cut each other's throats, until our enemy comes and takes away a fine country, of which, by such madness, we had rendered ourselves unworthy? Would it not be much better policy to trace back all our wrong steps of passion and revenge, and making hearty friends again, and joining our forces against the common enemy, drive him out of our country; and then by establishing a free government, and encouraging agriculture and commerce, and learning, and religion, make ourselves a great and happy people again; would not this, I say, be the true policy?

S. Why yes, I confess, general Marion, it would be a noble thing, and very desirable, if it could be done. But I cannot bear to think of being the first to make terms with the tories, after they have been burning, and plundering, and murdering our best friends. It is too hard, sir, for mortal flesh and blood.

M. It is a great trial, I confess; but "the heavier the cross the brighter the crown," you know, sir. And as to the difficulty of the undertaking, that's the very thing that should make us jump at it; the glory of showing ourselves wiser and better men than our enemy. And besides, let us recollect that the glory of this exploit all now lies with us: for if we do not pluck up courage and do it, it will never be done.—The tories are, generally, an ignorant people; and therefore not much of wise or good is to be expected from that quarter. They have also, in many instances, acted a very savage part by us: their consciousness of this can have no tendency to make them court reconciliation with us. Since, then, but little is to be expected from them, it seems incumbent on US to do the more. We have better information, and we have also a much better cause. These are great advantages which God has given us; and now it becomes us to improve them, to his glory and to our own honor, by showing a conciliatory and magnanimous spirit towards our enemies. And though it should cost us labor to win such a victory, yet, I am confident, that when won, it will appear to us the most glorious that we ever achieved. To conquer an enemy by the sword, is, no doubt, honorable; but still it is nothing in comparison of conquering him by generosity. As arguing both superior virtue and courage, it commands higher admiration from the world, and is reflected on by ourselves with far more self-esteem and applause. And then, sir, only consider how such conduct will gild the future scenes of life. This unfortunate quarrel betwixt us and our countrymen, the tories, is not to last forever. It was only the act of a wicked ministry, attempting, by an unconstitutional tax to enslave an affectionate part of the nation. God can never suffer such an attempt to prosper. It must be but a momentary quarrel; and we ought to accustom ourselves to think of it as such, and to look beyond it to the happy days that are to succeed. And since the storm of war is soon to subside into the calm of peace, let us do nothing now, that may throw a cloud over the coming sunshine. Let us not even talk of 'exterminating war'! that unnatural crime which would harrow up our souls with the pangs of remorse, and haunt our repose with the dread of retaliation—which would draw down upon our cause the curse of heaven, and make our very name the odium of all generations. But, far differently, let us act the generous part of those who, though now at variance, are yet brothers, and soon to be good friends again. And then, when peace returns, we shall be in proper frame to enjoy it. No poor woman that we meet will seem to upbraid us for the slaughter of her husband; no naked child, for robbing him of his father; no field will cry against us for a brother's blood. On the contrary, whenever the battles which we are now fighting, shall recur to our thoughts, with the frightened enemy grounding their arms and crying for quarter, we shall remember how we heard their cries and stopped the uplifted sword. Joy will spring in our bosoms, and all around will smile with approbation.—The faces of the aged will shine upon us, because we spared their sons; bright-eyed females will bless us for their surviving husbands: and even the lips of the children will lisp our praises. Thus with a heaven of delighted feeling in our hearts, and the smiles both of God and man on our heads, we shall pass the evening of our days in glorious peace. And when death shall call us to that better world, we shall obey without reluctance. Conscious of neither dread nor hate towards any of the blessed people that dwell there, we shall go in strong hope of witnessing the bright realities of that state, where all is immortality and love. Perhaps we shall there meet many of those whom it has been our sad destiny to fight with here; not in their present imperfect state, but in their state of exaltation, clad in robes brighter than the stars, and their faces outshining the sun in his noonday splendors. Perhaps at sight of us, these glorious spirits may rush with new-flushed beauties, to embrace us, and in the presence of crowding angels, recount our kindness to them in the days of their mortality; while all the dazzling throngs, listening delighted, shall fix on us their eyes of love, inspiring those joys which none but strong immortals could sustain. Are not these, O my friends, hopes worth contending for? Is revenge to be cherished that would rob us of such honors? Can generosity be dear that would ensure to us such so great rewards? Then let us not think benevolence was enjoined in vain, which is to conduct us to such immortal felicities."

As Marion spoke these words, his countenance, which in general was melancholy, caught an animation beyond the reader's fancy to conceive.

The charms of goodness, and the bright rewards which await it, were painted in such living colors on his face, that not even the stranger could have beheld it unmoved. On me, who almost adored Marion for his godlike virtues, its effects were past describing. My bosom heaved with emotions unutterable, while the tear of delicious admiration swelled in my eyes. As to captain Snipes, he appeared equally affected. His eyes were riveted on the general, and towards the close of the speech his breath seemed suspended; his color went and came; and his face reddened and swelled; as under the powerful eloquence of the pulpit.

CHAPTER XXVII

Marion and Lee attack and take fort Watson and fort Motte—
interesting anecdotes.

*F*rom Georgetown, Marion proceeded with colonel Lee to attack
the British post on Scott's lake, generally called fort Watson. The situation
of this fort was romantic and beautiful in the extreme.—Overlooking the
glassy level of the lake, it stood on a mighty barrow or tomb like a mount,
formed of the bones of Indian nations, there heaped up from time
immemorial, and covered with earth and herbage.—Finding that the fort
mounted no artillery, Marion resolved to make his approaches in a way
that should give his riflemen a fair chance against their musqueteers. For
this purpose, large quantities of pine logs were cut, and as soon as dark
came on, were carried in perfect silence, within point blank shot of the
fort, and run up in the shape of large pens or chimney-stacks, considerably
higher than the enemy's parapets. Great, no doubt, was the consternation
of the garrison next morning, to see themselves thus suddenly overlooked
by this strange kind of steeple, pouring down upon them from its blazing
top incessant showers of rifle bullets. Nor were they idle the while, but

returned the blaze with equal fury, presenting to us, who lay at a distance, a very interesting scene—as of two volcanoes that had suddenly broke out into fiery strife, singeing the neighboring pines.

Though their enemy, yet I could not but pity the British, when I saw the great disadvantage under which they fought. For our riflemen, lying above them and firing through loopholes, were seldom hurt; while the British, obliged, every time they fired, to show their heads, were frequently killed.—Increasing still the awkwardness of their situation, their well, which was on the outside of the fort, was so entirely in the reach of our rifles, that they could not get a pail of water for coffee or grog, without the utmost hazard. After a gallant resistance, they surrendered themselves prisoners of war; one hundred and twenty in number.

This fort had been very judiciously fixed in a country exceedingly fertile, and on a lake abounding with fine fish, and from its contiguity to the river Santee, forming an admirable deposite for their upland posts. From their military storehouse, which was on the outside of the fort, the British attempted, at the commencement of our attack, to get out their goods, and to roll them up into the fort. But in this exposed state, their men were picked off so fast by our sharpshooters, that they were soon obliged to quit such hot work.

The sight of their casks and bales, rolled out and shining so richly on the side of the hill, set the fingers of our ragged militia-men on such an itch, that there was no resisting it. And presently a squad of three of them were seen pushing out, without leave or license, to attack a large hogshead, that lay very invitingly on the outside of the rest. The enemy seeing the approach of our buccaneers, reserved their fire until they had got pretty near up to the intended prize; then all at once cut loose upon them with a thundering clap, which killed one, crippled a second, and so frightened the third, that he forgot the cask, and turning tail, thought of nothing but to save his bacon! which he did by such extraordinary running and jumping, as threw us all into a most immoderate laugh.

Presently up comes my black waiter, Billy, with a broad grin on his face, and says, "Why, master, them militia men there, sir, are tarnal fools: they do not know nothing at all about stealing. But if you will please, sir, to let me try my hand, I can fetch off that hogshead there, mighty easy, sir."

"No, no, Billy!" said I, shaking my head, "that will never do, my lad. I value you much too highly, Billy, to let you be knocked on the head, so foolishly as all that comes to."

"Lord bless you, sir," replied he, smiling, "there is no more danger in it, than in eating when a body is hungry. And if you will only please let me try my hand, sir, if you see any danger, why then, master, you may call me back, you know, sir."

Upon this he started. Fortunately for him, our riflemen, seeing what he was after, made a noble diversion in his favor, by throwing a galling fire into the fort. On getting within thirty yards of the hogshead, he fell flat on his face, and dragged himself along on his belly until he reached it. Then seizing the hogshead with a hand on each chine he worked it backwards and backwards, like an alligator pulling a dog into the river, until he had fairly rolled his prize to the brink of the hill, where, giving it a sudden jerk by way of a start, and at the same time jumping up, he ran with all his might down the precipice, the hogshead hard after him, and was soon out of all danger. Numbers of shots were fired at him, but not one touched him, which gave great joy to our encampment, who were all anxious spectators of the transaction, and seemed to take a deep interest in Billy's success. And no wonder; for he was a most noble-hearted fellow, and exceedingly useful in camp. Officers or soldiers, cadets or colonels, no matter who they were, that asked Billy a favor, they were sure to have it done for them; and with such a cheerful air, as did them more good than the service itself. So that I much question, whether there was a man in all our camp, whose good luck would have given more general satisfaction than his.

On opening Billy's hogshead, which indeed was no hogshead, but rather a puncheon, as big as two hogsheads, there was a prodigious stare among our men at the sight of so much wealth.

100 strong white shirts for soldiers,

50 fine do. do. for officers,

50 camp blankets,

100 black stocks,

100 knapsacks, and

6 dragoon cloaks,

were the valuable contents of Billy's cask. The native genius of the poor fellow instantly broke out in a stream of generous actions, which never stopped, until the hogshead was completely emptied. First of all, he began with me, to whom he presented half a dozen of the fine shirts and black stocks, with a dragoon's cloak. Then to the general he made a present, also to the officers of his family. To his fellow-servants, who messed with him, he gave two shirts a-piece. But what pleased me most in Billy's donations, was his generosity to the two men who had miscarried in their attempt on the same cask. Seeing that they were much mortified at their own failure, and a little perhaps at his success, he desired them to come and help themselves to what they liked. Hearing him then express a wish that he knew what to do with the balance, I told him that many of our dragoons were poor men, and much in want of shirts. "Aye, sure enough," said he, and immediately handed them out a shirt a-piece, until all were gone.

For this generosity of Billy's, general Marion dubbed him "captain Billy," a name which he went by ever afterwards. Nothing was ever more seasonable than this supply, purchased by Billy's valor; for before that, we were all as ragged as young rooks. There was not an officer in camp, except colonel Lee and his staff, who was so rich as to own two shirts. I am very sure that Marion's aids had but one a-piece. And yet so independent of wealth is cheerfulness, that I have often seen our officers in their naked buffs, near a branch, singing and dancing around their shirts, which they had just washed, and hung on the bushes to dry.

From the reduction of fort Watson, we set out immediately in high spirits, for the still nobler attack on fort Motte. For the sake of fine air, and water, and handsome accommodations, the British had erected this fort in the yard of Mrs. Motte's elegant new house, which was nearly enclosed in their works. But alas! so little do poor mortals know what they are about! the fine house, which they had rudely taken from poor Mrs. Motte, proved to the British, what his gay shirt did to Hercules. It wrought their downfall. For, after a fierce contest, in which many valuable lives were lost on both sides, through the sharp shooting of the yaugers, and the still closer cutting of our riflemen, it struck Marion that he could quickly drive the enemy out of the fort, by setting the house on fire. But poor Mrs. Motte! a lone widow, whose plantation had been so long ravaged by the war, herself turned into a log cabin, her negroes dispersed, and her stock, grain, &c. nearly all ruined! must she now lose her elegant buildings too? Such scruples were honorable to the general; but they showed his total unacquaintedness with the excellent widow. For at the first glimpse of the proposition, she exclaimed, "O! burn it! burn it, general Marion! God forbid I should bestow a single thought on my little concerns, when the independence of my country is at stake.—No sir, if it were a palace it should go." She then stepped to her closet and brought out a curious bow with a quiver of arrows, which a poor African boy purchased from on board a Guineaman, had formerly presented her, and said, "Here, general, here is what will serve your purpose to a hair." The arrows, pointed with iron, and charged with lighted combustibles, were shot on top of the house, to which they stuck, and quickly communicated the flames. The British, two hundred in number, besides a good many tories, instantly hung out a white flag in sign of submission.

The excellent Mrs. Motte was present when her fine new house, supposed to be worth six thousand dollars, took fire; and without a sigh, beheld the red spiry billows prevailing over all its grandeur.

The day after the destruction of her house, she invited general Marion with all the officers, British as well as American, to dine with her. Having now no better place of accommodation, she entertained us under a large arbor built in front of her log cabin, where, with great pleasure, I observed that the same lady could one day act the Spartan, and the next the Parisian:

thus uniting in herself, the rare qualities of the heroine and the christian. For my life I could not keep my eyes from her. To think what an irreparable injury these officers had done her! and yet to see her, regardless of her own appetite, selecting the choicest pieces of the dish, and helping them with the endearing air of a sister, appeared to me one of the loveliest spectacles I had ever beheld. It produced the happiest effect on us all. Catching her amiable spirit, we seemed to have entirely forgotten our past animosities; and Britons and Americans mingled together, in smiles and cheerful chat, like brothers. I do not recollect a transaction in the whole war, in which I can think that God looked down with higher complacency than on this. And to the day of my death, I shall believe, that God enabled us to beat the British in arms, because we had so far beaten them in generosity. Men, who under such cruel provocations, could display such moderation as we did, must certainly have given our Maker good hope, that we were equal to the glorious business of self-government; or in other words, of living under a republic, which must certainly be his delight, because both implying and producing more wisdom and virtue, than any other government among men.

The name of the British commandant, our prisoner, was Ferguson; and a very pleasant gentleman he was too, as I found on getting acquainted with him, which I soon did. After talking over our various adventures in the war, he asked me if I did not command the cavalry, in the late skirmishing between Watson and Marion. I told him I did. "Well," replied he, "you made a very lucky escape that day: for do you know that we were twelve hundred strong, owing to colonel Small's joining us in the march?"

"Then truly," said I, "if that were the case, I made a lucky escape, sure enough."

"And where were you," he asked again, "when general Marion so completely surprised our guard at Nelson's old fields: were you there?"

I told him I was not, but that my brother, Hugh Horry, was.

"Well," continued he, laughing heartily, "that was my lucky day. I had a command there that morning of about thirty men, as an advance. We had not left the guard more than five minutes before the Americans charged and swept all. The moment we heard the firing and the cries of our people, we squatted in the high grass like so many rabbits, then running on the stoop, till we gained the woods, we cleared ourselves." I laughed, and asked how many men he supposed Marion had that morning."

He replied, he really did not know, but supposed he must have had three or four hundred.

"Well, sir," said I, "he had exactly thirty."

The reader may perhaps conceive Ferguson's astonishment: I cannot describe it.

Soon as the dishes were removed, we were presented with a spectacle to which our eyes had long been strangers, a brave parade of excellent wine: several hampers of which had been received at the fort the very day before we commenced the attack. To poor soldiers like us, who, for years, had hardly quenched our thirst on any thing better than water or apple brandy grog, this was a sight immensely refreshing. Whether it was owing to the virtues of this noble cordial, with the recollection of our late glorious victories; or whether it was the happy result of our generosity to the enemy, and of their correspondent politeness to us, I do not know; but certain it is, we were all very gay. But in the midst of our enjoyments, which none seemed to relish with a higher glee than general Marion, a British soldier came up and whispered to one of their officers, who instantly coming round to the general, told him in a low voice, that the Americans were hanging the tories who had been taken in the fort!

In a moment he sprang up, in a violent passion, and snatching his sword, ran down towards our encampment. We all followed him, though without knowing the cause. On turning the corner of the garden which had concealed their cruel deeds, we discovered a sight most shocking to humanity, a poor man hanging in the air to the beam of a gate, and struggling hard in the agonies of death. "Cut him down! cut him down!" cried the general, as soon as he had got near enough to be heard, which was instantly done. Then running up, with cheeks as red as fire coals, and half choked with rage, he bawled out, "In the name of God! what are you about, what are you about here!"

"Only hanging a few tories, sir," replied captain Harrison of Lee's legion.

"Who gave you a right, sir, to touch the tories?"

To this, young M'Corde, of the same corps, replied, that it was only three or four rascals of them that they meant to hang; and that they had not supposed the general would mind that.

"What! not mind murdering the prisoners. Why, my God! what do you take me to be? do you take me for a devil?"

Then, after placing a guard over the tories, and vowing to make an example of the first man who should dare to offer them violence, he returned with the company to Mrs. Motte's table.

Of the three unfortunate tories that were hung dead, one was named Hugh Mizcally. The name of the person so timely cut down was Levi Smith, a most furious tory. This title produced him such respect among those degenerate Britons, that they appointed him gatekeeper of Charleston, a circumstance that operated much against the poor whigs in the country. For Smith soon broke up a pious kind of fraud, which the wives and daughters of the tories had for some time carried on at a bold rate.

To the immortal honor of the ladies of South Carolina, they were much more whiggishly given than the men; insomuch that though married to tories, they would be whigs still.

These fair ladies, in consequence of their relation to the tories, could, at pleasure, pass into Charleston; which they never left without bringing off quantities of broad cloth cut and jumped into petticoats, and artfully hid under their gowns. The broad cloth, thus brought off, was for regimentals for our officers.—Things went on swimmingly in this way for a long time, till Smith, getting one day more groggy and impudent than usual, swore that some young women who were going out at the gate, looked much bigger over the hips than they had need, and insisted on a search. The truth is, these fair patriots, preparing for a great wedding in the country, had thus spoiled their shape, and brought themselves to all this disgrace by their over greediness for finery. But Mr. tory Smith affected to be so enraged by this trick, which the girls had attempted to play on him, that he would never afterwards suffer a woman to pass without first pulling up her clothes.

He carried his zeal to such length, as one day very grossly to insult a genteel old lady, a Mrs. M'Corde.

Her son, who was a dragoon in Lee's legion, swore vengeance against Smith, and would, as we have seen, have taken his life, had not Gen. Marion interposed.

In the Charleston papers of that day, 1781, Smith gives the history of his escape from Marion, wherein he relates an anecdote, which, if it be true, and I see no reason to doubt it, shows clear enough that his toryism cost him dear.

In his confinement at Motte's house, he was excessively uneasy. Well knowing that the whigs owed him no good will, and fearing that the next time they got a halter round his neck, he might find no Marion to take his part, he determined if possible to run off. The tories were all handcuffed two and two, and confined together under a sentinel, in what was called a 'bull-pen', made of pine trees, cut down so judgmatically as to form, by their fall, a pen or enclosure. It was Smith's fortune to have for his yoke-fellow a poor sickly creature of a tory, who, though hardly able to go high-low, was prevailed on to desert with him. They had not travelled far into the woods, before his sick companion, quite overcome with fatigue, declared he could go no farther, and presently fell down in a swoon. Confined by the handcuffs, Smith was obliged to lie by him in the woods, two days and nights, without meat or drink! and his comrade frequently in convulsions! On the third day he died. Unable to bear it any longer, Smith drew his knife and separated himself from the dead man, by cutting off his arm at the elbow, which he bore with him to Charleston.

The British heartily congratulated his return, and restored him to his ancient honor of sitting, Mordecai-like, at the king's gate, where, it is said, he behaved very decently ever afterwards. Smith's friends say of him, that in his own country (South Carolina) he hardly possessed money enough to buy a pig, but when he got to England, after the war, he made out as if the rebels had robbed him of as many flocks and herds as the wild Arabs did Job. The British government, remarkable for generosity to their friends in distress, gave him money enough to return to South Carolina with a pretty assortment of merchandise. And he is now, I am told, as wealthy as a Jew, and, which is still more to his credit, as courteous as a christian.

CHAPTER XXVIII

The author congratulates his dear country on her late glorious victories—recapitulates British cruelties, drawing after them, judicially, a succession of terrible overthrows.

*H*appy Carolina! I exclaimed, as our late victories passed over my delighted thoughts; happy Carolina! dear native country, hail! long and dismal has been the night of thy affliction: but now rise and sing, for thy "light is breaking forth, and the dawn of thy redemption is brightening around."

For opposing the curses of slavery, thy noblest citizens have been branded as 'rebels,' and treated with a barbarity unknown amongst civilized nations. They have been taken from their beds and weeping families, and transported, to pine and die in a land of strangers.

They have been crowded into midsummer jails and dungeons,* there,

---

* All Europe was filled with horror at the history of the one hundred and twenty unfortunate Englishmen that were suffocated in the black hole of Calcutta. Little was it thought that an English nobleman (lord Rawdon) would so soon have repeated that crime, by crowding one hundred and sixty-four unfortunate Americans into a small prison in Camden, in the dogdays.

unpitied, to perish amidst suffocation and stench; while their wives and children, in mournful groups around the walls, were asking with tears for their husbands and fathers!—

They have been wantonly murdered with swords and bayonets,* or hung up like dogs to ignominious gibbets.—

They have been stirred up and exasperated against each other, to the most unnatural and bloody strifes. "Fathers to kill their sons, and brothers to put brothers to death!"

Such were the deeds of Cornwallis and his officers in Carolina! And while the churches in England were, everywhere, resounding with prayers to Almighty God, "to spare the effusion of human blood," those monsters were shedding it with the most savage wantonness! While all the good people in Britain were praying, day and night, for a speedy restoration of the former happy friendship between England and America, those wretches were taking the surest steps to drive all friendship from the American bosom, and to kindle the flames of everlasting hatred!

But, blessed be God, the tears of the widows and orphans have prevailed against them, and the righteous Judge of all the earth is rising up to make inquisition for the innocent blood which they have shed. And never was his hand more visibly displayed in the casting down of the wicked, than in humbling Cornwallis and his bloody crew.

At this period, 1780, the western extremities were the only parts of the state that remained free. To swallow these up, Cornwallis sent Col. Ferguson, a favorite officer, with fourteen hundred men. Hearing of the approach of the enemy, and of their horrible cruelties, the hardy mountaineers rose up as one man from Dan to Beersheba. They took their faithful rifles. They mounted their horses, and with each his bag of oats, and a scrap of victuals, they set forth to find the enemy. They had no plan,

* A brother of that excellent man, major Linning, of Charleston, was taken from his plantation on Ashley river, by one of the enemy's galleys, and thrust down into the hold. At night the officers began to drink and sing, and kept it up till twelve o'clock, when, by way of frolic, they had him brought, though sick, into their cabin, held a court martial over him, sentenced him to death, very deliberately executed the sentence by stabbing him with bayonets, and then threw his mangled body into the river for the sharks and crabs to devour.

no general leader. The youth of each district, gathering around their own brave colonel, rushed to battle. But though seemingly blind and headlong as their own mountain streams, yet there was a hand unseen that guided their course. They all met, as by chance, near the King's mountain, where the ill-fated Ferguson encamped. Their numbers counted, made three thousand. That the work and victory may be seen to be of God, they sent back all but one thousand chosen men.

> *A thousand men on mountains bred,*
> *With rifles all so bright,*
> *Who knew full well, in time of need,*
> *To aim their guns aright.*

At parting, the ruddy warriors shook hands with their returning friends, and sent their love. "Tell our fathers," said they, "that we shall think of them in the battle, and draw our sights the truer."

Then led on by the brave colonels Campbell, Cleveland, Shelby, Sevier, and Williams, they ascended the hill and commenced the attack. Like Sinai of old, the top of the mountain was soon wrapped in smoke and flames; the leaden deaths came whizzing from all quarters; and in forty minutes Ferguson was slain, and the whole of his party killed, wounded or taken.

To avenge this mortifying blow, Cornwallis despatched colonel Tarleton with thirteen hundred and fifty picked troops, against Morgan, who had but nine hundred men, and these more than half militia. At the first onset, the militia fled, leaving Morgan with only four hundred to contend against thirteen hundred and fifty, rushing on furiously as to certain victory. What spectator of this scene must not have given up all for lost, and with tears resigned this little forlorn, to that unsparing slaughter which colonel Tarleton delighted in? But, contrary to all human expectation, the devoted handful stood their ground, and, in a short time, killed and captured nearly the whole of their proud assailants!—

Raging like a wounded tiger, Cornwallis destroys all his heavy baggage, and pushes hard after Morgan. The pursuit is urged with unimaginable fury: and Cornwallis gains so fast upon the Americans, encumbered with their prisoners, that on the evening of the ninth day he came up to the banks of the Catawba, just as Morgan's rear had crossed at a deep ford. Before the wished-for morning returned, the river was so swollen by a heavy rain, that Cornwallis could not pass. Adoring the hand of Heaven, the Americans continued their flight. On the morning of the third day, Cornwallis renewed the pursuit with redoubled fury, and by the ninth evening, came up to the banks of the Yadkin, just as Morgan's last rifle corps was about to take the ford. Presently the rain came rushing down in torrents, and by the morning light the furious river was impassable! Who so blind as not to acknowledge the hand of God in all this?

Soon as he could get over, the wrathful Cornwallis renewed the pursuit; but before he could overtake them at Guilford Courthouse, the Americans, joined by their countrymen, gave him battle, and killed one third of his army. Cornwallis then, in turn, fled before the Americans; and as he had outmarched them before, he outran them now, and escaped safely to Wilmington. With largely recruited force he returned to Virginia, where four hundred deluded men, (tories) under colonel Pyles, came forward to join him. On their way they fell in with Col. Lee and his legion. Mistaking them for Tarleton and his cavalry, they wave their hats and cry out, "God save the king! God save the king!" Lee encourages the mistake, until they are all intermixed with his dragoons, who at a signal given, draw their swords and hew the wretches to pieces. Only one hundred make their escape. These fall in, the next day, with colonel Tarleton, who, mistaking them for what he called "damned rebels," ordered his troops to charge, which they did; and regardless of their repeated cries, that "they were the king's best friends," put most of them to death.

Thus wonderfully did God baffle lord Cornwallis, and visit a sudden and bloody destruction upon those unnatural wretches, who were going forth to plunge their swords into the bowels of their own country.

After this, being joined by all the British troops in that quarter, he rolled on like an angry flood to Williamsburg and York, where God sent his servant Washington, who presently captured him and his fleet and army, near ten thousand strong.

CHAPTER XXIX

The British evacuate Charleston—great joy of the citizens—
patriotism of the Charleston ladies.

As when a lion that has long kept at bay the fierce assaulting
shepherds, receives at last his mortal wound, suddenly the monster trembles
under the deadly stroke; and, sadly howling, looks around with wistful eye
towards his native woods. Such was the shock given to the British, when
the sword of heaven-aided justice struck down the bloody Cornwallis. With
him fell the hopes of the enemy throughout our state.

In Charleston, their officers were seen standing together in groups,
shaking their heads as they talked of the dreadful news. While those who
had marched up so boldly into the country, now panic-struck, were every
where busied in demolishing their works, blowing up their magazines,
and hurrying back to town in the utmost dismay. Hard pressing upon the
rear, we followed the steps of their flight, joyfully chasing them from a
country which they had stained with blood, and pursuing them to the very
gates of Charleston. As we approached the city, our eyes were presented
with scenes of desolation sufficient to damp all hearts, and to inspire the
deepest sense of the horrors of war. Robbed of all animal and vegetable

life, the neighboring plantations seemed but as dreary deserts, compared with what they once were, when, covered with sportive flocks and herds, and rice and corn, they smiled with plenteousness and joy. In the fields, the eyes beheld no sign of cheerful crops, nor in the woods any shape of living beast or bird, except a few mournful buzzards, silently devouring the unburied flesh of some poor wretched mortals, who had fallen in the late rencontres between the English and Americans. Indeed, had those days continued, no flesh could have been saved; but blessed be God, who shortened them, by chastising the aggressors (the British) as we have seen.

On the memorable 14th of December, 1782, we entered and took possession of our capital, after it had been two years seven months and two days in the hands of the enemy. The style of our entry was quite novel and romantic. On condition of not being molested while embarking, the British had offered to leave the town unhurt. Accordingly, at the firing of a signal gun in the morning, as agreed on, they quitted their advanced works, near the town gate, while the Americans, moving on close in the rear, followed them all along through the city down to the water's edge, where they embarked on board their three hundred ships, which, moored out in the bay in the shape of an immense half moon, presented a most magnificent appearance.

The morning was as lovely as pure wintry air and cloudless sunbeams could render it; but rendered far lovelier still by our procession, if I may so call it, which was well calculated to awaken the most pleasurable feelings. In front, were the humble remains of that proud army, which, one and thirty months ago, captured our city, and thence, in the drunkenness of victory had hurled menaces and cruelties disgraceful to the British name:— And close in the rear, was our band of patriots, bending forward with martial music and flying colors, to play the last joyful act in the drama of their country's deliverance; to proclaim liberty to the captive; to recall the smile on the cheek of sorrow; and to make the heart of the widow leap for joy. Numbers, who, for years, had been confined to a single room in their own elegant houses, could now throw open their long-locked doors, and breathe and walk at large in these beloved apartments, from which they had been so long excluded. Numbers, who, for years, had mourned their separation from children, wives, and sires, were now seen rushing, with trembling joy, to the long-coveted embrace. Oh! it was a day of jubilee indeed! a day of rejoicing never to be forgotten. Smiles and tears were on every face. For who could remain unmoved, when they saw the little children running with outstretched arms to embrace their long absent fathers; when they saw the aged trembling with years and affection, clasping their warrior sons, glorious in arms, and those sons, with pleasure-sparkling eyes, returning the pious embrace, and congratulating the deliverance of their fathers; while all along the streets, as we moved in clouds of joy-rolling dust, nothing was to be heard but shouts of, liberty and America forever; and nothing was to be seen but crowds of citizens shaking hands and thanking God for bringing them to see that happy day. And to crown all, on both sides of us, as we marched in shining rows, stood our beauteous countrywomen, mingling their congratulations. The day was precious to all, but none I believe enjoyed it so highly as did the ladies of Charleston. Being, great numbers of them at least, women of fortune and liberal education, they had early discovered the deformity of lord North's enslaving principles, "unconditional taxation," which they abhorred worse than the yaws; and hating the measure, they could not but dislike the men who were come to execute it. In common with their sex, they were sufficiently partial to soldiers of honor. But alas! they were not permitted the pleasure to contemplate the British in that prepossessing light. On the contrary, compelled to view them as mere 'fighting machines,' venal wretches, who for pay and plunder, had degraded the man into the brute, the Briton into the buccaneer, how could they otherwise than detest them?

Nor were the manners of the British officers at all calculated to remove those antipathies. Coming to America, under the impression that the past generation were 'convicts,' and the present 'rebels,' they looked on and treated their daughters only as 'pretty Creoles,' whom it was doing great honor to smile on!

But this prejudice against the British officers, founded first on their sordidness, then, secondly, fed by their insolence, was, thirdly and lastly, matured by their cruelty. To see the heads of their first families, without even a charge of crime, dragged from their beds at midnight, and packed off like slaves to St. Augustine; to see one of their most esteemed countrymen, the amiable colonel Haynes, hung up like a dog before their eyes; and to hear continually, from all parts, of the horrid house-burnings and murders committed by Rawdon, Tarleton, Weymies, and their tory and negro allies, filled up the measure of female detestation of the British officers. They scorned to be seen in the same public walks with them; would not touch a glove or snuff-box from their hands; and in short, turned away from them as from the commonest felons or cut-throats. And on the other hand, to be treated thus by 'buckskin girls,' the rebel daughters of convict parents, was more than the British officers could put up with. The whig ladies, of course, were often insulted, and that very grossly too; and not only often threatened, but actually thrown into the provost or bastile. No wonder then that they were highly delighted to see such rude enemies, after repeated overthrows in the country, chased back to town, and thence, covered with disgrace, embarking to leave the country for ever. No wonder that, on hearing of our line of march that morning, they had decked themselves in their richest habits, and at the first sound of our drums, flew to their doors, windows, and balconies, to welcome our return.

Never before had they appeared half so charming. Sweet are the flowers of the field at every season of the year, but doubly sweet, when, after long icy winter, they spread all their blossoms to the spring-tide sun. Even so the daughters of Charleston, though always fair, yet never seemed so passing fair as now, when after sustaining the long wintry storms of British oppression, they came forth in all their patriot charms to greet the welcome beams of returning liberty. And never shall I forget the accents of those lovely lips, which, from behind their waving handkerchiefs, that but half concealed their angel blushes, exclaiming, "God bless you, gentlemen! God bless you! welcome! welcome to your homes again!"

CHAPTER XXX

Marion returns to his plantation—is appointed a member of the legislature—some valuable anecdotes of him—his marriage—and retirement.

After the retreat of the British from Carolina, Marion sheathed his sword for lack of argument, and went up to cultivate his little plantation in St. John's parish, where he was born. But the gratitude of his countrymen did not long allow him to enjoy the sweets of that rural life, of which he was uncommonly fond. At the next election, he was in some sort compelled to stand as a candidate for the legislature, to which, by an unanimous voice, he was sent, to aid with his counsel, the operations of that government, to whose freedom his sword had so largely contributed. The friends of humanity were all highly pleased with his call to the legislature. From his well known generosity to his enemies, during the war, they fondly hoped he would do every thing in his power to extinguish that horrid flame of revenge, which still glowed in the bosoms of many against the tories. Nor did Marion disappoint their hopes. His face was always, and undauntedly, set against every proposition that savored of severity to the tories, whom he used to call his "poor deluded countrymen." The reader may form some idea of general Marion from the following anecdote, which was related to me by the honorable Benjamin Huger, Esq.

During the furious contests in South Carolina, between the British and Americans, it was very common for men of property to play 'jack of both sides,' for the sake of saving their negroes and cattle.—Among these, a pretty numerous crew, was a wealthy old blade, who had the advantage of one of those very accommodating faces, that could shine with equal lustre on his victorious visitants, whether Britons or buckskins. Marion soon found him out; and as soon gave him a broad hint how heartily he despised such 'trimming;' for at a great public meeting where the old gentleman, with a smirking face, came up and presented his hand, Marion turned from him without deigning to receive it. Everybody was surprised at this conduct of the general, and some spoke of it in terms of high displeasure. However, it was not long before they caught the old weathercock at one of his tricks, and, soon as the confiscation act was passed, had him down on the black list, fondly hoping, no doubt, to divide a large spoil. Marion, who was then a member of the legislature, arose to speak. The aged culprit, who also was present, turned pale and trembled at the sight of Marion, giving up all for lost.—But how great, how agreeable was his surprise, when instead of hearing the general thundering against him for judgment, he heard him imploring for mercy! His accusers were, if possible, still more astonished. Having counted on general Marion as his firmest foe, they were utterly mortified to find him his fastest friend, and, venting their passion with great freedom, taxed him with inconsistency and fickleness that but illy suited with general Marion's character.

"It is scarcely eighteen months, sir," said they, "since you treated this old rascal with the most pointed and public contempt, on account of the very crime for which we wish to punish him. And here, now, instead of taking part against him, you have declared in his favor, and have become his warmest advocate with a legislature."

"True, gentlemen," replied Marion, "but you should remember that it was war then; and therefore my duty to make a difference between the real and pretended friends of my country. But it is peace now, and we ought to remember the virtues of men, particularly of the old and timid, rather than their follies. And we ought to remember too, that God has given us the victory, for which we owe him eternal gratitude. But cruelty to man is not the way to show our gratitude to heaven."

Of the same complexion was his behavior in a large party at governor Matthew's table, just after the passage of the famous act to confiscate the estates of the tories. "Come, general, give us a toast," said the governor. The glasses were all filled, and the eyes of the company fixed upon the general, who, waving his bumper in the air, thus nobly called out—"Well, gentlemen, here's damnation to the confiscation act."

The following anecdote of Marion I have heard from a thousand lips, and every time with that joy on the countenance, which evinced the deep interest which the heart takes in talking of things that are honorable to our countrymen. While Marion was a member of the legislature, a petition was presented to the house for an act of amnesty of all those arbitrary measures which the American officers had been obliged to adopt during the war, in order to get horses, provisions, &c. for the army. The petition was signed by the names of all the favorite officers of the state, and among the rest, by that of our hero. Some of his friends, it seemed, had done it for him, on the supposition that he needed such an act as well as the rest. But Marion, who had listened very attentively to the reading of the petition, on hearing his name mentioned as one of the subscribers, instantly arose, and insisted that his name should be struck off from that paper. He said "he had no manner of objection to the petition; on the contrary, he most heartily approved of it, and meant to vote for it; for well did he know, he said, that during the war, we had among us a world of ignoramuses, who, for lack of knowing their danger, did not care a fig how the war went, but were sauntering about in the woods, popping at the squirrels, when they ought to have been in the field fighting the British; that such gentlemen, since they did not choose to do any thing for their country themselves, might well afford to let their cattle do something; and as they had not shed any of their blood for the public service, they might certainly spare a little corn to it; at any rate he had no notion, he said, of turning over to the mercy of these poltroons, some of the choicest spirits of the nation, to be prosecuted and torn to pieces by them; but that, nevertheless, he did not like to have his name to the petition, for, thank God, he had no favors to ask of them. And if, during the war for his country, he had done any of them harm, there was he, and yonder his property, and let them come forward, if they dare, and demand satisfaction."

And I never heard of any man who ever accused him of the least injury done him during all the war.

Marion continued a member of the legislature, until orders were issued to repair and put in commission Fort Johnson, to the command of which he was appointed, with the pay of about twenty-two hundred dollars per annum. Though this salary had been voted him chiefly because of his losses during the war, yet it was not continued to him longer than two or three years, when it was reduced to less than five hundred dollars annually. Numbers of people had their feelings greatly hurt on this occasion, and, I dare say, much worse than his own. For he was a man who cared very little for money; and besides, about that time he entered into matrimony with that excellent and wealthy lady, Miss Mary Videau, who, with her affections, bestowed on him a fortune sufficient to satisfy his utmost wishes, even though they had been far less moderate than they were. Seeing now no particular obligation on him to continue longer in the public service, he gladly yielded to his sense of what he owed to a generous and beloved companion, and with her, retired to his native parish of St. John's, where, amidst the benedictions of his countrymen, and the caresses of numerous friends, he spent the short remnant of his days, participating every rural sweet with the dear woman of his choice, feasting on the happy retrospect of a life passed in fighting for the rights of man, and fondly cherishing the hopes of a better.

CHAPTER XXXI

The author's last visit to Marion—interesting conversation on the importance of public instruction—free schools shown to be a great saving to a nation.

I often went to see Marion. Our evenings were passed as might have been expected between two old friends, who had spent their better days together in scenes of honorable enterprise and danger. On the night of the last visit I ever made him, observing that the clock was going for ten, I asked him if it were not near his hour of rest.

"Oh no," said he, "we must not talk of bed yet. It is but seldom, you know, that we meet. And as this may be our last, let us take all we can of it in chat. What do you think of the times?"

"O glorious times," said I.

"Yes, thank God!" replied he. "They are glorious times indeed; and fully equal to all that we had in hope, when we drew our swords for independence. But I am afraid they won't last long." I asked him why he thought so.

"Oh! knowledge, sir," said he, "is wanting! knowledge is wanting! Israel of old, you know, was destroyed for lack of knowledge; and all nations, all individuals, have come to naught from the same cause."

I told him I thought we were too happy to change so soon.

"Pshaw!" replied he, "that is nothing to the purpose. Happiness signifies nothing, if it be not known, and properly valued. Satan, we are told, was once an angel of light, but for want of duly considering his glorious state, he rebelled and lost all. And how many hundreds of young Carolinians have we not known, whose fathers left them all the means of happiness; elegant estates, handsome wives, and, in short, every blessing that the most luxurious could desire? Yet they could not rest, until by drinking and gambling, they had fooled away their fortunes, parted from their wives, and rendered themselves the veriest beggars and blackguards on earth.

"Now, why was all this, but for lack of knowledge? For had those silly ones but known the evils of poverty, what a vile thing it was to wear a dirty shirt, a long beard, and ragged coat; to go without a dinner, or to sponge for it among growling relations; or to be bespattered, or run over in the streets, by the sons of those who were once their fathers' overseers; I say, had those poor boobies, in the days of their prosperity, known these things as they now do, would they have squandered away the precious means of independence and pleasure, and have brought themselves to all this shame and sorrow? No, never, never, never.

"And so it is, most exactly, with nations. If those that are free and happy, did but know their blessings, do you think they would ever exchange them for slavery? If the Carthagenians, for example, in the days of their freedom and self-government, when they obeyed no laws but of their own making; paid no taxes, but for their own benefit; and, free as air, pursued their own interest as they liked; I say, If that once glorious and happy people had known their blessings, would they have sacrificed them all, by their accursed factions, to the Romans, to be ruled, they and their children, with a rod of iron; to be burdened like beasts, and crucified like malefactors?

"No, surely they would not."

"Well, now to bring this home to ourselves. We fought for self-government; and God hath pleased to give us one, better calculated perhaps to protect our rights, to foster our virtues, to call forth our energies, and to advance our condition nearer to perfection and happiness, than any government that was ever framed under the sun."

"But what signifies even this government, divine as it is, if it be not known and prized as it deserves?"

I asked him how he thought this was best to be done?

"Why, certainly," replied he, "by free schools."

I shook my head.

He observed it, and asked me what I meant by that?

I told him I was afraid the legislature would look to their popularity, and dread the expense.

He exclaimed, "God preserve our legislature from such 'penny wit and pound foolishness!' What sir, keep a nation in ignorance, rather than vote a little of their own money for education! Only let such politicians remember, what poor Carolina has already lost through her ignorance. What was it that brought the British, last war, to Carolina, but her lack of knowledge? Had the people been enlightened, they would have been united; and had they been united, they never would have been attacked a second time by the British. For after that drubbing they got from us at fort Moultrie, in 1776, they would as soon have attacked the devil as have attacked Carolina again, had they not heard that they were 'a house divided against itself,' or in other words, had amongst us a great number of Tories; men, who, through mere ignorance, were disaffected to the cause of liberty, and ready to join the British against their own countrymen. Thus, ignorance begat toryism, and toryism begat losses in Carolina, of which few have any idea.

"According to the best accounts, America spent in the last war, seventy millions of dollars, which, divided among the states according to their population, gives to Carolina about eight millions; making, as the war lasted eight years, a million a year. Now, it is generally believed, the British, after their loss of Burgoyne and their fine northern army, would soon have given up the contest, had it not been for the foothold they got in Carolina, which protracted the war at least two years longer. And as this two years' ruinous war in Carolina was owing to the encouragement the enemy got there, and that encouragement to toryism, and that toryism to ignorance, ignorance may fairly be debited to two millions of loss to Carolina.

"Well, in these two extra years of tory-begotten war, Carolina lost, at least four thousand men; and among them, a Laurens, a Williams, a Campbell, a Haynes, and many others, whose worth not the gold of Ophir could value. But rated at the price at which the prince of Hesse sold his people to George the Third, to shoot the Americans, say, thirty pounds sterling a head, or one hundred and fifty dollars, they make six hundred thousand dollars. Then count the twenty-five thousand slaves which Carolina certainly lost, and each slave at the moderate price of three hundred dollars, and yet have seven millions five hundred thousand. To this add the houses, barns, and stables that were burnt; the plate plundered; the furniture lost; the hogs, sheep, and horned cattle killed; the rice, corn, and other crops destroyed, and they amount, at the most moderate calculation, to five millions.

"Now, to say nothing of those losses, which cannot be rated by dollars and cents, such as the destruction of morals and the distraction of childless parents and widows, but counting those only that are of the plainest calculations, such as,

1st.	Carolina's loss in the extra two years' war.	}	$2,000,000
2d.	For her four thousand citizens slain in that time,	}	600,000
3d.	For twenty-five thousand slaves lost,	}	7,500,000
4th.	For buildings, furniture, cattle, grain, &c. &c. destroyed,	}	5,000,000
			$15,100,000

Making the enormous sum of fifteen millions and odd dollars capital; and bearing an annual interest of nearly ten hundred thousand dollars besides! and all this for lack of a few free schools, which would have cost the state a mere nothing."

I sighed, and told him I wished he had not broached the subject, for it had made me very sad.

"Yes," replied he, "it is enough to make any one sad. But it cannot be helped but by a wiser course of things; for, if people will not do what will make them happy, God will surely chastise them; and this dreadful loss of public property is one token of his displeasure at our neglect of public instruction."

I asked him if this were really his belief. "Yes, sir," replied he, with great earnestness, "it is my belief, and I would not exchange it for worlds. It is my firm belief, that every evil under the sun is of the nature of chastisement, and appointed of the infinitely good Being for our benefit. When you see a youth, who, but lately, was the picture of bloom and manly beauty, now utterly withered and decayed; his body bent; his teeth dropping out; his nose consumed; with foetid breath, ichorous eyes, and his whole appearance most putrid, ghastly, and loathsome, you are filled with pity and with horror; you can hardly believe there is a God, or hardly refrain from charging him with cruelty. But, where folly raves, wisdom adores. In this awful scourge of lawless lust, wisdom discerns the infinite price which heaven sets on conjugal purity and love. In like manner, the enormous sacrifice of public property, in the last war, being no more, as before observed, than the natural effect of public ignorance, ought to teach us that of all sins, there is none so hateful to God as national ignorance; that unfailing spring of national ingratitude, rebellion, slavery, and wretchedness!

"But if it be melancholy to think of so many elegant houses, rich furniture, fat cattle, and precious crops, destroyed for want of that patriotism which a true knowledge of our interests would have inspired, then how much more melancholy to think of those torrents of precious blood that were shed, those cruel slaughters and massacres, that took place among the citizens from the same cause! As proof that such hellish tragedies would never have been acted, had our state but been enlightened, only let us look at the people of New England. From Britain, their fathers had fled to America for religion's sake. Religion had taught them that God created men to be happy; that to be happy they must have virtue; that virtue is not to be attained without knowledge, nor knowledge without instruction, nor public instruction without free schools, nor free schools without legislative order.

"Among a people who fear God, the knowledge of duty is the same as doing it. Believing it to be the first command of God, "let there be light," and believing it to be the will of God that "all should be instructed, from the least to the greatest," these wise legislators at once set about public instruction. They did not ask, how will my constituents like this? won't they turn me out? shall I not lose my three dollars per day? No! but fully persuaded that public instruction is God's will, because the people's good, they set about it like the true friends of the people.

"Now mark the happy consequence. When the war broke out, you heard of no division in New England, no toryism, nor any of its horrid effects; no houses in flames, kindled by the hands of fellow-citizens, no neighbors waylaying and shooting their neighbors, plundering their property, carrying off their stock, and aiding the British in the cursed work of American murder and subjugation. But on the contrary, with minds well informed of their rights, and hearts glowing with love for themselves and posterity, they rose up against the enemy, firm and united, as a band of shepherds against the ravening wolves.

"And their valor in the field gave glorious proof how men will fight when they know that their all is at stake. See major Pitcairn, on the memorable 19th of April, 1775, marching from Boston, with one thousand British regulars, to burn the American stores at Concord. Though this heroic excursion was commenced under cover of the night, the farmers soon took the alarm, and gathering around them with their fowling pieces, presently knocked down one-fourth of their number, and caused the rest to run, as if, like the swine in the gospel, they had a legion of devils at their backs.

"Now, with sorrowful eyes, let us turn to our own state, where no pains were ever taken to enlighten the minds of the poor. There we have seen a people naturally as brave as the New Englanders, for mere lack of knowledge of their blessings possessed, of the dangers threatened, suffer lord Cornwallis, with only sixteen hundred men, to chase general Greene upwards of three hundred miles! In fact, to scout him through the two great states of South and North Carolina as far as Guilford Courthouse! and, when Greene, joined at that place by two thousand poor illiterate militia-men, determined at length to fight, what did he gain by them, with all their number, but disappointment and disgrace? For, though posted very advantageously behind the corn-field fences, they could not stand a single fire from the British, but in spite of their officers, broke and fled like base-born slaves, leaving their loaded muskets sticking in the fence corners!

"But, from this shameful sight, turn again to the land of free schools; to Bunker's Hill. There, behind a poor ditch of half a night's raising, you behold fifteen hundred militia-men waiting the approach of three thousand British regulars with a heavy train of artillery! With such odds against them, such fearful odds in numbers, discipline, arms, and martial fame, will they not shrink from the contest, and, like their southern friends, jump up and run! Oh no; to a man they have been taught to read; to a man they have been instructed to know, and dearer than life to prize, the blessings of freedom. Their bodies are lying behind ditches, but their thoughts are on the wing, darting through eternity. The warning voice of God still rings in their ears. The hated forms of proud merciless kings pass before their eyes. They look back to the days of old, and strengthen themselves as they think what their gallant forefathers dared for liberty and for them. They looked forward to their own dear children, and yearn over the unoffending millions, now, in tearful eyes, looking up to them for protection. And shall this infinite host of deathless beings, created in God's own image, and capable by virtue and equal laws, of endless progression in glory and happiness; shall they be arrested in their high career, and from the freeborn sons of God, be degraded into the slaves of man? Maddening at the accursed thought, they grasp their avenging firelocks, and drawing their sights along the death-charged tubes, they long for the coming up of the British thousands. Three times the British thousands came up; and three times the dauntless yeomen, waiting their near approach, received them in storms of thunder and lightning that shivered their ranks, and heaped the field with their weltering carcasses.

"In short, my dear sir, men will always fight for their government, according to their sense of its value. To value it aright, they must understand it. This they cannot do without education. And as a large portion of the citizens are poor, and can never attain that inestimable blessing, without the aid of government, it is plainly the first duty of government to bestow it freely upon them. And the more perfect the government, the greater the duty to make it well known. Selfish and oppressive governments, indeed, as Christ observes, must "hate the light, and fear to come to it, because their deeds are evil." But a fair and cheap government, like our republic, "longs for the light, and rejoices to come to the light, that it may be manifested to be from God," and well worth all the vigilance and valor that an enlightened nation can rally for its defence. And, God knows, a good government can hardly ever be half anxious enough to give its citizens a thorough knowledge of its own excellencies. For as some of the most valuable truths, for lack of careful promulgation, have been lost; so the best government on earth, if not duly known and prized, may be subverted. Ambitious demagogues will rise, and the people through ignorance, and love of change, will follow them. Vast armies will be formed, and bloody battles fought. And after desolating their country with all the horrors of civil war, the guilty survivors will have to bend their necks to the iron yokes of some stern usurper, and like beasts of burden, to drag, unpitied, those galling chains which they have riveted upon themselves for ever."

This, as nearly as I can recollect, was the substance of the last dialogue I ever had with Marion. It was spoken with an emphasis which I shall never forget. Indeed he described the glorious action at Bunker's Hill, as though he had been one of the combatants. His agitation was great, his voice became altered and broken; and his face kindled over with that living fire with which it was wont to burn, when he entered the battles of his country. I arose from my seat as he spoke; and on recovering from the magic of his tongue, found myself bending forward to the voice of my friend, and my right hand stretched by my side; it was stretched to my side for the sword that was wont to burn in the presence of Marion when battle rose, and the crowding foe was darkening around us. But thanks to God, 'twas sweet delusion all. No sword hung burning by my side; no crowding foe darkened around us. In dust or in chains they had all vanished away, and bright in his scabbard rested the sword of peace in my own pleasant halls on Winyaw bay.

CHAPTER XXXII

The death of Marion—his character.

> *"Next to Washington, O glorious shade!*
> *In page historic shall thy name have place.*
> *Deep on thy country's memory are portrayed*
> *Those gallant deeds which time shall ne'er erase.*
>
> *Ah! full of honors, and of years farewell!*
> *Thus o'er thy tomb shall Carolina sigh;*
> *Each tongue thy valor and thy worth shall tell,*
> *Which taught the young to fight, the old to die."*

*T*he next morning, I set out for my plantation on Winyaw bay. Marion, as usual, accompanied me to my horse, and, at parting, begged I would come and see him again soon, for that he felt he had not long to stay. As the reader may suppose, I paid but little heed to this expression, which I looked on as no more than the common cant of the aged. But I soon had cause to remember it with sorrow. For I had been but a few weeks at home, before, opening a Charleston paper, I found in a mourning column, "The Death Of General Marion." Never shall I forget the heart-sickness of that moment; never forget what I felt when first I learned that Marion was no more. Though the grave was between us, yet his beloved image seemed to appear before me fresher than ever. All our former friendships, all our former wars returned. But alas! he who was to me the soul of all the rest; the foremost in every battle; the dearest at every feast; he shall return no more! "Oh Marion, my friend!" my bursting heart seemed to say, "and art thou gone? Shall I no more hear that voice which was always so sweet; no more see that smile which awakened up such joy in my soul! Must that beloved form be lost forever among the clods in the valley. And those godlike virtues, shall they pass away like the empty visions of the night!"

From this deep gloom which strong atheistic sorrow had poured over my nerves, I was suddenly roused, as by an angel's touch, to the bright hopes of religion. The virtues of my departed friend all flashed at once upon my kindling thoughts: his countenance so stern with honor; his tongue so sacred to truth; that heart always so ready to meet death in defence of the injured; that eye ever beaming benevolence to man, and that whole life so reverential of God. The remembrance, I say, of all these things, came in streams of joy to my heart.

"O happy Marion!" I exclaimed, "thou art safe, my friend; thou art safe. No tears of mine shall doubt thy blissful state. Surely if there be a God, and that there is, all nature cries aloud through all her works, he must delight in virtue, and what he delights in must be happy."

Then it was, that I felt what a benefactor Marion had been to me. How dear his company while living; how sweet his memory when dead. Like the sun travelling in brightness, his smiles had ever been my joy, his example my light. And though now set in the grave, yet has he not left me in darkness. His virtues, like stars, are lighted up after him. They point my hopes to the path of glory; and proclaim, that, though fallen, he is not extinguished.

From the physicians and many others who attended him in his last illness, I learned that he had died as he had lived, a truly great man. His chamber was not, as is usual with dying persons, a scene of gloom and silent distress, but rather like the cheerful parlor of one who was setting out on an agreeable journey. "Some," said he, "have spoken of death as a leap in the dark; but for my part, I look on it as a welcome resting place, where virtuous old age may throw down his pains and aches, wipe off his old scores, and begin anew on an innocent and happy state that shall last for ever. What weakness to wish to live to such ghastly dotage, as to frighten the children, and make even the dogs to bark at us as we totter along the streets. Most certainly then, there is a time when, to a good man, death is a great mercy even to his body; and as to his soul, why should he tremble about that? Who can doubt that God created us to be happy; and thereto made us to love one another? which is plainly written in our hearts; whose every thought and work of love is happiness, and as plainly written as the gospel; whose every line breathes love, and every precept enjoins good works. Now, the man who has spent life in bravely denying himself every inclination that would make others miserable, and in courageously doing all in his power to make them happy, what has such a man to fear from death, or rather, what glorious things has he not to hope from it?"

Hearing one of his friends say that the methodists and baptists were progressing rapidly in some parts of the state, he replied, "Well, thank God for that; that is good news." The same gentleman then asked him which he thought was the best religion. "I know but one religion," he answered, "and that is hearty love of God and man. This is the only true religion; and I would to God our country was full of it. For it is the only spice to embalm and to immortalize our republic. Any politician can sketch out a fine theory of government, but what is to bind the people to the practice? Archimedes used to mourn that though his mechanic powers were irresistible, yet he could never raise the world; because he had no place in the heavens, whereon to fix his pullies. Even so, our republic will never be raised above the shameful factions and miserable end of all other governments, until our citizens come to have their hearts like Archimedes' pullies, fixed on heaven. The world sometimes makes such bids to ambition, that nothing but heaven can outbid her. The heart is sometimes so embittered, that nothing but divine love can sweeten it; so enraged, that devotion only can becalm it; and so broke down, that it takes all the force of heavenly hope to raise it. In short, religion is the only sovereign and controlling power over man. Bound by that, the rulers will never usurp, nor the people rebel. The former will govern like fathers, and the latter obey like children. And thus moving on, firm and united as a host of brothers, they will continue invincible as long as they continue virtuous."

When he was near his end, seeing his lady weeping by his bedside, he gave her a look of great tenderness, and said, "My dear, weep not for me, I am not afraid to die; for, thank God, I can lay my hand on my heart and say, that since I came to man's estate, I have never intentionally done wrong to any."

These were nearly his last words, for shortly after uttering them, he closed his eyes in the sleep of death.

Thus peaceful and happy was the end of general Francis Marion, of whom, as a partisan officer, general Greene has often been heard to say, that "the page of history never furnished his equal." And if any higher praise of Marion were necessary, it is to be found in the very remarkable resemblance between him and the great Washington. They both came forward, volunteers in the service of their country; they both learned the military art in the hard and hazardous schools of Indian warfare; they were both such true soldiers in vigilance, that no enemy could ever surprise them; and so equal in undaunted valor, that nothing could ever dishearten them: while as to the still nobler virtues of patience, disinterestedness, self-government, severity to themselves and generosity to their enemies, it is difficult to determine whether Marion or Washington most deserve our admiration. And even in the lesser incidents of their lives, the resemblance between these two great men is closer than common. They were both born in the same year; both lost their fathers in early life; both married excellent and wealthy ladies; both left widows; and both died childless.

The name of Marion continues dear to the people of the south; and to this day, whenever his amiable widow rides through the country, she meets the most pleasing evidences, that her husband, though dead, is not forgotten. The wealthy, everywhere, treat her with the respect due to a mother; while the poor, gathering around her carriage, often press to shake hands with her, then looking at each other with a sigh they exclaim—"That's the widow of our glorious old Marion."